A PRACTICAL COURSE
IN SUCCESSFUL SELLING

WAR DEPARTMENT EDUCATION MANUAL · EM 748

A Practical Course in Successful Selling

by *Harry Simmons*

PUBLISHED FOR THE UNITED STATES ARMED FORCES INSTITUTE
BY HARPER & BROTHERS

WAR DEPARTMENT

WASHINGTON 25, D. C., 10 July 1944

EM 748, *A Practical Course in Successful Selling* is published for
the information of all concerned.

[A. G. 300.7 (10 July 44).]

BY ORDER OF THE SECRETARY OF WAR:

G. C. MARSHALL,
Chief of Staff.

OFFICIAL:
J. A. ULIO,
Major General,
The Adjutant General.

DISTRIBUTION: X

(Additional copies should be requisitioned from USAFI,
Madison, Wisconsin, or nearest Overseas Branch.)

EDUCATIONAL SERVICES SECTION, STANDARDS AND
CURRICULUM DIVISION, TRAINING, BUREAU OF
NAVAL PERSONNEL, NAVY DEPARTMENT, WASHING-
TON, D. C.

10 July 1944   (Copies for Navy personnel should be requisitioned from Educational Services Section.)

CONTENTS

PREFACE

THIS special edition of *A Practical Course In Successful Selling* has been prepared exclusively for off-duty study by military personnel.

It has been the author's desire to take the subject of selling out of the realm of theoretical discussion and to substitute therefor the most practical kind of *working* information and knowledge, as derived from actual selling experiences in the field of hard knocks.

The material contained in the following chapters should be easily digested, understood and practiced by any student of high school, business school or college age, and by any other person interested in studying selling in its practical aspects.

If you are interested in selling as a profession and as a means of livelihood, this book is designed for *you*—no matter what you intend to sell or how you intend to sell it.

The seven hundred or more specific brass-tacks ideas, suggestions, talking points and selling points in the following pages are deliberately intended to function as "thinking points" to stimulate your mental activity and imagination.

When imagination can be stimulated and properly directed by a practical presentation of the hows, whys and wherefores of creative selling, extraordinary results become possible!

Being a salesman himself, the author knows other salesmen—their hopes, their fears, their problems, their ambitions. Having been also both prospect and customer on various occasions, he feels that he has been able to analyze the good and bad solicitations of the many salesmen who have worked on him.

All these things the author has endeavored to translate into simple, modern sales language with but one end in view—that you, the student or the salesman, may have further light and additional help in acquiring the one accomplishment that will provide you with all your future desires—*to wit*, the art and practice of Successful Selling!

END-OF-COURSE TEST AND CERTIFICATE

As you finish this course you should take an End-of-Course Test in order to qualify for a Certificate. If you received this book for individual study through enrollment in the United States Armed Forces Institute, you may obtain the End-of-Course Test by sending an *Application for Institute Test or Examination* to the Commandant, United States Armed Forces Institute, Madison 3, Wisconsin, or to the Commandant of the nearest branch Institute. If you obtained this book for study through your membership in a class, you may obtain the End-of-Course Test from your instructor. In either case be sure to apply for the test before you finish the course, in order to avoid delay in obtaining your certificate.

CHAPTER I

Introduction To Selling

WHETHER we realize it or not, we are all of us constantly sales-minded, from the cradle to the grave.

The baby sells its mother (by force of noise) on the idea of a meal. The boy sells his father (by persistence) on the idea of buying him a bicycle. The adolescent youth sells his girl friend (by persuasion) on the idea of a date. The man sells his employer (by extra efficiency) on the advisability of retaining his services. The politician sells his constituency (by exhortation) on the desirability of retaining him in office.

In every avenue of life—regardless of what we do or how we do it—there is always an idea waiting to be sold; and the man who sells it is either a good salesman or a poor one, according to how thoroughly he does his selling job.

No one wants to be a novice at anything—least of all in selling. Anyone may be able to make just a nominal sale of any idea, but the man who sells constantly and in ever-increasing quantities is the successful salesman who has learned his lessons in the school of experience.

Brass-tacks selling is the type of selling that holds to the ground and sticks to fundamentals, without paying too much attention to theories and experiments. It is practical selling of the most intense type—aggressive, hard-hitting and factual. The prospect is not beguiled into a series of psychological reactions and studied under a microscope. He is shown the product or merchandise; given the facts in simple, forceful manner; and solicited for the order without beating about the bush.

This is the kind of selling that will be discussed in these pages. Frankly, after more than twenty years of selling experience in one form or another, it is the only kind of selling I know that is really practical and resultful. It is the type of selling that is used currently by the majority of successful salesmen on the firing line.

After all, we salesmen are in business to get the business! The only evidence that counts with the sales manager is the customer's name on the dotted line. The only business that does us any good is the good business we can corral in sufficient volume to justify our salaries, our drawing accounts, and our commissions.

I feel that I am talking to people who know what this is all about, because you are evidently interested in learning more about the all-important subject of selling. You may have been on the firing line yourselves. You know something about people and human nature, how they act and react under the pressure of all kinds of selling; and you know something about the various selling methods. You know that the only selling that brings home the bacon most of the time is the brass-tacks type that gets right down to earth and "talks turkey!" That is the only kind of selling worth studying and worth talking about.

With our enlarged modern vision, and with a full appreciation of the salesman's importance in modern business, we look ahead with salesmanship to a new day and age—a day of greater opportunity and an age of increasing competition. On every side and in every branch of industry and commerce, the salesman forges ahead with renewed vigor and vitality, concentrating his attention on the one end result of his efforts, the only desired climax—how to get the order and how to make more sales!

There are so many facets to successful salesmanship that no salesman should ever dare to claim his graduation. Regardless of how long he functions as an active member of the selling profession, he remains—if he is wise —a permanent undergraduate in a most exacting institution of learning—the school of practical business.

From day to day he gathers more knowledge and develops new selling points; he stalks his prospects and acquires additional friendships; he builds up a still more interesting and convincing sales presentation; he spends more and more of his time watering the roots of desire; and he strives constantly to perfect his efficiency and to increase his percentage of success in closing sales.

To keep himself abreast of the best men in the selling profession, he is constantly on the alert—openminded and broadminded in learning new methods to solve both old and new problems; in discovering new ways to overcome sales resistance; and in picking up effective bits of modern strategy to shatter old inhibitions against new products, new ideas and new services.

Incidentally, it is interesting to discover that almost everything we have ever learned in our entire experience of life and living is at some time or other likely to be of help and benefit in our daily job of selling.

In our constant contacts with human beings we are called upon to exercise every ounce of resourcefulness, training and initiative that we can develop. The lessons we learned at home and on the playground; the courses we took at school; the experience we acquired in the office and out in the field—every single bit of experience we have ever picked up combines to build up within us a background of ingenuity and stability that stands us in extraordinarily good stead in our work of selling the average human being the necessities and luxuries of life!

A selling job is not the easiest job in the world, but it is certainly the most interesting. It is interesting because of its infinite variety of daily contacts, its constant demands on our mental equipment, its incessant calls on our quick wits and good judgment, its never-ending urge for initiative and aggressiveness; and its grateful satisfactions and rewards in both friendships and money for a job well done.

What does the modern salesman concern himself with in trying to get the order?

After he has studied his entire line of merchandise and discovered his prospects, he is concerned continually with uncovering the most effective ways and means of initiating the interview, opening the sale, building up the various stages of interest and desire, and finally closing the sale.

With the exclusive aim of helping you to become successful salesmen, the following pages will be devoted to a detailed presentation of practical methods, constructive suggestions, and workable ideas that have been tried, tested and perfected in the daily rounds of actual sales experience. These will be drawn from personal experience and from the experience of successful salesmen in every part of the country and in all kinds of business. They will be discussed only from the practical viewpoint of the everyday salesman in the field, *by* a practical field man!

It must be borne in mind that while every thought and

suggestion presented naturally cannot be aimed directly at your individual business or your personal problems, nevertheless in the aggregate you will find many suggestions and ideas that can be adapted, in whole or in part, in principle or in form, to your requirements.

After all, adaptability is one of the most important attributes of a good salesman. The most successful salesman is he who can easily adapt himself to conditions, as well as change the conditions to suit his own ideas and preferences. Methods of individual selling and applicability of ideas and suggestions may vary considerably according to the demands and requirements of different types of business, but fundamental selling principles remain constant and unalterable.

One of the first fundamentals of all selling is a thorough knowledge of the product, or the merchandise, or the service you are trying to sell. Nothing can take the place of this knowledge—not even a first-class attempt to "bluff" your way through to a sale.

Nothing impresses a prospect or customer so much as full and complete information about the product you are trying to get him to buy. You should always be able to tell him how it is made, what it is made of, how much service it will give, how much abuse it will stand, what it will do for him, and most important of all, how much more efficient it might be or how much money it might save him over some older model or some competitive product.

It is the fundamental principles of selling that we shall endeavor to bring forward in the chapters that follow.

Test Questions

1. Can you mention anyone who is not salesminded?
2. Do you think a good salesman is one who sells only merchandise?
3. What do you think is the final test of a good salesman?
4. What do we mean by "brass-tacks" selling?
5. What part do you think theory plays in practical salesmanship?
6. What part do you think salesmanship plays in modern business?
7. In what way do you think your educational and worldly background may help you in a selling job?
8. Do you think there are compensations for the difficulties of a selling job? What are they?
9. What does the modern salesman concern himself with in trying to get the order?
10. Why would you like to become a salesman?

Study Suggestions

1. Discuss the question of theory and practice in modern selling. Where do you think each finds its proper place?
2. As between the man who sells an idea, a service, or a specific piece of merchandise, which salesman has the easiest job—and why?
3. Discuss the difference, as you see it, between selling a tangible product and an intangible idea.
4. Give three illustrations each of tangible selling and intangible selling.
5. Give a specific illustration of how your education or personal experience might help you in selling a particular product.

CHAPTER II

What Is Salesmanship?

To BE short and sweet about it—salesmanship is the art of selling! There may be—and probably are—various degrees of artistry in your selling and mine, but nevertheless it is an art. No one can ever convince me to the contrary so long as I can induce a prospect, through the power of knowledge, enthusiasm, and persuasion, to buy some product or merchandise he did not want to buy or had no idea of buying, or when I can develop a casual once-in-a-while buyer into a good friend and thus make a good customer out of him at the same time.

Selling is a profession! It is not a game, or a pastime, or a racket—it is a full-fledged profession, the members of which include many of the biggest business men in the country. It is a profession you can be proud of because of its high standards of ethics and service, and you can help to maintain its high standards as you go on with your selling. In fact, you will have to, or else you will soon be out of the selling profession.

There are four types of salesmen. First, there is the order-taker. He is the type who gravitates through a territory, stopping in here and there to pick up orders that his regular customers have ready for him. He asks them "how much they need today," and makes a note of their requirements. If they don't need anything this trip his stock reply is: "Well, I'll be seeing you next trip." If something occurs to keep the salesman from making his rounds, his customers mail the orders in to headquarters; and if something should prevent the salesman from ever coming back, his customers could probably be handled by mail just as effectively. This man's part in the picture has been just that of an occasional caller. He makes no constructive suggestions to his customers. His stock salutation is: "Hello, how's business?" He is not capable or thoughtful enough to hand out ideas and suggestions to help his customer's business—and thus help his own. He does no thinking and no planning. He works as an automaton, taking what is given to him and thanking his customers for their generosity He is an order-taker!

Second, there is the traveling-man type of salesman. He travels through his territory much as a tourist would. He enjoys himself, has a good time "on the road," and eventually acquires the reputation of being a glad-hander, a good fellow, and a good mixer. He takes all the orders he can get and occasionally goes out of his way to "buy" all the business he can. He is a good entertainer and knows all the "bright spots" that his customers enjoy visiting with him. The size of his orders is frequently measured by the amount of money he spends and the amount of good cheer he spreads. With his expense account and his genial personality, he cuts a wide swath in his territory, and when he passes out of the picture he is mourned as a good fellow and a generous spender rather than as a constructive type of salesman. He is the traveling man!

Third, there is the high-pressure salesman. Despite the fact that high-pressure selling has been a thing of the past for many years, certain types of this selling still exist. The high-pressure salesman is the man who claims to be able to sell anything and everything to anyone, regardless of whether they need it or not. He uses every bit of driving force that he can develop in his talk. He builds up his presentation to a grand climax of enthusiasm and sweeps his prospect before him in a wave of hysteria. He sells all he can, on a one-time basis, regardless of whether it fits in with his prospect's needs, or desires, or policies, or future benefits. He is not the type that is welcomed back and given repeat orders. He is the type that has been out of fashion, lo, these many moons. He is the high-pressure salesman!

Fourth, and finally, there is the creative salesman. He is the man who is really entitled to be called a salesman. He is the man who goes out into his territory and builds it up as a permanent, substantial enterprise on a constructive business basis. He continually looks for "suspects" and creates "prospects" out of them. Through the force of his creative ability he transforms his prospects into customers. He carefully implants in the minds of his prospects the thought that a particular want does exist and that he, the creative salesman, is the man who can most satisfactorily and most efficiently fill that want. He builds up his customers gradually but surely by *low-pressure* selling methods—methods that bear the mark of good business, good ethics, and common sense. He is constantly at hand with ideas and suggestions that will help to increase his customer's business, because he understands that this is the only way to increase his own business. As he helps his customer his customer helps him, and as his customer's confidence grows in him he gets more and more of his customer's business. Not satisfied to stand still, he keeps his eyes open for new contacts and new prospects, and thus constantly adds new blood to his customer list. He is the man who becomes the really successful salesman and helps to maintain the high standards of the selling profession. He is the man who eventually advances into the executive ranks of business. He is the highest type of salesman in our modern chain of distribution. He is the creative salesman!

The creative salesman is the modern ambassador of business and the advance agent of prosperity. As the Babson Institute says in one of its sales bulletins, he is "the soldier, in the service of his firm, who knows that no business can succeed without selling.

"He restocks empty shelves.

"He reclothes those who have become shabby and worn.

"He replaces dilapidated automobiles and threadbare tires.

"He builds new homes.

"His battle is fierce—he must break down sales resistance, old-fashioned prejudices, sharp competition.

"He really fills the pay envelopes.

"He takes unemployed off the streets.

"He feeds the hungry.

"He restores joy to the discouraged.

"He is the missionary of good times.

"Without him the wheels of industry must stop. . . .

"Let every salesman realize his importance, and realizing this let him also know his responsibilities . . .

"Salesmanship must be helpful rather than pestiferous, welcome rather than unwelcome, informative rather than flamboyant, engineered rather than ballyhooed, researched rather than strong-armed, and serviced rather than forced."

I am not one of those who believe in inspirational selling as pure and simple inspiration alone. To me, inspiration by itself has always seemed rather sickly sweet and usually elicits the familiarly sarcastic refrain of: "Oh yeah?" However, there is a kind of inspiration that I most certainly do believe in—and that is *practical* inspiration —the kind that urges and inspires you to sell through the practical knowledge of *how* to sell. When you have learned how to sell, and have acquired a certain proficiency in the art of selling, then you naturally are eager to learn how to sell more. You want to learn how to go about finding more prospects, how to make more friends, how to sell more customers, and, most important of all, how to sell more to each customer!

As you learn how to increase your sales per customer, and thus make big customers out of little ones, you multiply your income and your value to your company and to yourself. After all, a customer is like a gold mine— the more you dig and the deeper you go, the more prospect you have of getting close to him; and the closer you get to him, the more you will sell him. A customer either likes you or doesn't like you. If he doesn't like you, he won't buy from you. But if he happens to like you, he buys everything he can and occasionally he goes out of his way to buy more from you. To have a customer who likes you is a great tribute, not to your powers of personal attraction, but to your attitude, your knowledge, your ability to serve him efficiently and satisfactorily.

While I do not believe in inspiration alone, I do believe that all selling is inspirational. Certainly it is the greatest satisfaction and inspiration in the world to see an "expect" develop into a "suspect"—a "suspect" into a "prospect"—and a prospect into a customer. Then there is that greatest thrill of all, when you begin to realize that the customer is yours—and yours alone—and that no one can take him away from you so long as you continue to take care of him!

Proficiency in the art of selling can be acquired only through experience. In selling, as in every other art and profession, "practice makes perfect." It is from actual experience in the field that we gradually acquire the proficiency that comes from constant practice and that eventually transforms us into good salesmen.

To help us in our selling we must constantly draw upon and develop every ounce of our mental, moral, and physical equipment. Everything we have ever learned in our entire experience of life and living is at some time or other apt to be of help and benefit in our daily jobs.

For guidance and consideration, therefore, let us discuss briefly this check list of

25 PERSONAL QUALITIES DESIRABLE FOR SELLING

1. Knowledge

Certainly we can repeat again and again the well-known platitude that "Knowledge is Power." To be a good salesman you must know your merchandise, know your customer, and know yourself. You cannot know too much about your merchandise; most salesmen do not know half enough about what they sell. Nothing is so destructive of the customer's confidence as to be constantly forced to admit that you "do not know." And, in the same measure, nothing is so helpful as to be able to answer his queries fully, intelligently, and interestingly. To guide you in your selling, you must know your customer's business, his potentialities, his possibilities, and his desires. And to help you in making your mark, you must know yourself, your limitations, your powers, and your capabilities. The man who knows, and knows that he knows, has the prospect in the palm of his hand!

2. *Enthusiasm*

Are you genuinely enthusiastic about your job and about your merchandise? If not, how can you expect to get your prospect excited about that sale? Enthusiasm breeds enthusiasm. With it, you can move mountains of prejudice and resistance; without it, you become insipid and your efforts absolutely impotent. If you cannot become enthusiastic about your job, better change to one that you can; you will never get anywhere in a lackadaisical frame of mind.

3. *Helpfulness*

What can you do to help your prospect or your customer? Can you present a new idea or a good suggestion, or offer some special service? A spirit of helpfulness is one of the most helpful assets you can have. Customer-appreciation expands rapidly in an atmosphere of helpfulness, and the contrary is true in the same degree. Customers are human beings; they appreciate the little things you try to do for them, particularly those that seem unselfish and that have no "catch" to them. The more you can do for your customer, the more he will do for you!

4. *Imagination*

As Napoleon once said, "Imagination rules the world." The power of imagination makes it possible for you to help your prospect visualize the profit in your line, the value in your merchandise, and the desirability of your cooperation. Constructive imagination has a dramatic force that sweeps away the minor arguments of sales resistance and draws the prospect into your fold. With this vital quality, you are miles ahead of your competitor; without it, he may be ahead of you. Develop your imaginative powers to the utmost and they will develop your sales figures in proportion.

5. Constructiveness

The ability to act and talk constructively, as opposed to destructively, is a valuable asset in selling. It builds up respect in the mind of the prospect and adds to his feeling of confidence in you. Never offer a criticism if you cannot offer a remedy at the same time. Never tear anything to pieces if you cannot follow by building it up. Anyone can criticize; not everyone can offer constructive suggestions. If your prospect has the wrong type of merchandise, show him why; if his sales plan is impractical, suggest a better one; if he is buying hand-to-mouth, show him how he can make money by giving you larger commitments; if his publicity brings him the wrong type of buyers, show him how another merchant does the job correctly. A constructive attitude makes you a welcome caller; the opposite finds the prospect constantly "too busy" to see you!

6. Creativeness

Creative ability in a salesman is the *ne plus ultra* of all selling. The man who can create a desire has the first opportunity to fulfill that desire. The man who can create a spirit of optimism to replace a feeling of pessimism is usually the first to benefit from the change. The man who can create a practical sales plan for his prospect or customer is the salesman who sells the merchandise for that plan. The man who creates a receptive attitude on the part of the prospect is in the best position to make the sale. Build up your creativeness and your creativeness will build up your sales volume!

7. Friendliness

This is one of the most important qualities in a salesman's personal equipment. However, friendliness must not be confused with the familiarity that breeds contempt. It is rather the outward evidence of a cheerful willingness on the part of the salesman and eventually begets a similar friendliness on the part of the customer. As was written by an old English poet, Sir Philip Sidney, "There is nothing so great that I fear to do it for my friend; nothing so small that I will disdain to do it for him." In that line is a powerful sermon of service for every salesman! In that one line lies the entire key to friendship in business!

8. Courtesy

It is inconceivable that a salesman should be discourteous in his dealings with a prospect or a customer; and yet, occasionally, a man will violate the rules of common courtesy without realizing it. Entering a private office with his hat on, or while smoking; speaking in a loud, aggressive tone of voice; failing to keep appointments promptly or to apologize for such failures; neglecting any of the courtesies that one gentleman should accord another. Your prospect should be accorded the same courtesy, deference, and respect that you yourself would like to receive.

9. Diplomacy

Call it tact, good taste, judgment, or what you will, diplomacy is a necessary attribute of the successful salesman. It enables him to say the right thing at the right time, and to avoid saying the wrong thing at the wrong time. It enables him to handle prospects with a finesse that keeps clear of embarrassing situations. It helps him to answer sales objections without argumentation and to pass around organization obstacles without conflict. Tact in handling prospects; good taste in what is done; good judgment in what is said—all these combined in one man result in diplomacy of the highest order—and very frequently help to get the order!

10. Sincerity

Sincerity produces an earnestness of tone and attitude that convinces the prospect you know what you are talking about and that you mean what you say. Without the note of true sincerity, your sales argument may sound affected and false—than which there is nothing more dangerous to your success. In the words of Confucius, "Sincerity and truth are the basis of every virtue." Surely, there can be no virtue without sincerity, just as there can be no sincerity without truth.

11. Confidence

To sell your prospect, your presentation must reflect absolute confidence in your merchandise, your firm, and yourself. Lack of confidence in the slightest detail is soon evident in your speech or manner and is quickly reflected in similar lack of confidence on the part of the prospect. Without confidence, you are apt to find yourself floundering in a sea of embarrassment; with confidence, your battle is half won. Can there be any question about what your feeling should be?

12. Persistence

It takes persistence to break down resistance! The prospect worth having is the one worth following up. Don't be afraid to make repeat calls. Repetition, with variations, will eventually weaken the resistance of the toughest prospect, providing you keep your eyes open for the breaks. You may have called on your prospect half a dozen times, and he is all ready to buy on the seventh call—but you dropped him. Isn't it just too bad!

13. Persuasion

The power of persuasion is one of the finest forms of selling. Whether it is the persuasion of your argument, of your manner, of your service, of your quality, of your prices or terms—persuasiveness in selling is one of the important ingredients of success. When you have reached the point where you can persuade your prospect to buy or try something he doesn't want, you have finally become a salesman!

14. Initiative

A man of initiative keeps moving forward. He initiates action with his prospect just as he initiates the selling idea that assures his interest. Initiative is the quality that keeps a salesman looking around and looking ahead to the unexpected things he can do without waiting to be told to renew the prospect's interest and to cinch the sale. A salesman with initiative has a two-to-one chance of keeping ahead of his competitor!

15. Aggressiveness

There is an *agreeable* aggressiveness that injects a spark of snap and force into a sales talk or presentation.

This is the type that adds the salt of interest to a contact and indicates to your prospect that you are on your toes and ready to take care of his needs with the well-known "vim, vigor, and vitality." An aggressive salesman is ready to go places and knows how to get there!

16. Courage

It is highly desirable for a man to have the courage of his convictions, even though he may not always consider it advisable to stand up for them. It is true that you must learn to agree with your customer, rather than disagree. In the last analysis, however, the man who has the courage to stand up for his firm, his merchandise, and his ideas is the man who eventually gains the respect of the prospect and, more often than not, gets the business.

17. Determination

The resolve to make good supplies the force of determination that gets the business. Determination is the quality that sets one's face toward a job and pushes on until it is completed. It is the "will to win" and "do or die" spirit so vitally important in many contacts that seem hopeless or impossibly difficult, and that frequently accomplishes the impossible.

18. Dependability

There is nothing that impresses a customer more than the quality of dependability. Are you in the habit of keeping your word? Do you keep the promises you make, or do you make promises too freely? Can he depend upon your doing the things he asks you to do, or do you forget easily and cover yourself up with alibis? How many times have you slipped up on the information he asked you to get from your factory, or the samples, or advertising material, or window display pieces, or what-have-you?

19. Adaptability

A good salesman can adapt himself to any conditions. The only thing certain about any selling job is that conditions are always uncertain. One must be prepared for the unexpected at all times—particularly the whims and fancies of a changeable prospect. Your ability to adapt yourself to his moods and ideas, even though you may not always agree, is the quality that frequently flatters him into submission!

20. Thoughtfulness

In selling, just as in anything else, it is frequently the little things that count. Have you ever thought of doing any of the personal things that make a hit with every human being? Have you ever invited him to lunch or to a game? Have you ever written him a little note from your office passing on a new idea? Have you ever noticed his secretary or his assistant? Have you ever thought of his family? Have you ever called his attention to some new development in his industry? Why not? What have you got to lose? And how much more chance have you to gain?

21. Judgment

Judgment is forced upon us by experience and teaches us when and how to use all our qualities in selling. It is compounded largely of common sense and diplomacy. It tells us when to talk and when to listen; when to argue and when to agree; when to be aggressive and when to fade out of the picture. It is the judgment we develop from our daily contacts that gives us our reputation for good or bad salesmanship.

22. Personality

Personality is the combination of enthusiasm, intelligence, smartness—tied up with the elusive sparkle of magnetism. It is a "heads up" attitude that captures your prospect "hands down." If you've got it, you're just that much ahead of the procession; if you haven't, you work a little harder to develop it. It is easily understood that smartness of appearance is also an asset. In calling on prospects, first impression is important; you don't always get a second chance to correct a bad first impression.

23. Integrity

The man of integrity makes a salesman who can be depended upon to resist all temptations of unethical dealing. It needs no argument to assure you that integrity is one of the essential qualities of good salesmanship. The lack of it soon becomes noticeable and develops mistrust in the prospect, while the possession of it develops a confidence that often overcomes all competition and keeps you in exclusive charge of the business!

24. Loyalty

Both your firm and your customer demand absolute loyalty—and they are both entitled to it. No man will permit a customer to run down his firm; neither will he permit his firm to take advantage of his customer. It takes a man of balance and good judgment to steer a clear course between customer and company loyalty; but the better you can do it, the better your position and reputation with both.

25. Industry

The life of a salesman calls for work, and more work—but its compensations more than make up for your efforts. Regardless of what your hopes and your objectives may be, it takes hard work to bring them about. The quality of industry looms large in the selling profession—and a great part of it is good old-fashioned leg work. Of course, leg work never takes the place of brain work, but it does make your brain work possible. After all, in the daily round of selling there is no substitute for calls, and more calls!

TEST QUESTIONS

1. Why would you call salesmanship an art?
2. Why could you call selling a profession?
3. Mention four types of salesmen.
4. In what way does selling become inspirational?
5. Mention five important personal qualities desirable for selling.
6. How much knowledge do you think you need in selling?
7. What is the difference between Imagination and Creativeness?
8. What is the difference between Persistence and Persuasion?
9. What is the difference between Initiative and Aggressiveness?
10. What is the difference between Dependability and Adaptability?

STUDY SUGGESTIONS

1. Discuss an actual example of both the "order-taker" and "traveling-man" type of salesman and weigh them in the economic scale.

2. Which salesman do you think is of the modern school, and why—the high-pressure or low-pressure type?

3. Give a complete example of creative salesmanship; how a "creative" salesman would operate, as against the "order-taker" type.

4. Construct a specific sales situation and describe the part that "inspiration" plays for and with the salesman.

5. Give as complete a description and explanation as you can of "personality" and the part it plays in salesmanship.

CHAPTER III

What Makes a Good Salesman Better?

EVERY one of us in the selling profession is constantly seeking for some way to better his salesmanship. We are always open to suggestion—constructive suggestion—on how to do a better job today than we did the day before.

Every little while we hear of someone who is a better salesman than we are. It may be the sales manager who throws it up to us, goading us on to further effort. It may be the star salesman on the force who boasts about his big volume, his new customers, his commission checks. It may be a competitive salesman who sells the man we couldn't make an impression on. It may even be the customer, who tells us what a fine salesman Bill Jones is and how much he does for him.

Whoever it is, we go through the same old process of laughing it off—and then wondering about it. Is Bill Jones really so much better than we are? How does he get his reputation for being a star salesman? What are the things he does that we do not do? How did he finally manage to sell old man Brown, and, wonder of wonders, actually make a friend out of the old crank? Was it just a lucky break, or does Bill Jones really know so much more about selling than we do? And if he really does know more than we do, how did he get that way? Ah, there's the question that starts us thinking—*how did he get that way?*

Yes, we agree that practice makes perfect, in selling as in everything else. But there must still be something else, some short cut, some simple formula, some easy-to-learn hocus-pocus combination that, once acquired, will take us by the hand and lead us along some royal road to success.

Well, there *is* a combination that will make better salesmen out of us, but it is none of the simple things we hoped for. It is a combination of *Plus Values* in selling; Plus Values that, thoroughly developed, industriously perfected and properly applied, will eventually lead us to the rainbow's end and make star salesmen out of *us*! These Plus Values are the things that the beginner never hears about and that the average salesman never thinks about. They are the things we do unconsciously almost every day to some extent, except that here they are projected to an uncommon degree of perfection.

Study this list carefully. I don't mean that you must have all these attributes *today*—but you should have them some day. Analyze those you think you have and see how you can carry them to a higher degree of perfection. Check up on those you know you have not, and decide what you need to do to develop them. To make up for those you lack today, play up harder than ever the attributes that you do possess.

After all, these are the Plus Values that make *any* salesman stand out from the crowd in a class by himself. They stamp him unmistakably as an extraordinary salesman— a superior human being—the kind of man that other businessmen respect and enjoy knowing and working with. These Plus Values are the means to a gloriously satisfying end—the gradual acquirement of *uncommon* success in the selling profession!

15 Plus Values That Make a Good Salesman Better

1. *He Does the Usual Thing in an* Unusual *Way*

The quality that sets one man apart from another is the quality of being different. Not different to a ridiculous extreme, but to the extent of being slightly more clever and considerably more interesting and constructive in whatever he does. While a dozen men will handle a matter of detail in the same style of routine, the thirteenth salesman will add to his handling a touch of individuality, an iota of brilliance, a flash of distinctive character that make him stand out like the proverbial sore thumb. Whatever that man does, he attaches to it the quality of dynamic interest; and so actively intrigues the attention and admiration of the customer that he immediately steps into the limelight of premier consideration.

When this uncommon salesman is asked to show a sample, he is not satisfied merely to take it out of his bag and lay it casually before the customer. He produces it with an air of showmanship; he builds up an atmosphere of distinction with a few well-chosen phrases that play up its particular attractiveness; he lays it carefully, almost lovingly, on his customer's desk or counter, as if it were a precious jewel of unusual luster.

When he writes a customer a letter, it is not just an ordinary conglomeration of words, but an interesting succession of thoughts laid out in unusual style. When he is called upon to supply a quotation, he is not content merely to set down the price; he adds to it a logical set of reasons for the price varying one way or the other and he frequently answers an objection in advance. When he calls on his customer, his is not the usual entrance of an ordinary mortal; his pleasant greeting, plus an attitude of restrained enthusiasm and a definite statement on a pertinent topic of mutual interest, sets him apart as a salesman of interest and authority in his line and one to whom the customer can listen with confidence and respect. When he loses an order, he doesn't slink out of the customer's sight with his spirits drooping; he is sportsman enough to take his temporary loss with a cheerful smile and a constructive expression for the future.

The quality of being different is one of the most sought-after qualities in the art of selling. Every good salesman can develop this important attribute still further by continual study and thought of the worth-while things he can do that the average man never even dreams of. This additional effort pays tremendous dividends!

2. He Constantly Plans How to Help His Customer

A good salesman sells merchandise not by intrinsic value alone, but frequently by the addition of personal service features that make him more desirable and more valuable than an ordinary salesman in the eyes of his customer.

When you have a good customer who buys from you regularly, that customer is entitled not only to the best merchandise you can give him, but also to your personal cooperation in the matter of passing along suggestions and ideas picked up from other customers in your territory that might be of help to him. A salesman who is on his toes and keeps his eyes and ears open constantly acquires such information and catalogues it in his mind for distribution to needy customers elsewhere.

After he has learned something about his customer's business, he may become capable of suggesting new grades or types of merchandise, new price lines, new uses, new ideas in publicity or display, improvements in ordering that will save time or money, more convenient methods of packing or shipping. Personal service of this character, offered with tact and intelligence, keeps the salesman before his customer in the most favorable light possible; and proves to him concretely that the salesman is interested in his welfare as well as in his orders. No customer living can permanently withhold his admiration and appreciation of this high level of salesmanship; and his most frequent type of response is in the assurance that their relationship shall continue indefinitely. Just try to get a customer away from a salesman who gives him this kind of helpful personal service!

3. He Constantly Analyzes His Customer's Possibilities

To develop a strong sales argument for additional orders, and to decide whether or not the customer is worth the service he gives him and the time he spends on him to build him up properly, every good salesman analyzes the customer's possibilities.

By carefully studying his customer's methods of distribution, the salesman may discover latent possibilities for additional lines of higher grade merchandise or for larger quantities of lower priced grades. He may discover that by shipping direct to branch offices or branch houses he can sell his customer a larger volume and save him more money. He may find that in comparison with another organization, his customer is not distributing as much of his merchandise as he should; and he will ferret out the reason for the deficiency and present it to his customer as a constructive suggestion.

Analysis of this kind is not necessarily accomplished at one time; it may be carried on coincidentally with the development of the customer; but this analysis does tell you very frequently how to build up your sales argument and how much future business you can logically expect. Like any good businessman, you can then set up your own budget of hopeful effort, and time, and personal promotion expense.

4. He Keeps in Close Touch with His Customers

Continual contact is the essence of salesmanship. And there are a number of effective methods of maintaining the necessary contact with your customers. A little further on, in Chapter XXIV, under the caption "How to Multiply Your Effectiveness," you will find several suggestions on practical methods of maintaining these contacts.

It is desirable here to suggest that the more closely you can keep in touch with your customer and his requirements, the more closely does he keep in touch with you and the reminders of your merchandise. Naturally, however, keeping in touch with your customer does not mean pestering him to death with unnecessary calls. Contacting must be done with good judgment—when there is a good reason, a specific need, a regularly expected visit, or a definite service to be performed. Don't forget that there is just as much danger of unselling by making a pest of yourself, as there is of underselling by not calling often enough. You must strike a happy medium between the two extremes.

The principal reason for keeping in touch is to be "Johnny on the spot" when your customer needs your merchandise or your services; and also to offset any intervening calls by competitive salesmen. The principal danger from keeping too closely in touch is that you may waste your customer's time unnecessarily and develop a dangerous indifference to your presence. Fortunate is the salesman who can become so friendly with his customer that he receives a cheerful warning in advance when he approaches either extreme.

5. He Has an Uncommon Spirit of Service

An attitude of willingness in the service of the customer is one of the finest guarantees of a customer to serve! When your customer wants something, he wants it right now, and he is in no mood to be argued out of it, or ignored, or neglected.

As was quoted in the previous chapter as a sermon of service, "There is nothing so great that I fear to do it for my friend; nothing so small that I will disdain to do it for him." The finest expression of friendship in business is that which makes a customer feel perfectly free to call on you for items of service that may or may not be connected with your business.

The customer rightly takes it for granted that you will be willing and delighted to perform any necessary service in connection with your business. But when a customer becomes so friendly that he calls on you for some personal service unrelated to business, you can accept it as a compliment and rejoice in the development of his confidence and esteem. The more friendly he becomes, the more often he may call on you for such service—and vice versa. Which is a consummation devoutly to be desired by every farseeing salesman, and one that we all hope for. It is the unconscious expression of a relationship that becomes increasingly difficult for a competitor to break. The more you can serve your customer, the more he will serve you—in business!

6. He Has a Valuable Experience to Draw On

Certain pessimists to the contrary notwithstanding, everything in your past experience may some day prove valuable in your job as a salesman. Various lines of business may differ in detail, but business principles are the same in all business practice.

Your last job may have given you experience that is valuable to one of your customers right now. The job you had before that may have given you experience suitable for another customer. Don't be backward about applying your past experience to your present selling job. Don't be bashful about telling your customer of your past experience in solving his particular type of problem. In most cases, he will be glad to know about it and he may gather increased confidence in your selling efforts and in your suggestions.

As an old Roman poet has written, "That man is wise to some purpose who gains his wisdom at the expense and from the experience of another." You and your customer can both benefit from each other's experience, and neither one of you need be ashamed to admit it. Your experience may qualify you to offer valuable suggestions to your customer on matters pertaining to methods, merchandise, or policies. In offering occasional advice, with tact and diplomacy, you may work yourself more and more into his regard. Eventually, as he finds your experience valuable to him, he may come to look upon you as a part of his organization; and the closer he draws you to him, the more it is bound to react to your benefit and advantage.

7. He Has a Fine Consideration for Subordinates

Wherever the salesman goes and whomever he calls upon, he must frequently contact subordinate clerks, secretaries, assistants, as well as the executive principal. Needless to say, he must be exceedingly careful to show no changed front or spirit of condescension in his contacts with subordinates.

In many organizations the principal entrusts his subordinate with large responsibility and leans a great deal on his judgment and reports. If you should fail to treat him with proper respect and consideration, you may suffer in these reports. On the other hand, many a salesman has benefited immeasurably from his courteous treatment of a principal's assistant or secretary; he has had appointments arranged for him; he has had tips passed on to him; he has had his merchandise strongly recommended; he has had his own personal stock built up with the principal; and in many other ways his considerate treatment of employees has brought him direct and indirect returns of great value.

I have seen salesmen walk into a store or reception room and treat employees with the grossest discourtesy and condescension; and yet they have complained bitterly about their inability to make the right contacts or to make any headway in the organization. On the other hand, under the impetus of decent treatment I have often seen employees go considerably out of their way to perform a genuine service for a salesman that he would never receive otherwise. These are the things that count heavily in a salesman's final appraisal.

8. He Is Continually Dissatisfied with His Accomplishments

No salesman, building for the future, is ever satisfied with what he has accomplished today. As he visualizes the potentialities of his job, and realizes how much there is to do in the future, he begins to understand that today's accomplishment is but a small opening wedge to the possibilities ahead. He has so many more prospects to find, so many more friendships to make, so many more customers to develop, so much more merchandise to sell that he must keep constantly moving upward and continually building ahead.

I once knew a salesman who, no matter how big an order he got, always said to himself, in substance: "You ain't seen nothin' yet; wait till I get really started with this customer." He was never satisfied with what he got, although of course he didn't say so to his customer. In his own mind he kept constantly planning how to do a little more than he did yesterday, how to sell a bigger order to the same man next time, how to make him a little more friendly on his next visit. He kept comparative records of all his sales; he kept a mailing list of all his accounts; he kept a separate list of all his business friends; and that week-end was a failure in which he couldn't add healthy figures and additional names on every sheet. He was his own hardest taskmaster and his own quota-pusher; with the result that he was always at the top of the list in volume and earnings. But most important of all, he had the largest number of individual customers and the longest list of personal contacts and friends of any man on the force. Whenever there was a special quota to make, or a contest figure to meet, he always knew where to go to get those last few orders that are so hard to get and that put him over the top.

9. He Has a Large Capacity for Friendship

The ability to make friends—and keep them—is one of the greatest assets in modern business. The great majority of business today is done through friendships; and it is invariably the truth that the salesman with the most friendships is the man with the most business. The greater your capacity for making friends, the greater your capacity for making money. The two are inseparable.

Friendship in business is simply the business of making friends for your company and yourself. The man who thoughtlessly says there is no friendship in business is usually the first man to call on his friend when he needs something. Many people like to act blasé and say that business is just a cold-blooded transaction of dollars and cents. But the salesman who builds a customer relationship into an enduring friendship; the customer who "waits until next week" for a friendly salesman to make his regular visit; the "cold-blooded" businessman who calls a trusted counselor in to do an important job for him and will not use another man who may be even better trained; the small buyer who mails his order in to a friendly individual at the factory and feels cheated when it is handled by someone else—all these daily occurrences prove that business is really a series of warm-hearted contacts between trusted friends.

The smart salesman is he who thinks of business only in terms of friendly relationships and builds his friendships as constructively and as regularly as possible from every conceivable contact. He is the man who realizes that this is a small world indeed, and that his ever-widening circle of friendship is the only circle worth traveling in!

10. He Has a Keen Understanding of Human Nature

The study of human nature is a study that never ends. It develops from the broadening experience of innumerable contacts and gives us the ability to make our way in the world with the smallest amount of conflict and the greatest amount of pleasure and profit. It enables us to meet and to handle human beings pleasantly and efficiently; and to gain our own selfish ends with mutual benefit. It teaches us to recognize the many-sided facets of the human mind and to steer clear of the worst and play up to the best sides of our prospects and customers. It spotlights the truth in the old familiar rhyme: "There is so much good in the worst of us and so much bad in the best of us, that it hardly behooves any of us to talk about the rest of us."

An understanding of human nature helps us to analyze the inner workings of the average prospect's mind; and in so doing we eventually learn to use better judgment in adapting our selling style to different types of prospects and customers. No salesman can use the same method of attack on every prospect; he must gradually learn to change his approach, his sales talk, and his closing punch to fit the differing mentalities he encounters. One prospect may be slow to make a decision, and it is necessary to build him up carefully; another may have a procrastinating nature, and a little extra pressure is indicated to push him over the top; still another prospect may be technically-minded, and he may require a more careful expounding of facts, figures, and reasons. Every prospect shows a different reaction to sales effort; and the more the salesman knows about human nature and the different types of minds, the more he benefits from his activities.

11. He Is a Student of Business Organization and Efficiency

In this modern day and age, the student of modern business practices has a great advantage over the salesman who relies mainly upon the "push-and-pull" type of selling. As you develop your knowledge of business efficiency and organization, you acquire a number of talking points you would not have otherwise; you discover increased avenues and outlets for the distribution of your line; you recognize the value and effectiveness of new-fangled ideas and methods; and your selling attitude gains in broadmindedness, in impressiveness, and in prestige.

The modern salesman sells modern merchandise along modern lines to modern buyers. As a consequence, he must be familiar with modern methods of manufacture and the latest developments and trends in distribution; he must know as much as possible about modern sales, advertising, and merchandising practices; and he should know something about the requirements and preferences of the ultimate consumer. The first teaches him *how* to sell his line; the second tells him *where* to sell it; and the third advises him *what* to sell!

The average prospect or customer has little difficulty in assessing the value and scope of your general business training. It is only natural that his confidence in you increases in direct proportion to the amount of knowledge you possess and to the way you use it for his benefit.

12. He Is an Interesting and Intelligent Talker

If a salesman is an interesting talker, he is pretty sure to be intelligent; if he is intelligent, he is apt to be interesting; and if he is both interesting and intelligent, he is certain to be convincing!

The prospect usually considers the salesman interesting when he says something that appeals to him personally—to his pride, his pleasure, or his purse. The salesman demonstrates his intelligence when he discusses only the things that are certain to interest his prospect; in this way he has an opportunity to convince the prospect of the merit of his proposition. He is a wise salesman who selects from his regular sales talk the points that will appeal to the particular prospect, and who so dresses them up that the prospect becomes interested by the very manner and meaning and personality of the salesman's presentation.

Talk is cheap, but the effect may be expensive! As an old writer has well written: "It is a sad thing when men have neither the wit to speak well, nor judgment to hold their tongues. The more ideas a man has, the fewer words he takes to express them. Wise men never talk to make time; they talk to save it." If you don't know what to say, and are not sure how to say it—save your reputation and don't say it!

13. He Is a Good Leader and Organizer

The better-than-average salesman betrays a quality of leadership that is a distinct asset to the company he represents and of definite value to his customer. He is easily recognized as being beyond the run-of-the-mine type of salesmen; and his customer frequently avails himself of his leadership and organizing ability in working with his other executives or employees. In this capacity, the salesman has an opportunity to lead the thinking of the customer's executives into directed channels, and to organize his employees' preferences for the particular product or merchandise under consideration.

The wise salesman welcomes such opportunities to work with the customer's organization. At times, he may have the privilege of contacting them in sales meetings and at conventions, or out in the territory, or in branch offices or stores. Most of the time he suggests and creates such opportunities himself; and his spirit of leadership and initiative is never more valuable to him than when he can arrange such contacts. It is by this method that he becomes closer and more indispensable to his customer, and that his services develop greater appreciation.

14. He Is an Indefatigable Worker

It goes without saying that to become a better-than-average salesman, you must be a better-than-average worker. Nothing worth while is ever attained without hard work; and in the selling profession hard work, properly directed, brings a reward that the average salesman can only envy. In working for your company and for your customer, you are only working for yourself; and if you are going to be satisfied with less than hard work, your company is apt to become satisfied with less than you!

Your working effort is closely tied up with your time management. A recent Salesman's Bulletin issued by the Babson Institute discusses the salesman who works hard enough but loses out through poor Time Management. It charts the available working time in a year as 2,920 hours, with only 920 hours per year actually spent with prospects! It goes on to say:

"There are several ways, however, in which the salesman can increase his actual Selling Time. A great many men do not work Saturdays. If such men worked even four hours on Saturdays, this would increase their working time by 200 hours. On an average a third of this time is lost between calls, thus giving about 135 additional hours in the presence of prospects—an increase of 15 per cent in the time so spent.

"Many salesmen will find that they are working only six hours a day. If they would increase this to eight hours, this would add 460 hours to their Selling Time, or an additional 307 hours in the presence of their prospects—an increase of 33 per cent above the present average time so spent.

"Of course, many salesmen work a few hours on Saturday anyway; and others work eight hours a day instead of six. There is still another way, however, in which most men can increase the time spent with prospects. This is by cutting down the time spent between calls, which averages a full third of their total sales time.

"To do this a salesman must, of course, be more systematic. He must plan his day's work in advance. We fully realize that the salesman is dependent more or less upon the convenience of his prospects, but nevertheless careful planning will enable him to cut down on this lost time between interviews. Perhaps he can arrange a certain number of interviews at a definite time; perhaps he can plan his calls so as not to make such big jumps from one interview to another; perhaps experience or information shows him that certain prospects can best be seen at certain times.

"There are many ways to increase the Time when you are in the presence of your prospect—the Time you are *exposing yourself to a sale.* The extent by which you can increase this time will pretty closely represent the extent by which you can increase your sales and earning power."

15. *He Keeps His Eyes Open and Takes Advantage of Every Break*

The average salesman envies the successful salesman and alibis himself by saying that the other fellow "got the breaks." The better-than-average salesman needs no alibi; he goes out and *makes* the breaks; and he does it largely by keeping his eyes open and taking advantage of every possible opening in the prospect's armor.

If the prospect shows the slightest sign of weakening, the salesman rushes in with his sales argument and pounds him harder than ever. If there is the slightest opening in the lines of merchandise now stocked, the salesman steps into the gap prepared to fill it. If he hears any news on the outside or gets any comment on the inside, he develops it into an argument for his product. If there is a new development in the industry or a new buying trend on the part of the consumer, he presents it to his prospect tied up to his suggested product. Wherever he goes and whatever he does, he keeps his eyes wide open and takes full advantage of every favorable happening. In short, as was said previously, his is a "heads up" attitude that captures his prospect "hands down"!

TEST QUESTIONS

1. What does the term "Plus Value" mean to you as applied to a salesman?
2. How many Plus Values can you remember?
3. What would you consider the three most important Plus Values, and why?

4. What value do you think there is in being uncommon?

5. Mention three ways of giving a customer uncommon service.

6. In what way could your own experience be of help to your customer?

7. As between courtesy, consideration and friendliness, which quality would you consider most important, and why?

8. Why bother with the study of human nature?

9. Why would you think an easy talker is necessarily a good salesman?

10. In what way can a salesman occasionally make his own "breaks"?

Study Suggestions

1. If you were to tell another man how to become a better-than-ordinary salesman, what would you suggest? Write down at least six of your suggestions.

2. Discuss the value of friendship in business. How would you make friends; what would you expect to do for them; and what would you expect them to do for you?

3. Discuss in some detail how a wider knowledge of general business methods and practices could be of help to you as a salesman.

4. In what way do you think good leadership and organizing ability might affect you?

5. Consider that you are called upon to work 48 hours a week as a salesman in some specific business of your own choosing. How would you divide your time—how many days—how many hours a day—morning, afternoon or night?

CHAPTER IV

How to Develop Sales Imagination

CALL it vision, creation, romanticism, castle-building, what you will—by any other name it is still Imagination, one of the most important dimensions in selling! The power and performance of imagination transcend all other forms of competition. Selling must be saturated with imagination—it starts with it, carries on with it and closes with it.

A sales solicitation without imagination is like a sermon without end—dull, dry, tiresome. It lacks the emotion that gives it life. It needs the vital spark of inspiration and the subtle touch of romance to lift it out of the rut of mediocrity and start it off on the road to a sale.

Imagination is a talking point that tells a selling story on the way to the cash register! While it may reach to the stars in its effort to be interesting and intriguing, it must still hold its feet on the ground and be practical, constructive and specific—no rambling permitted!

The question is, how can we transfuse the life-giving blood of imagination into the system of the salesman at the point of sale? What are the features and talking points of cold-blooded industrial and commercial products that lend themselves to the magical touch of imagination? And how can these talking points be used to set the prospect on fire with desire?

Here are 12 ways in which the "fourth dimension" of selling tells a story, paints a picture—and rings the bell!

1. The Love of Romance

No matter how practical or commercial we may think we are, it is a well-known fact that we are all more or less susceptible to the romantic approach. And every industry, every business, every service has inherent possibility somewhere along the line for a story with romantic appeal. The trick is to put our finger on the spot and make the proper selection of the angle that will lend itself to the building-up process of imagination.

It may concern the invention of the product, the origin of the key materials, the genesis of the idea, the difficulties of manufacture, the adventures of distribution, the development of acceptance, the romance of success—any vital keynote that will help us to transform the usual into the unusual and draw a curtain of romance over an otherwise cold, calculating business proposition. The world-wide love of romance is a gesture of escape from an otherwise bleak and uninteresting situation; so why not cash in on this complex of the human race and paint a picture in terms and tones that people will grasp with outstretched hands?

2. The Urge of Quality

We are a nation taught to discriminate continuously in favor of the finest quality merchandise that money can buy. Temporary conditions may place quality beyond our reach for a time; but when the emergency passes we revert to type and hold out our hands for better things. Regardless of whether they are genuine silk shirts, de luxe accommodations, genuine leather accessories, finer foods or better automobiles, both the mass and class of these United States provide a coast-to-coast market of eager acceptance.

If we will attune our selling efforts to the quality urge of all the people all the time, we will reach a harmony of results that will chime in with the steady tinkle of the cash register. No man or woman can actually prefer inferior grades after being shown and sold on better merchandise. It is up to the salesman to present and tie in his line with the constantly prevailing urge of quality!

3. The Comparison of Value

How many salesmen present a higher priced product to the customer and justify it by merely saying: "This is a better buy!" Why don't we paint a vivid picture of how it is a better buy and why it is worth a little more money and what it will give the customer in longer and finer service? Why don't we learn to actually take the value *out* of the merchandise; build it up dramatically as a separate entity; compare the value with that of inferior grades—in other words, paint a dynamic comparison picture of it to the customer, so that even he who runs may easily be able to understand why it is worth more to him than the lower priced product?

The more effectively we can build up this comparison picture of merchandise values, the more successfully do we sell the better items in our line. Modern creative salesmanship puts the customer directly into the comparison picture with the merchandise, and makes the customer really see how much more this merchandise will do for him!

4. The Pride of Possession

Here is one of the strongest buying motives known to salesmanship; and yet how many salesmen ever think of building up the customer's pride of possession? The customer may not admit it, or may not even think of it until it is pointed out by the salesman—but the personal pride that he feels in buying and owning a better automobile, a better house, a better suite of furniture, a better radio, a luxurious rug is frequently all the urge that is necessary to get his signature on the salesman's order blank.

Unfortunately, too many salesmen seem to think that buying motives of this kind are all poppycock and baloney; they have to be shown and taught that basic human emotions such as these can be converted without too much trouble into the finest kind of selling points.

5. The Joy of Attractiveness

"A thing of beauty is a joy forever." Which is one of the reasons why practical, hard-headed business men learn to profit handsomely from the newer aspects of modern merchandising and selling. Styles and fashions changing from season to season bring us greater attractiveness in many of the things we use and wear every day of the year. Furniture moderne brought a new joy of attractiveness that was also carried over into many other articles. Modern packaging is injecting new beauty into old products. Streamlining brings new attractiveness to physical aspects that are old and worn.

All these are but the reflection of age-old human desires; and the rapid acceptance of these new developments indicates the value we place upon the inherent joy of attractiveness. The salesman who recognizes the existence of this human characteristic and builds part of his sales attack around it finds a strong and hearty selling point made to order for him!

6. The Thrill of Enthusiasm

Building enthusiasm for his line is one of the first problems of every salesman. People develop enthusiasm in varying degrees; it is the salesman's task to calculate the amount of effort and enthusiasm necessary to breed a like enthusiasm in his customer; and then to strike while the customer is hot and before his enthusiasm has an opportunity to recede.

No man can instil enthusiasm into a customer who doesn't feel the thrill of it himself. It is a difficult thing to make someone else see what we cannot see ourselves. But the salesman who can become genuinely enthusiastic about his line has a two-to-one chance of getting his customer to react favorably to his own enthusiasm, and to translate that thrill of enthusiasm into the thrill of a sale! Watch human reactions and then watch your sales figures jump!

7. The Pleasure of Prestige

Volumes have been written about our propensity for "beating the Joneses." People in every walk of life and in every capacity find themselves, consciously or unconsciously, following this strongly accented American practice. It can be readily translated into the pleasure of prestige that comes from better names and better reputations connected with our daily purchases. Well-known houses and nationally known products spend much time, effort and money building up this prestige asset, and cashing in on the known pleasure that human beings feel in owning and boasting of possessions with this prestige glamour.

Manufacturers with definite prestige use this force in every available avenue of selling; and those on the way up endeavor to build up their prestige in every possible channel of distribution. The pleasure of prestige is a legitimate and potent sales weapon which, when wielded by a shrewd, understanding salesman will eventually build up his own prestige on the sales force.

8. The Efficiency of Application

Yes, the word efficiency, like service, has been well worn and abused, but only because it has been used in so many instances where it was far-fetched and over-done. To the salesman who uses it in its proper place, with the proper reserve as well as emphasis, the efficiency of application has considerable potency for sales leverage.

If an article is ideal in the use for which it is designed; if it has a double use, or possibly many uses; if it is designed to replace an article more expensive, more inconvenient to handle, more cumbersome in size, more dangerous to use, more unpleasant in its results; if it has a health, safety or adornment application—the salesman with sufficient imagination can build up his sales talk around a series of talking points that aim in a direct line at the only conclusion possible—the actual sale!

9. The Virtue of Durability

How long will it last? What kind of service will it give me? How often will it break down? How about replacement parts? How quickly can I get them and what will they cost me? Can repairs be made easily? Will it become shabby long before it is worn out, or will it retain its good appearance to the very end? Will it look old-fashioned or become outmoded shortly and have to be replaced with new models, or has it a stability that will enable me to get full value out of it?

Answer these questions to the customer's full and complete peace of mind and you answer in advance many serious objections that he might raise and thus shorten the path to an order. Durability, after all is said and done, is a virtue that holds a prominent place in the customer's mind; and if his concern on that score can be put to rest an extremely important hurdle has been taken successfully.

10. The Charm of Desirability

The article that becomes most desirable in the eyes of the customer is the article he will buy—no matter what the cost! How, then, can we build up the charm of desirability to the customer?

We cannot merely say it is a nice product or a good thing for him to have. He has gone blasé on ordinary selling talk. It is up to us to apply a little showmanship to our product and dramatize the specific points that are essential, interesting and desirable. As we build up the impressiveness of these specific points, we stimulate the desirability of the product in the eyes of the customer. In a human being, it is sex appeal; in a product, it is desirability; in either case it is a charm that must be discovered. And when we can instil the charm of desirability into the customer's mind, we have arrived at the ultimate goal of all selling.

11. The Elation of Suitability

It is one thing to tell a customer that our product is just the thing for him—it is another thing to prove it. But when we can take the product and—by the presentation of special samples made to fit his exact requirements in suitable shades or shapes or sizes, with the technical perfections or improvements that his present product may lack, with an efficiency of application that is new to him, with a quality appeal that intrigues him—when we can prove to him by his own admission that it is particularly well suited to his needs, then we arrive at a condition that can be called the elation of suitability.

Almost every customer is delighted to find a product that can effectively supersede an older article. Especially when it is one that provides greater suitability or increased efficiency, that is within the range of his ability to pay, and that he can easily re-sell or effectively use, as the case may be. When we can submit such a product to such a customer and develop a tacit admission of suitability, we frequently manage to add them up to a sale! At least, as long as we try hard enough, we haven't lost anything by trying.

12. The Relish of Satisfaction

To satisfy or not to satisfy—that is the question. The customer who is entirely satisfied with our merchandise and our service is the man whom we must keep continually sold in order to be certain that he is continually satisfied. It does not pay to take a customer's permanent satisfaction too much for granted; there are too many slips between one salesman and another. The customer whom we know is not entirely satisfied is the man whom we usually watch most carefully and on whom we expend the most effort. It is between these two types of customers that our imagination must keep working overtime!

The relish of satisfaction is a mutual feeling between the salesman and the customer. On the one hand, the salesman has the keen relish of satisfaction that comes from the knowledge of a job well done and a customer well sold; on the other hand, the customer experiences his satisfaction from the merchandise he has received, the price he has paid, and the service he has been given by the salesman. The two are inseparable and indivisible. And the keener they become, the greater is the spirit of service, the feeling of friendship, and the building of repeat business and a permanent relationship!

TEST QUESTIONS

1. In what way can Imagination help you in selling?
2. Do you think selling is an emotional or unemotional process, and why?
3. In selling a prospect, how far do you think we may go with our Imagination?
4. Do you think it is silly to consider Romance in selling?
5. What types of prospects do you think could be swayed by such things as Romance, Attractiveness, Desirability?
6. What types of prospects do you think could be swayed by such things as Quality, Value, Durability?
7. How could you instil "Pride of Possession" into a prospect?
8. What value would you place on Enthusiasm in selling?
9. What types of products do you think you could sell by using the argument of Prestige?
10. What is the difference between Suitability and Satisfaction?

STUDY SUGGESTIONS

1. Select your own product; pick your own type of prospect; and show how Imagination can paint a picture that will help you to sell.
2. What types of products do you think can be sold more easily without Imagination? Explain why and how.
3. In what way do you think Sales Imagination can be applied "to set the prospect on fire with desire?"
4. Select four entirely different products and set down

opposite each one the principal imaginative quality that
would make it easier to sell.

5. From memory, write down as many of the twelve imaginative qualities as you can recall, and set down opposite each one the product, type of merchandise, idea or
service that it could help to sell.

CHAPTER V

How to Find Prospects

IT IS self-evident that to get more *customers*, you must find more *prospects*. To find more *prospects*, you must find more people whom you can *suspect* of becoming interested in your product, merchandise or service. To obtain these *suspects*, you must go where you can logically *expect* to find them.

The final acid test of any good salesman is not only how he develops and builds up his current customers, but also how many new prospects he can find and develop into good customers!

If your organization, whatever it is, were to sit back and depend for its future growth upon the business of the customers it has today, it would eventually reach a point of stagnation and begin to slip backward. That is why sales managers are constantly urging their men to keep their eyes open and to locate new prospects who can be built up to supplement present customer lists, and to take the place of customers who drop out of the parade in the natural course of mortality and evolution. Without such new prospects, we cannot develop new customers.

The more prospects you can locate and add to your list of good accounts, the more valuable you will become to your company and to yourself—and the more surely will your value be recognized by your executives!

Gold-mining for Prospects

In the process of transforming a mere suspect into a customer, the prospect occupies a key position of vast importance! A "suspect" is merely an "*expect*"—but a "prospect" has been qualified definitely for probable transmutation into customer status. The perpetual scramble for good prospects forces every sales-minded individual to the limits of ingenuity in acquiring and developing additional contacts that hold potential sales value.

Salesmen are like waiters. There are good waiters and dumb waiters. For every good salesman we know, we can probably point out another man who struts down the street like a mechanical figure—the outward shell appears to be perfect, but the inner compartment is a vacuum. Yet some salesmen can never understand why the other fellow always seems to get the "breaks" and beat them to a new lead and a new customer!

In the good old days, prospects almost fell into your lap. These days, they are in the lap of the gods. And before you can do any lapping at the spring of sales, you are going to be called upon for a bit of sleuthing, a little headwork and a lot of footwork.

The man who uses his backbone to support his head, instead of using his hips to support his backbone, is the salesman who can be expected to benefit most from the approaching prosperity. He is the man who will keep his eyes open for the unexpected breaks; who will discover sales tips and leads in the apparently monotonous routine of his everyday job; and who will pyramid the little things that count up into the big things that mount up!

How do you acquire new prospects to work on? Do you

wait, hope and pray for them to come in (if they do) through regulation channels? Or do you try to develop your manhunting abilities and go out after them through *unusual* channels?

Here are seventeen channels to follow. How many do *you* follow—and how many can you add?

1. News Item Leads

Reams have been written about tips that can be gleaned from almost every sort of news item—and yet the last word can never be said.

It all depends upon the capacity for mental incubation on the part of the reader. One man *sees* an item in a superficial daze and it creates no mental response. Another man *reads* the same item and finds in it a direct lead to a new account and a profitable customer. A third man never even wastes (?) his precious leisure to look over the news items!

Every day of the year, wherever we go and whatever we do, we are literally surrounded by new items that are gold nuggets in disguise. Newspapers, magazines, trade journals, house organs bring to our seeing and unseeing eyes an untold number of tips and leads on new companies, new products, new uses, new equipment, new systems; personnel changes, reorganizations, new offices, new branches, new departments, new territories opened; dividend notices, removal notices, business increases, new bond issues, profit and loss statements, vital statistics, increased employment and increased potentials in practically every industry.

Has one of your customer friends taken a new job? Hooray! You've got a friend in a new concern, possibly one you have never sold before. Has he been transferred to another branch, or another department, or promoted to a better position? What a wonderful excuse to write him a little note of congratulation! He won't think any less of you for it.

Has your friend acquired an addition to his family? Is he going on a long trip? Has he done something in his business or public life to merit public notice? Has he written an article? Has he won a prize? All these are first-rate excuses for contacting your man. Even if he is someone you have never met—but would like to—a diplomatically phrased letter might lead to a contact that will develop a prospect.

Our friend Bill Foster has gone to a new company . . . there's a chance to break into a new account. The old Jones & Remler Company is building an extension to their factory . . . there's some supply business in sight. The Franklin Mill is renewing dividend payments and talking about a new bond issue for modern equipment; a couple of new branch stores just opened in Watertown; a new road is being pushed into Falls City; old man Jones is reorganizing his factory office and installing new systems; new distributors are being found in the drug industry for an item that was formerly merchandised exclusively through specialty dealers; and any number of business organizations prove by their statements of increased earnings that they are good prospects for new supplies or new equipment. Literally a gold mine of profitable information for wide-awake sales detectives who don't need to be told a second time how to go after business and beat the other fellow to the front door!

Many salesmen keep clipping files in which they put these items away for future use at the right time. I know one man whose wife clips these items for him. Another man tells his stenographer to watch for them. Still another man I know does his own clipping—files them away in a file folder, an envelope, or a notebook—and every now and then he rummages through his clippings and does something about them. Just another way of making your headwork save you footwork!

2. Customer Leads

Here is another prolific source of leads that many men are a bit timid about using. They seem to feel that a customer will be offended if he is approached for a lead to another prospect.

As a matter of fact, the opposite is not far from the truth. Many customers wonder why salesmen are not a bit keener to pump them for more leads in their own line of business. Sometimes they even volunteer the information. They are frequently delighted to pass on a name or two that the salesman can go to work on; occasionally they will even go so far as to arrange for the interview, by telephone or by mail.

You're a lucky man (or a good salesman) if you have a fair number of customers so well sold on you and your line that they themselves provide you with occasional leads to new prospects. They are in a splendid position to do so—if they will; and you are in an excellent position to capitalize on them—if they do.

What finer talking point and selling opportunity could you desire than a satisfied customer who sends you, apparently of his own volition, to other branches of his own company, or to friends and acquaintances in other firms, or who gives you even cold leads to other people who *should* buy your product! He knows your product from firsthand experience and he knows who else can use it to similar good advantage. You know *your* advantage in using his name as the strongest kind of sales leverage.

What do you do to get such leads from your customer? Do you ever suggest this method of cooperation, diplomatically? Do you ever actually *ask* him to suggest other names? Strange how many men are timid about actually *asking* for something. What are you afraid of? Don't you realize that every human being enjoys the sensation of doing something for someone he likes? Frequently, all he needs is the slightest suggestion from you.

I have known salesmen who have never really had to go out into the cold world to find new prospects. They play their old customers for all they are worth! They build up their entire list of new customers from the valuable prospect leads obtained from old-customer friends. As a result of this method of operation, they find new prospects comparatively easy to sell, because when they get the name of a prospect from an old customer, they use the prestige of the customer's name so adroitly and so effectively that the prospect's resistance is cut down to a minimum.

Every road to a customer should be double-tracked— one prospect track leading into the customer's office and another track leading out to another prospect therefrom! Every salesman who builds up a good customer and fails to profit from his good-natured willingness to help along further, is overlooking an effortless and valuable method of cashing in on all his opportunities. There are enormous possibilities here for building up what actually amounts to an endless chain of good business, on a prospect-customer-prospect bill of lading! What the chain letter did for dimes, the wide-awake salesman can build up legitimately in his own business.

3. Advertising Leads

As a rule, your most prolific source of leads is your company's advertising. This should always result in a certain number of inquiries. When these are turned over to you, your first job is to separate the legitimate inquiries from curiosity seekers; then you must qualify the remaining inquiries into various degrees of emergency, location, credit rating, and general desirability in accordance with your knowledge of conditions.

The most gratifying leads, naturally, are repeat inquiries from customers, who are practically sold even before you call on them. Then there are the general merchandise inquiries from the trade at large in your territory, whom you probably have a better-than-even chance to sell because of their own interest. These general inquiries are the ones that test your salesmanship and your value to the firm. The greater your percentage of closures, the better your standing at the main office. Lord help you when your failures begin mounting above your sales; you better have a good alibi ready, or your boss will have a better one!

A good salesman keeps after his main office to send him all the leads possible. When he gets these leads, he goes after them before they get "cold." He makes prompt, intelligent reports on them back to the main office, and in that way encourages them to continue sending him leads. Nothing gets a salesman "in Dutch" so easily as to neglect the inquiries he receives. As soon as the main office gets an idea that the salesman pays no attention to the leads they send him they are likely, first, to stop sending leads at all; and second, to call him in "on the carpet." Inquiries cost money, and your company has a right to expect prompt action and reports on those they send you!

The man who reads general advertisements gets a lot of information about what is happening in his own and related lines of business. He will discover possibilities for selling or distributing allied lines; suggestions for co-operative campaigns; ideas for benefiting from or tieing in with other types of advertising; talking points or sales objections picked up from competitive advertising or from advertising in other lines; new methods of approach and new arguments that can be used on prospects; good leads to other types of prospects that were never before considered.

Publicity stories often contain sales leads that point an arrow directly at the subject. News stories about the activities and movements of individuals; about the openings of new stores, new public developments, new public buildings and institutions; spectacular happenings or catastrophes that might call for new supplies or for additional requirements in your line . . . all these are available for the mere effort of looking intelligently over the headlines.

Direct mail advertising, incidentally, can be worked in the same way as publication news items. Many interesting and valuable notices and announcements come in through the mails; many leads to the doors of actual prospects can be culled from a discriminative reading of direct mail during the course of time.

4. Calls on Similar Businesses

Other businesses in similar and allied lines may present valuable tips on our own business. For example, the Red Book classified telephone directories and other similar classified mediums present fairly complete lists of names that can be checked against current customer lists.

Whatever you are selling, it is certainly good business to call on a long list of firms in the same line of business. Particularly valuable is this rule when you already have a customer or two in that line.

Every customer you have can be the means of getting you another. There is no stronger sales incentive than other customers in the same line of business as Bill Jones. Bill usually wants what the other fellow has, and the next fellow will want what Bill is using. Play them against each other for all they are worth—and frequently they are worth a lot. This is perfectly legitimate and smart selling, so long as it is done honestly and ethically.

The most effective way to break into an industry is to sell one of its recognized leaders; the rest should be duck soup for any salesman who knows his way about. And if you don't know anything about it, check into the number of men in the same line who are using your competitor's products. If your competitor can do it, you can do it! . . . Or can you?

I once knew a salesman who had the job of introducing a new brand of ginger ale on the Pacific Coast. He first sold an opening order to one store in as many different lines of business as he could induce to take it on. Then he went back into the territory and worked each line of business thoroughly, using his first sale as a talking point and as an entering wedge. Believe me, that salesman sold ginger ale!

5. Calls on Allied Industries

We may find that we are confronted with the anomalous situation of sometimes being strong in similar-business contacts but weak in allied businesses. It may be that salesmen do not always possess the imagination that will carry them over from one type of business to another.

When you have exhausted your leads in one industry, it is not a bad idea to check into the possibilities that may be lying dormant in some other industry allied more or less closely to your own. Why not try to capitalize on the gains you have already made in one industry and try to carry over into the other? One does occasionally get into the rut of working only one or two lines of business, when there may be astonishing potentialities for additional volume in some other industry not heretofore considered.

Many an industry dovetails into one or two others. Bridging the gap from one to another is not so difficult if you have a record of previous sales and a list of friends to use as talking points. To say nothing of having the right kind of merchandise to talk about! Using your head to make additional headway is better than using your legs for extra footwork. However, the two cannot be permanently divorced; the leads you develop by using your head, you must close by using your legs. Regardless of how clever you may be, there is still no substitute for calls!

6. Cold Canvass Calls

Here is probably the toughest way of adding new prospects to your list. At the same time, it is a valuable procedure because it gives you an insight into your business acceptance that you will never get any other way; and because the prospects you qualify in this way are generally your own property and will not get away from you so easily.

A hard-to-get prospect is usually a hard-to-lose customer. You are not apt to have so much competition on cold canvass calling, because few salesmen can stand the gaff. Those who do it successfully are performing a priceless services for themselves and their firms, because in this way they supplement the regular channels of inquiries with prospects they would never get a lead on. Also, they bring in the new blood that every business needs to keep it from getting into a rut. Salesmen who appreciate the full value of such prospects frequently devote a specified amount of their time to making cold canvass calls, even though they get a regular supply of leads from other sources. These are the men who are looked upon by the firm as valuable new-business-getters.

Yes, I know that a great many business houses do their best to discourage the man who calls "without an appointment." Between receptionists and secretaries who have the job of trying to keep you out—and executives who cold-shoulder you after you get in—you'll make a number of calls before you get a break. But the law of averages is still with you! Every now and then you will meet a "regular fellow" who won't high-hat you to death; who will be surprisingly open-minded to new ideas and new products; who will be as helpful and understanding as he can be; and who more than counteracts the discouraging calls that preceded him.

It is this "regular fellow" that you want to be mighty sure to play up to, for he is the man who is going to make your cold canvass calling worth while! He is the man who is going to bring up your average; who is going to give you an order, or help you to get an order, that will spur you on to making additional calls and getting more business. *That* man is the silver lining to the shadow of selling!

7. *Active Customers*

By far the most valuable prospects you have on your entire list are your active customers! No matter how little or how much you have sold them in the past, they are always good prospects for repeat orders on the same merchandise. In addition, they represent your most fertile field for the presentation of new products, new models, new styles, new deals.

If you would cultivate your most certain source of income, cultivate your customer. Play with him, plead with him, talk with him, live with him. Indulge him in his whims, build up his ideas, and serve him with his needs on a silver platter. In your business he is your all-in-all; he can make you or break you; and if you will never forget him, he will never forget you!

It is unthinkable that a customer should be overlooked in the daily round of prospecting; and yet I have seen salesmen who never stopped in to call on a customer between orders! They never knew how their product was selling; when he was running low on stock; when he would need more. After an order was delivered, they never checked up to see if it was okay; or whether he needed any help, any advice, or any information; or whether he could use additional sizes, or styles, or colors; or whether he was a prospect for another one of their family of products. Shortsighted selling of this kind builds up no dollar signs on your sales reports.

Most unfortunate of all, this kind of selling gives the salesman the reputation of being only a "fair-weather salesman"—the kind who calls only when there is an order on tap. To have your customer think well of you and bear you constantly in mind, you should call on him occasionally

even when there is no order in sight. You never can tell—
he may want to discuss something with you that will give
you an opportunity to develop something with him.

8. Inactive Customers

If only one-fourth of the inactive customers in your
territory could be brought to life again, your job would
be a bed of roses! Inactive accounts are the bugbear of
every business and the opportunity of every salesman.
There is always a reason for the inactive customer—and
every such reason is a challenge to your salesmanship.

Maybe he didn't like the last order you sold him—and
he was too busy, or too timid, or too disgusted to complain.
Why didn't you check him up? Maybe the man whom you
succeeded couldn't get along with him, or vice-versa. Have
you given him a good chance to look *you* over? Maybe your
prices are wrong, your delivery uncertain, your quality
spotty, your styles out of date, your dealer help lacking,
your publicity deficient.

Whatever the reason, *there* is your chance to clean up
a sore spot and to build up a customer for yourself! If you
are looking for additional prospects, here they are—made
to order for you. Insist on your main office giving you a
complete list of inactive accounts; and if you want to do
some prospecting for real gold, carry the list around with
you and make these calls a part of your regular job.

I know a lot of shortsighted salesmen take it for granted
that inactive customers are "dead ones." But perhaps they
never stop to wonder how they got that way! After all,
every one of these so-called "dead ones" is buying from
some salesman today. Why not from you? Possibly, as
Postum says, "There's a Reason." *There* is a real challenge
to your ability!

9. Contact Letters

An excellent method of "warming up" cold canvass calls is through the medium of the mails. Letters written to cold canvass prospects might call attention to your intended visit; or to specific talking points about your product; or to concrete examples of use by a well-known customer; or to the adaptability of your product to a certain industry; or to the experience of your firm or yourself in solving particular problems; or to the satisfaction of using a quality product; or to the economic advantages of your price line; or to your mutual friendship with another man who buys your line.

Almost any sensible subject that will provide an interesting point of contact between yourself and the man you have never met will go a long way toward reducing the atmospheric chill when you finally make your call. Anything you can do to warm up a cold canvass call cuts down the possibility of chilblains and builds up the probability of good-will. Uncle Sam's mailman can be one of your most important links in the selling chain; why not use him in every possible way?

I know a salesman who jots down in his notebook the name of every likely looking firm he sees in his travels. Before he leaves a town, he spends a nickel for a telephone call and asks their operator for the name of their sales manager, advertising manager, or whatever executive he calls on. Twice a month he makes it a point to write a personal letter to these men—and really marks it "Personal." Next time he is in the neighborhood he stops in and makes his call. Occasionally, he even receives a written invitation to call—usually in reply to his definite request for "the courtesy of an interview to discuss a product (or an idea) of benefit and advantage to yourself and your firm."

You would be surprised to know how many wide-awake and open-minded executives there are who really see and answer letters of this kind "to their benefit and advantage!" They are usually the type of executives who keep their private office doors as wide open as their minds. They are always looking for new ideas, new products, new merchandise—and they are the men who usually give you the entrées you hope for.

10. Sidewalk Leads

To one man a walk down a business street is just part of the daily grind. To another man, it is an interesting part of the exciting adventure of business. The one salesman might just as well tap his way along with a white cane; the wideawake salesman keeps open the lines of communication between his eyes and his brains and makes a mental note of everything he sees that might be used in his business.

Attractive window displays and store fronts—and sometimes those not quite so attractive—provide sales leads that open the way to the cagey mind of a hitherto uninterested prospect. Methods of displaying merchandise; painted or illuminated signs on the outside; hanging signs on the inside; merchandising point-of-sale signs on counters or display cases; store decorations inside and out; all these apparently trivial details and many more like them sometimes give one a tip that leads the way straight to a new account.

Did you ever watch a "pitch man" operate a sidewalk stand, and notice the showmanship in his build-up? Notice how he wraps up his merchandise in the atmosphere of an interesting story and yet succeeds in tieing it in with his climax!

Do you ever watch the passing show to note how people wear their clothes and handle their accessories; to figure out what stops them at a particular store and draws them inside; to see what pulls them across the street apparently out of their way; to analyze the general appearance of the crowds and to attempt to guess their purchasing trends?

Do you ever dawdle in front of new construction jobs, not just from idle curiosity, but in an attempt to figure out the many sources of supplies and equipment that may go into the building by the time it is fully leased and opened? Did you ever get the idea that the line you are selling might be just the one to fit that location and that business?

11. Exhibitional Leads

Exhibits, fair, conventions, business and industrial shows of various kinds suggest new slants and broaden old perspectives. Many a man has stopped in at a business show or even a county fair and come away with his cranium filled with new perspectives, new ideas about selling his line, new names to call on, new uses and new applications to talk about, new ideas about human nature and their likes and dislikes.

It is pitiful to run into a man occasionally who says he cannot afford to waste time on affairs of this kind. He is so busy trying to force through his old and outmoded selling plans that he hasn't any time to pick up new ones—at least until such time as he himself is recognized as being outmoded by men with new minds and new ideas!

Every man who has anything at all to do with selling

should be forced to attend occasional affairs and promotions of this type, so that he may keep in touch with the continual advances in his line and with the constant developments in selling technique—to say nothing of the developments in buying technique! The only man who cannot benefit from contacts of this character is the mechanical man who has no mind.

12. Seasonal Leads

The only leads I know of that are practically automatic and effortless are those that pertain to the changing seasons. And yet even those are sometimes overlooked, which proves again that the simplest things are not always the most obvious.

A great many men sell products and merchandise that are seasonal to a greater or less degree. Unfortunately, some men ride along with the seasons and make not the slightest effort to change their values. They take it for granted that this season is slow and that season is big. But what do they do in the so-called big seasons to build up, carry over and cash in on an over-supply of leads for slow seasons? Fortunately, seasonal changes are not as sharp and severe as they used to be, because every sales executive recognizes the need for extra effort in straightening out the tapering-off curve.

There is a more pronounced tendency for sales executives and salesmen to approach these seasonal changes with a greater supply of sales tips and leads, such as suggested in this chapter, and to apply a little more effort behind these leads. One of the things that should help tremendously to offset the slow-season complex is the steady development of the endless-chain idea discussed under the heading of "Customer Leads."

13. Current Events Leads

Nothing is too far fetched for the real salesman to consider. It matters not whether an event is of local, national or international significance; whether it is political, civic, industrial or commercial—if it has some relation to the salesman's product it is worth placing under the microscope.

A national convention or an international regatta; a civic affair, such as the opening of a new transit line or a new park; a political argument that involves competitive parties; an industrial event, such as the opening of a new factory; a commercial event of local or national significance, such as the promotion of an exhibit or of a big fair —all these are grist to the salesman's mill.

It is up to the thinking salesman to locate the application to his own personal product; and much of the time the application is there—it needs only to be ferreted out. Social events, too, may present direct or indirect opportunities for sales. All that is necessary is the ability to use one's head and the energy and activity to follow through.

14. Social Contacts

There is no law against selling your friends, provided you can do it tactfully and ethically.

Whatever club you belong to includes some members who can be approached carefully and considerately, so as not to give offense or to violate any rules. Whether it is a business club, a fraternal organization, a bridge club, or a golf club—there is always a 19th hole—and friendship and good fellowship cover a multitude of selling sins. Without doing business on the golf course, you can make your golf game help your business; and the same applies to your bridge game or your luncheon club.

Fellowship friends are also business men. Some of them can be good prospects for your product; and diplomatic solicitations can be made and still kept within the bounds of good taste and good judgment. No good business man need ever resent a sales solicitation when it is coated and larded with tact and consideration for the social amenities; and no good salesman who can use his head will permit himself to be stymied by a "No Solicitation" rule.

If you had a cigar for every legitimate sale made in clubs and fraternal organizations in your territory in spite of a "No Solicitation" rule, you could open a store and sell cigars at retail! It is all a case of doing it tactfully and properly.

15. Conversational Leads

Smoking-car gossip out in the territory occasionally brings interesting sidelights, names, conditions and facts to the surface where they can be picked up by the wide-awake listener and put to work on the selling line. More than one man on his way to a distant city has been given valuable information in advance by a talkative unsuspecting competitor. It brings us back to the old saying that there are many times when "silence is golden."

The same opportunities exist in social contacts, whether they are clubs, meetings, parties or smaller gatherings. It cannot be considered improper or unethical to keep one's ears open when other people are willing to talk. Even in talks with prospects' and customers' personnel you are occasionally apt to pick up tips and leads that can be followed up without acting improperly or betraying a confidence. If there is any danger of the latter, you can usually obtain permission to use a tip or a lead that has been divulged.

All these little things resolve themselves into just one

big thing—is the salesman on his toes? Is he awake to his opportunities? Does he know how to respond when opportunity knocks on his door? If he doesn't, he is doomed to be always just a cub salesman. If he does, he is on his way to stardom and no one can stop him!

16. New Business Houses

There are new stores, new branches, new offices, new firms, new factories opening every day. How do you get to know about them?

Read the advertisements in the newspapers and magazines; check the news items, especially on the financial page; listen to the conversations of your friends at home, on the street, at your club; keep your eyes open on your daily rounds and note what is going on all over your territory—whether you walk, ride, or drive.

Some of these new business houses make mighty good prospects for whatever you have to sell. They have to buy it from someone—why not from you? It is usually just a case of keeping your wits about you and beating your competitor to the front door!

17. New Industry Developments

No modern industry keeps standing still. It is constantly moving forward into newer fields and newer developments.

The business standards and concepts of an entire industry may change within a comparatively short time—and overnight old equipment is replaced with new! The increasing efficiency of trade associations has had a rejuvenating effect on many old industries. Modern research has opened new markets, brought forth new products, developed new styles, new sizes, new models—all with their accompanying needs for still more of what you have to sell.

Trade journals of various industries paint vivid pictures of the newest trends—and tell a profit story that you cannot afford to overlook. Keep your eye on the trends and the trends will keep you on top of your sales quota. Above all, keep your eyes open—wide open!

Test Questions

1. Describe briefly the order and development of prospects, suspects, expects and customers into *regular* customers.
2. Why do you think "prospecting" is necessary in the selling process?
3. Explain the significance of the phrase: "Gold-mining for prospects."
4. How many different types of printed publications can you mention that might provide you with prospect leads?
5. How could you develop an endless chain of prospects?
6. Name three ways in which advertising can help you to find prospects.
7. Explain, first, the similarity—and second, the difference, between "similar businesses" and "allied industries."
8. Name six general ways in which you can find prospects.
9. Which would you consider the most valuable type of prospect leads, and which the toughest way to get leads?
10. In your opinion, what would be the three easiest ways to get prospect leads—and why?

Study Suggestions

1. Let us suppose that you have acquired about twenty-five clippings with prospect leads in six different cities of your territory. How would you benefit from them and what would you do?
2. Let us imagine you are a salesman confined to only one city, and yet you acquire good prospect leads in other

cities. How would you benefit from them and what would you do?

3. Let us analyze the inquiries you might receive from your firm's advertising. How would you separate the wheat from the chaff and qualify them for follow-up work?

4. You have been given two prospect leads by one of your regular customers. Exactly how would you follow them up; what would you do and what would you say; and after you have sold them, what would be your next step?

5. Of what value is friendship in supplying prospect leads; that is, how would you get friendship leads, what good would they be, and how would you introduce yourself to them?

CHAPTER VI

How to Handle Your Prospects

IF I were asked what, in my opinion, is the most desirable and most essential of all qualities in the handling and cultivating of prospects, I should reply with one word —Tact!

Webster defines tact as "the ability to deal with others without giving offense." From the viewpoint of the salesman, I should add to that, "while actively soliciting, interesting, selling, and closing the prospect." It is the *activity* surrounding all this effort that calls for so much tact.

The tactful handling of prospects is the most ticklish part of selling. Certainly, no one can get far in life without the quality that acts as a lubricating agent in all our contacts. In the entire category of human relations, no other ingredient is so vitally necessary and indispensable to the salesman. You may manage to do fairly well with a limited amount of knowledge of your product, by covering it up with enthusiasm or aggressiveness; or with a nominal amount of initiative, or constructiveness, or helpfulness; but you will not get far without a plentiful supply of tact. The skillful application of tact frequently covers a multitude of other sins in selling; but without it your sins will surely find you out.

The development of tact must be one of the first principles and requirements of every salesman. It is not so difficult to acquire as it may seem. After all, tact is the skillful use of consideration, artfulness, thoughtfulness, and timeliness—all falling under the general head of Diplomacy. The application of tact is merely the application of the Golden Rule—"Do unto others as you would have others do unto you." To acquire and develop tact, then, means merely to acquire and develop a keener sense of what constitutes the Golden Rule.

With prospects, as with everything else, it "takes all kinds of people to make a world." In your selling activities, you will encounter as many different kinds of prospects as there are different kinds of human minds—far too many to classify—but the following list will give you 25 of the most important and the most frequently recurring types, with suggestions on how to handle them:

1. The Technical Prospect

This man usually has the exact, scientific type of mind. Some people may call him "finicky" because he is so intent on details. In most cases, however, he is interested in a technical explanation of the product rather than in the merchandising aspects. This man must be given careful, accurate, exhaustive information about your line from the technical side, stressing such things as materials, laboratory tests, machinery, manufacturing processes, etc.—all developed constructively and interestingly as an approach to the merchandising angle.

2. The Argumentative Prospect

You've got to watch out for this man. He takes to argument as easily as a duck to water. He likes nothing better than to get you involved in arguments pro and con, for the sake of the argument itself. Keep out of personalities and try to keep your statements confined strictly to the merits of your proposition, without going too far afield. Above all, don't try too hard to *win* an argument with this kind of prospect, because if you win an argument with him you are apt to lose the sale.

3. The Procrastinating Prospect

He never believes in ordering today what he can put off until next week or until next trip. The only way to overcome this man's tendency to procrastinate is to treat his order as an emergency matter. Show him what will happen to him if he doesn't order today; he will run out of stock; he will pay more next time you come around; he will lose sales and profits; he will lose customers and prestige. With this man you must bring to bear every bit of pressure you can develop in order to push him over the top. With this one type of man, you must practically "high pressure" him into an order.

4. The Hot-headed Prospect

He flies into a rage at the slightest provocation and acts as if you were deliberately trying to bait him. The only remedy for him is the "soft answer that turneth away wrath" and a shipload of tact. You must make haste slowly with this man and study every word you say. Not a single statement must be open to argument or misunderstanding. Occasionally, you may even have to smooth him down temporarily and leave him until next visit. It doesn't do to push him too far.

5. The Suspicious Prospect

Yes, there are people in the world who doubt everyone, themselves included. The only way to do business with this kind of prospect is to present undoubtable proof of every statement you make. Don't give him the slightest chance to pick your proposition to pieces. Don't leave any loose ends open to doubt. Tie up everything with the force of recognizable authorities and you may overcome his force of habit.

6. *The Good-natured Prospect*

This is the kind of prospect we all like to meet and make the most of; but don't get the idea that he is necessarily an easy mark. He is usually a fine fellow to do business with; but the best way to do business with him is to be outspoken in your optimism and let your good nature dovetail with his. Present your proposition constructively; lay all your cards on the table; and play up to his evident sense of fairness and decency. But don't let his good-naturedness kid you or talk you out of the order. He may be an expert at this kind of selling himself. It is up to you to keep *yourself* from being sold on the idea of leaving without the order!

7. *The Buck-passing Prospect*

Here is the man who thinks he can get rid of you by passing the buck to someone else. The best way to deal with him is to flatter him into submission. Tell him that regardless of the other fellow, you are most concerned with his approval and with his acceptance of your proposition. You are calling on him because *he* is the man you want to sell, and no one else. If you cannot tie him down that way, then talk frankly, tell him you realize he is trying to pass the buck to get rid of you, and appeal to his sense of justice and fair play. If necessary, I would rather be slightly hard-boiled with a man like this and take a chance on reaching his better side than be pushed out of the picture entirely; I have everything to gain and nothing to lose.

8. *The Wavering Prospect*

This kind of prospect just cannot make up his mind to do one thing or the other. With this man, it is necessary to do his thinking for him and to lead him into the action he should take. Present your proposition from his angle, just as if he himself were doing the thinking. Play up the many advantages of your product as against the few disadvantages, in such a way as to build up a tidal wave of proof that the only thing for him to do is to buy your product and put it in stock at once. Lead him to the proof; lead him to the decision; and lead his pen to the dotted line!

9. *The Silent Prospect*

This is a difficult type of man to work with because of his lack of response; but because he doesn't do a lot of talking is no proof that he doesn't do a lot of thinking! The only way to handle him is to present your proposition in a clear-cut, straightforward manner; and then by a few direct questions try to draw him out gradually as to his impressions or reactions. In this way you may get some statement from him which you can answer to his eventual satisfaction and in that way reach a decision. Don't try to talk him to death—you will only talk yourself out of his presence. The silent prospect is apt to be the thinking prospect; and a short, sensible sales talk will make more impression on him than a flood of conversation.

10. *The Shopping Prospect*

Here is the prospect who likes to shop around to his heart's content before he ever buys anything. It is up to you to stop him right here and now, by proving that he is wasting time and money in shopping around unnecessarily. You'll have to build up such a force of unanswerable proof and argument that he becomes overwhelmed with the desirability of your proposition and doesn't go any further. Parade your merchandise, your sales talk, your arguments, your authorities in such a sweep of logical presentation that the climax cannot be anything but favorable to you!

11. *The Curious Prospect*

Everyone has a certain amount of curiosity, but some have more than others. To the prospect who is overly curious, as indicated by his continuous questioning, you must present your sales talk in such a way as to retain his curiosity and yet feed him only enough to maintain his attitude. Don't give him everything you have; always retain something that you can use as a final closing punch when necessary to force him to a decision. A little mystery doesn't hurt; too much generosity in unloading your mind of everything you have doesn't do you any good; it leaves you without a comeback if he asks for more.

12. *The Self-important Prospect*

This is a trying type of prospect to handle. His high-hat attitude may cover only assumed importance, or it may cover a certain amount of real importance exaggerated to an unusual degree. In either case, you had better play up to his impression of himself and use flattery as tactfully as you can. Handle him with care if you care to handle him at all. The prospect who is really important usually shows a dignity of character and attitude which is not high-hat. With *this* man you can be natural and present your proposition as constructively as possible, from time to time offering valuable suggestions and ideas which might produce a favorable reaction.

13. *The Instinctive Prospect*

Here is the man who buys from his own personal "hunches" rather than from any logical sense of reasoning. He is usually superstitious about numbers, dates, quantities, etc., and is apt to place more reliance on good-fellowship than on good merchandise. If you can get on the right side of the instinctive prospect through the power of your personality, well and good; if not, your results with him will depend largely on the state of his illogical mind and much of your effort will be wasted. If you are on the wrong side, it may even be advisable not to put in too much effort.

14. *The Open-minded Prospect*

This is the finest type of prospect of all! Any time you have an idea that your prospect is the open-minded kind, congratulate yourself and go to work! Give him both barrels in every line of your presentation. He will be fair-minded enough to consider all the facts you lay before him; and if your proposition has any merit, he will be the first to admit it and either give you an order or tell you why he cannot. You usually know just where you are at with this man; and as a result you can meet him on his own ground and talk to him at his own level. If he says he cannot buy from you, he may give you a reason that you might be able to turn into a talking point for your own account. At any rate, he will probably be honest and fair with you and possibly give you an opportunity to develop his friendship.

15. The Copy-cat Prospect

Here is the type of prospect who can be turned to good use if you have an idea he is a copy-cat. All you need to tell him is that Bill Jones, down the street, carries your merchandise, and you can get an order from him. He is the man who buys only what someone else carries; he hasn't the nerve to put in a new line himself, or to inject a new idea into his organization, until someone else has started it. Then all you've got to do is show him who has it, and he goes on your customer list!

16. The Careless Prospect

The easygoing man who carelessly gives you an order, without being absolutely certain about just what he wants, is likely to be an expensive prospect. He may reject your shipment; or cancel the order; or find fault with the merchandise; or complain about the service—entirely without reason. He just "thought" he was getting something else and didn't bother to make sure. It is much safer and cheaper for you to make sure in the beginning that he knows just what he is ordering and just what he is going to get. Foresight with a prospect like this is much better than hindsight on an order that is rejected!

17. The Smart-aleck Prospect

Everyone occasionally runs into this type of prospect, although you would much prefer to run *over* him. The only thing to do is to humor him as far as you can. He is very susceptible to flattery; and he likes to be treated as if the responsibility of the world rests upon his shoulders. He is a difficult man to get along with, as a rule, because he becomes so irritating in his manner; the only possible way to handle him successfully is to carry along his idea of his own importance. If you cannot get along with him by flattery, it might become necessary to be somewhat hard-boiled and tone him down to a reasonable level. Naturally, that may involve losing the prospect and is to be used only as a last resort.

18. *The Enthusiastic Prospect*

The prospect who is too enthusiastic is just as dangerous as the one who is too skeptical. He may become very enthusiastic at first and let his emotions run away with him; but his enthusiasm wears off easily and he cools down quickly. His enthusiasm is neither sincere nor genuine; it is only a thin veneer which raises false hopes and then drops you with a dull thud. The only thing to do with the enthusiastic prospect is to get his official order right then and there; if you let him put it off until he cools down, you are lost. All your effort must be concentrated in the attempt to close him while he retains his enthusiasm; he is not dependable afterwards.

19. *The Skeptical Prospect*

Here is the man who disbelieves everything you say. No matter what your statement may be, he has an argument against it. The result is that you don't dare present anything to him that is not backed by the fullest force of proof and authority. Then you can stand up to him and force him to admit that he is all wrong and that your proposition is all right. Be careful about the things you claim, but claim everything you know you can prove!

20. The Timid Prospect

The man who is timid is always a problem. He is always afraid to do this or that; he is continually asking everybody's advice on what to do; he never dares to use his own judgment, unless it is supported by his wife or some friend. The salesman has the difficult job of trying to inject courage into the soul of the timid prospect. He must show him how useless it is to depend upon others' opinions, who know nothing of his problems. He must remind him that he is running his own affairs and is competent to make his own decisions. He must urge him to develop a spirit of pride in his own judgments. In short, he must bolster him up and make a man of him. Once built up, this prospect belongs to the man who developed him!

21. The Slow-thinking Prospect

This is the man who takes his time about making decisions. He cannot be hurried or pushed. He probably is willing to buy from you, but is exceedingly careful about saying so. He examines a proposition in tedious detail from every angle and eventually gives you his okay; but if you attempt to rush him into a decision you will probably lose him. You must watch out for this type of prospect; when you encounter him you must let him arrive at his own decision in his own sweet time; that is the only way you can do business with him.

22. The Cynical Prospect

Here is the confirmed pessimist, a dangerous species to contact because of what he might do to your own spirit of optimism. Nothing that you do or that anyone else does can be right. Nothing that you show him is any good. He can always prove that your line is no good; that your firm is on the wrong track; that you are wasting your time; and that he knows more about the whole proposition than you do. Any time you run across a prospect like this, and find that you cannot make any impression on him, you are better off dropping him cold. You can spend your time to much better advantage with a more hopeful type of prospect!

23. The Disagreeable Prospect

Fortunately, there are not many people in the world who are naturally disagreeable; but at rare intervals you will encounter a prospect so disagreeable that there is no hope for either of you in your contacts. This type of man I treat the same way as the Cynical Prospect—I drop him as quickly as I realize his disposition. Life is so short—and there are so many decent people in the world—that it is a waste of time and effort to try to do business with disagreeable people. And there is always the danger that they will embitter your own soul.

24. The Casual Prospect

He may be just looking around, but this may indicate sufficient interest to justify cultivating and following up. It is always possible that the casual prospect can be given a sales talk that will impress him sufficiently either to give you an order now or to remember you for the future. Many a casual prospect has been developed into a good customer through the force of a strong, interesting presentation of facts and a careful follow-up. No prospect is ever entirely out of the picture until you yourself drop him!

25. *The Hard-up Prospect*

You will encounter many prospects who like to place themselves in this category, but not all of them belong there. Most people who tell you how hard up they are hope to establish an alibi and thus get rid of you. The prospect who is really hard up isn't so proud of it that he spends all his time talking about it! With the former type of prospect, you have to destroy his alibi and show him how much better off he is than many others who are buying from you. With the latter type you can frequently arrange special billing and special terms that will enable him to take advantage of your proposition. Even if you cannot do this now, there is always a possibility of your doing it in the near future. In either case, here is a chance to add another name to your friendship list!

TEST QUESTIONS

1. What is your definition of Tact in selling?
2. Don't you think Aggressiveness might overcome any deficiency in your Tact? Why?
3. Don't you think it is rather silly to bother with the Golden Rule in selling?
4. How many different types of prospects can you remember?
5. What do you think is the most desirable quality in the handling of your prospects?
6. What would you consider the three most difficult types of prospects to sell?
7. What would you consider the three easiest types of prospects to sell?
8. What kind of picture does the term "Handling of Prospects" bring up in your mind?

9. At what stage in the selling process is the "Handling of Prospects" important?

10. Why is selling so much concerned with the subject of prospecting?

Study Suggestions

1. From the twenty-five prospect types listed, select five types that you think you could develop into permanent customers, and tell why.

2. List the different types of prospects you think you could develop into personal friends, and state why they have such possibilities.

3. List the prospect types you think might prove undependable, and indicate how you would handle them.

4. Select the toughest type of prospect in the list, and mention five things you might do to keep him interested.

5. Select the easiest type of prospect in the list, and mention five things you might do to develop his friendship for you.

CHAPTER VII

How to Warm Up the Prospect

PROSPECTS are human beings. They run both hot and cold, as well as lukewarm. Getting the prospect warmed up to your proposition, is the only way to manoeuver him into a receptive mood. And to get your sales message across, you must strike while the prospect is hot!

The smart salesman resorts to familiar strategy to remove the curse of chilliness from a lukewarm contact. The warming-up process is neither more nor less complicated than any similar effort we might make to transform a desirable casual acquaintance into a warm friendship, bearing in mind, naturally, that friendship in business is a highly profitable path to more business.

Quite properly, too. No one can criticize a salesman for intentionally building up a business friendship so long as the end result is not entirely selfish and so long as the building-up process contains the elements of mutual regard, respect and benefit. The difficult problem is to be able to steer a middle course between too much formality and too great familiarity.

Selling is a double-acting affair. No salesman makes a good sale unless he helps the buyer. No buyer makes a good buy unless he helps both himself and the salesman. The process of warming up the prospect is not only perfectly legitimate—it is absolutely indispensable in creative selling. It is the *mutuality* of the process that makes it good strategy, good salesmanship and good business!

There are many ways of warming up a lukewarm prospect. Here are just ten groups of different ideas. Many more can be added by salesmen during the course of their experience.

Constructive Calling

Too many salesmen wear out their welcome and cool off their prospect by making too many calls on him. Other salesmen accomplish the same misfortune by talking too much and wearing the prospect down. Both are excellent methods of committing sales suicide.

Making more and more calls on the same prospect is seldom good salesmanship. Fewer calls but more intelligent calls on the same man will develop more genuine warmth and build more constructive business. If the salesman has a definite creative reason for making a call, well and good. If he calls only to pass the time of day and "see what's doing," the chances are he is wasting the prospect's time and building up a source of irritation.

The man who opens his mouth and lets it run along like a cold water faucet, finds his prospect reaching the same temperature as the water. If he could only be made to realize that a *little* conversation is the shortest way to the dotted line, he would soon learn to talk much less but more skillfully. It doesn't take very much verbiage to talk yourself out of all prospects of an order, if you don't give your prospect an opportunity to think himself into a receptive mood!

Creative Selling

The experienced salesman sells a prospect in his mind long before he calls on him. He visualizes the prospect's need in the light of the product he has to sell. He originates the ideal combination of the two, and creates whatever adaptation is necessary of the one to the other. Then he presents his creative idea to the prospect as a specific solution of the condition to be corrected or the problem to be solved. If and when certain changes may be necessary, he is capable of suggesting such changes and again presenting his idea as a revised plan of his own creation.

That is creative selling—and that's the type of selling that has a better than fifty-fifty chance of warming up the prospect to the sparking point! Compare this with the kind of so-called selling that makes a number of casual calls on the off chance of striking an occasional buyer. Just a case of co-ordinated head-work as against haphazard foot-work!

Factory Contacts

Fortunate indeed is the salesman who has a constructive factory force to back up his work in the field. An occasional visit from a factory engineer; a letter that discusses the prospect's problems from the viewpoint of a dependable technical background; a circular that tells an interesting story of some new process that has direct application to the prospect's needs; all these things, and many more, have a warming influence on the prospect's mind and result in a keener receptiveness to the salesman's presentation.

The factory help that can be presented in specific individualized form proves a real help to both the salesman and the prospect. This is the kind of sales assistance that pays big dividends. The only pity is that more factories do not get the vision and do not back up their salesmen more effectively.

Product Personality

In these days of intense interest in modern design, we find that many products have distinctive personalities the same as human beings. Very frequently a prospect may be made interested in newly developed modern lines or styles or colors or uses of your product as against a competitive product. He may be intrigued with the idea of contemplated improvements or special designs for his own exclusive use. He may become interested in special samples made up and submitted to him. He may be offered the opportunity to incorporate his own ideas and suggestions in the product. To this extent it may reflect his own personality or the personality of his business.

There is nothing farfetched about this. Many a prospect has been brought into the fold by an offer of this kind extended by a salesman or by a factory man who has a quantity of creative vision and imagination as part of his sales equipment.

Personal Approaches

Probably the most warming of all influences on a prospect results from the salesman's personality and from the character and extent of his personal contacts.

Contacts develop into acquaintances; acquaintances develop into friendships. The more friendly a salesman can keep his contacts, the more surely does he push up his average of closings. The important thing for him to remember is that the contact is not an end in itself, but only the means to an end!

There are myriad ways for the tactful salesman to make the advances necessary to warm up his contacts with a prospect and eventually to strike up a friendship. The

telephone, local and long distance, keeps open the lines
of cordial contacting when personal calls are impossible
or undesirable. The mails offer a lane of communication
that runs the entire gamut from serious quotations and
specifications to the transmission of interesting ideas and
constructive suggestions, down to chatty personal notes
on a sociable level. The ripening of friendship between
salesman and prospect invariably includes valuable opportunity for more personal contacts at luncheons, meetings,
clubs, dinners, theaters, golf games, baseball games, foot-
ball games, etc., etc.

Opportunities and ideas for personal approaches are
not lacking. The difficulty lies in keeping oneself within
proper bounds. The salesman must be careful not to carry
his friendly advances to tactless extremes. It requires no
little diplomacy to strike a happy medium between the
formality that chills and the familiarity that breeds contempt.

Advertising Angles

Advertising portfolios have long been used to get the
prospect warmed up to a new line. This type of presentation is standard. It has no elements of novelty or newness.
It meets with varying success, with occasional misgivings,
and sometimes even with suspicion. As a result, to be entirely successful it should be more than just an average
advertising campaign.

The kind of advertising that gets a prospect more
easily interested, is that which has possibilities of a personal tie-up. Whether it be through the use of his signature slug, or through publicity stories, or radio announcements, or localized outdoor posters, or direct mail tie-ups,
the prospect warms up more certainly when he himself

has an opportunity to become individually connected with the advertising idea.

Present your advertising idea along this line and it may become the life-line that binds you to the prospect. Remember, if you can personify or personalize any of your publicity with the reflection of your prospect, the odds of getting him warmed up and sold are highly in your favor!

Sales Promotion Possibilities

There's a splendid way to get the prospect warmed up! Talk about the sales promotion possibilities of *your* line, and the sales possibilities in *his* line—and you are talking right down the prospect's alley.

Show him some of the point-of-sale material you have for him and some of the window displays you are using. If you have any plan for a demonstration campaign, either in the store or in the home, use it as a trump card and play it up strong.

Sales promotion plans designed to help the prospect sell *his* stock, are the type that will help you sell *your* stock. Remember, it is not how much *you* sell that counts, but how much the prospect can sell. If you can sell him on the idea that your sales promotion plans and ideas will help *him* sell *his* stock, you can take him out of the lukewarm class like forked lightning. And if your sales promotion plans *will* work that way, don't be bashful about getting the idea across with all your power, so that he cannot possibly forget it.

Marketing Aspects

Problems of distribution are constantly changing. New times and new conditions bring new methods of distribution, and these new methods are of intense interest to the prospect. It is up to the salesman to keep abreast of modern trends; to learn all he can about what is going on today so that he may be able to advise the prospect what might happen tomorrow.

What does it profit the salesman to sell a big bill of goods today, if the prospect's market is in the process of changing so that he cannot sell his goods readily? On the other hand, the salesman in his ignorance of market changes may sell the prospect only one dozen of an item where the new market possibilities may justify an order for a gross.

Modern methods of research; modern methods of extending and dovetailing markets; and new developments in distribution are constantly pushing market horizons backward and creating new zones of activity for both salesman and prospect. They should really be called new zones of *profit*. At the same time, they are profitable only to those who have the ability to find them and to recognize them. Constant study and alertness on the part of the salesman is bound to result in more substantial appreciation on the part of the prospect!

Customer Relations

It is the smart salesman who uses his good relationships with his customers to help bring his new prospects into camp. Use your good customers as brilliant beacons to light the way for your prospects.

No profit-seeking prospect ever closed his ears to the story of a competitor making good with your line! Play up your customers' good selling records and you'll naturally warm up the interest in your prospect's mind. He may say he is not interested, but don't let him kid you.

He may not admit it to you, but the chances are he may lie awake nights figuring out what his competitor is doing that he doesn't do.

Human nature is the same in every line of business. Build up your customer relationships, and then use them as a "bird dog" to trail new prospects and get them warmed up to the profit possibilities in your line. "Here you are, Mr. Prospect; if the Jones Store can do all this, you can do the same thing with the identical conditions in your store; and here's how. . . . !"

Psychological Aspects

The psychology of selling is nothing but common sense properly applied. Or perhaps I should say, uncommonly used. The same with the psychology of warming up a prospect.

Supplying him with the information he asks for, is only half the job. The salesman with experience will supply him also with the answers to the questions he does *not* ask. In many cases, this is more important than the former. The prospect's unuttered objections become stumbling blocks in his own mind when he quietly considers the few things you have told him. It is almost as dangerous to tell a prospect too little as to tell him too much. That's where the salesman's psychological aptitude enters the picture. That's where his experience stands him in good stead. Remember, it is not only what you tell the prospect that counts, but what he remembers!

Test Questions

1. What do we mean by "warming up" a prospect?
2. Describe the "mutuality" of the selling process.

3. What do you think is the difference between "constructive" and "destructive" calling?

4. In what way may a product have a personality?

5. What do you think is the one quality most important in making "personal approaches" to your prospect?

6. How can you get a prospect warmed up with advertising?

7. Why should a sales promotion idea be of help to you?

8. How can you develop your customer relationships into good "bird dogs"?

9. Give a short definition of the "psychology of selling."

10. What do you think are some of the psychological aspects of a selling job?

Study Suggestions

1. Select any product you desire, and give a detailed illustration of "creative selling."

2. Mention and discuss five ways in which your factory could be of help to you out in the field.

3. Tell us in detail how you would acquire new ideas for sales promotion plans, what you would do with them, and how they might help you to sell.

4. Select any product you desire, show how new methods of distributing such a product might be discovered, and mention some recent actual change in distribution methods that you know of.

5. Mention and discuss three different ways in which modern marketing research can be of help to you in your selling.

CHAPTER VIII

How to Build Your Sales Talk

Every good salesman has a double-track brain! One track receives frequent ideas and suggestions from his sales manager and from other executives of the organization, and stores them away for future use. The other track delivers these ideas to the prospect in the form of rapid-fire sales ammunition at the psychological moment. Your thinking apparatus must be in constant repair to keep both tracks functioning regularly, smoothly and effectively.

The average sales talk, whether a "canned" talk or a spontaneous talk made up on the spur of the moment, is merely a collection of good talking points built up in logical sequence to reach a climax that will, figuratively speaking, sweep a prospect off his feet and convince him of the soundness and desirability of your proposition. Every good sales talk has an attention-getting opening; an interesting follow-up; a spectacular demonstration; and an effective closing or climax.

However, the greatest drawback to some sales talks is that they are designed for delivery in long-winded gobs of indigestible conversation or argument. When the salesman gets through with his sales talk (if he does get through with it) the prospect may be so dizzy from the attack that he is "on the ropes" and unable or unwilling either to think or to act.

The ideal sales talk—as I have seen it in successful operation—is not designed for delivery as an uninterrupted speech, but is developed in a series of short, snappy, logically connected talking points and reasons why. It is so grouped and arranged that despite the constant interruptions of the average prospect (which almost always occur) the salesman does not lose his thread of thought or his continuity, but can pick up his prospect's interruption or argument, turn it into a talking point and carry on from that point to the next, smoothly and effectively. You cannot let yourself get flustered by your prospect's interrupting arguments or questions. You must learn to expect these. As a matter of fact, it is frequently desirable to invite such return arguments and questions at logical points in your sales talk, so that you may have the opportunity to shatter his objections as you advance in your presentation.

The finest mental equipment for every salesman is a large reserve collection of talking points that really "go places" in telling and selling the prospect. These talking points enable you to jump in at any point and answer your prospect's objection or argument with a definite, specific reply that will prove convincing and conclusive.

Talking points that point the way to the cash register are the best pointers for any salesman who expects to *sell*. And the best pointers are those that lead to ideas. Ideas stimulate thinking. Thinking develops new desires. New desires build new business. New business results in new profits. New profits develop still more ideas—and thus the circle of selling starts all over again!

There is never a business without an idea—sometimes a flock of ideas. The more ideas you can dig up, the more chances you have of "going places" with your prospect.

There is nothing that interests a prospect so strongly as a new idea, or even an old idea dressed up in new clothing. There are a number of ideas included in these

77 TALKING POINTS THAT GO PLACES IN TELLING AND SELLING THE PROSPECT

Check over these talking points and see how many you are not using. They may suggest new points that you can adapt to suit the varying moods and dispositions of your prospects. Go through these points with a blue pencil. Underline every talking point that seems applicable to your product, merchandise, or service. Then compile all the reasons that you know behind each point. Put these all down in your notebook under the various headings indicated, or under headings of your own preference, and when you have finished you will have a sales presentation that is much stronger than any you have ever had in the past.

Discuss the MERCHANDISE

QUALITY again occupies a position of importance in the buyer's mind. There is a gradual return to quality buying in all lines of business; and salesmen need no longer be timid about presenting higher grade lines. Good quality is cheaper in the long run—and it is the long run that counts! The CHARACTER of your product offers possibilities for interesting discussion. Is it distinctive? Has it features that your competitor's product does not possess? Is it in a class by itself? Has it a novelty appeal, or any unique characteristic that is uncommon? What is the ORIGIN of the product? Is it made of interesting or unusual materials from distant lands? What led to its creation and why does it have exceptional value? Does it fill

a specific need? Was it engineered for modern requirements? Can you weave an interesting story around its
beginnings? Is the STYLE up to the minute? Is it a fashion
that will have a considerable run, or just a fad that may
expire soon? Has it certain style advantages over your
competitor's line? Does it appeal to both sexes, or only
to children, or to all? Is it extreme, or conservative, or
in-between? Are its lines or texture especially pleasing?
Is it made of new and different materials? Will the SUIT-
ABILITY of the product create a place for itself? Does it
fit more exactly into your prospect's requirements? Can it
be used to better advantage or efficiency than some other
product? Why—and how? What is its measure of DESIRA-
BILITY? Will its ownership instill any pride of possession?
Does it supply an esthetic touch that has been lacking?
Will it do a better job, or be easier to handle, or simpler
to operate than something else? Has it intrinsic beauty
that will create joy, or pleasure, or satisfaction?

What is its PRICE class? Will it give better service at a
lower price, or at the same price? Does it justify its extra
price by some extra value? Is there a cash discount or
some special discount that will help put it across? Can
you offer a better price in quantity lots? Is price an important factor, or is it secondary to quality? Is the price
due to its intrinsic value, or to extra styling, convenience,
beauty, or efficiency? Has it the quality of EXCLUSIVE-
NESS? Has it a special feminine appeal for this reason?
Is it a rare pattern or design? Will its possession give
one a feeling of superiority? Is it available in individual
specifications? The question of DURABILITY is important.
Will it outlast another product, and thus add a premium
of greater service for slightly extra cost? Is it easily
destructible, or will it stand much wear and abuse? Is it

made with exceptional strength by using stronger materials?

What is its CONVENIENCE value? Does it solve an awkward handling problem at home or in business? Is it easy to use? Is it convenient to store when not in use? Does it allow more time for other duties or pleasures? Does it add anything to the buyer's convenience? Is it a PATENTED article? Won't the patent give your prospect a certain protection against imitation? Isn't it worth more because of this protection? Isn't the patent an added guarantee of its value? Can you protect your customers against infringement? If the government stands back of your patent, you can stand back of your customers! Is it a TESTED product? Have you a laboratory record to talk about? If not, how has it been tested and how can you prove the test? Has your factory provided you with facts and figures that you can talk about? Or have you an actual sample that you can test in the presence of your prospect?

Stress the Standing of Your COMPANY

Very frequently the AGE of your company makes a splendid talking point. If they have operated a long time, it is an indication of strength and stability. If they have operated a short time, and have accomplished many things, it is an indication of progressiveness. What is the REPUTATION of your company? Is their place in the industry near the top? Do they hold a position of leadership? Is there a strong goodwill value in the name? Have they arrived—or are they comers? How far ahead of the procession are they? And will they stay ahead? What is the SIZE of the company? How much larger than the nearest competitor? Is it impressive because of its size? Are they human and democratic despite their size? Is it a small company with a big reputation for quality; or a large company with a reputation for low price because of its volume?

What about the ORGANIZATION? Is it famous for its creative help, its experience, or its efficiency? Does it include any well-known names? Are they good merchandisers and sales promoters? Can they pass along their merchandising helps to their customers? Are they good mixers out in the field and can they help you with your prospects? Is their INTEGRITY unquestionable? Are they honest and fair in all their dealings with their customers? Do they go more than halfway with the customer? Are they liberal in their allowances and adjustments? What is their FINANCIAL standing? Have they ever been in difficulties? Do they meet their obligations promptly? Do they keep out of the courts? Is their rating an asset in your sales talk? Have they any plans for expansion worth talking about? What do the banks say about them? Is their financial position one of the best in the industry? What is their ETHICAL standing? Have they a strong sense of moral obligation? What was their position under the codes and what is it now? Are they known for their high principles and practices of fair competition? Do they take good care of their employees? Are they in good standing with their suppliers?

Talk About Your FACTORY

What is its SIZE? Is it large enough to be noteworthy? Does it occupy an important position in the industry because of its size? Is it a landmark, or is it just an average factory building? Is it a modern daylight plant with up-to-the-minute conveniences for its employees? How about the EQUIPMENT? Is it modernized and equipped with the latest developments in factory machinery? Is it equipped to do a large-capacity business? Can it turn out rush orders on a rush schedule? Is there an interesting development story in its beginnings and in its enlargements? Where is the LOCATION? Is it a convenient shipping point? Are low freight rates available because of its location? Is it an efficient distributing point for all sections of the country? How about the factory WORKERS? Are they especially skilled in their trade? Is there a large proportion of old-time craftsmen that you can talk about? Have they a good reputation in the industry as well as in the trade? Are they a happy crew, well taken care of? Are their working conditions something to talk about? Are they well paid for high-grade work? Are their working hours in accord with modern ideas? Are they free from labor troubles? Aren't these important points all reflected in the quality and reputation of your product?

What is their reputation for INVENTIVENESS? Have they a number of successful products to their credit? Are they constantly making improvements and developing new products? Can they solve the daily problems that arise in your trade? Do they carry a large INVENTORY? Can they ship on short notice? Can they fill in out-of-stock items in dealers' stores without delay? Or is their merchandise all made to order, with a considerable time-lag between shipments? How far ahead can you protect your customers? Can they manufacture special items quickly to help out? Are they inclined to be cooperative in this respect? Have they a good REPLACEMENT service? Can repair parts be shipped promptly? Are repair parts kept in stock or made to order? Are they furnished at reasonable charge? Aren't these important points with your customers? How about the PACKING service? Do they know their stuff when it comes to packing the merchandise for safety and convenience? Do their containers protect the merchandise better than your competitor's? Are their packages easy to handle and convenient to open? How about their SHIPPING service? Are they equipped to break down large shipments into small package lots for shipment to various points? Is this service an asset and a help to your customer?

Flatter Your CUSTOMER

Compliment him on his DISCRIMINATION in selecting your product. Point out the prestige of your company's name as it affects the development of his reputation among his trade. Build up his PRIDE OF POSSESSION in your quality merchandise among his family, his friends, his employees, his trade. Show him how the MODERNITY of your product will be reflected to his credit wherever he uses it. He should be glad to be up-to-date. Play up the question of PROFIT in your lines as against some other line with a smaller margin or with less consumer appeal. In asking him to stock your merchandise, use the personal FRIENDSHIP angle wherever you can. Everything else being equal, this is what frequently turns the trick. Mention his increased EFFICIENCY in the use of your product and show him how much time and money he can save. Comment on the extra APPEARANCE value of your product in his store or office, as against your competitor's product. Don't overlook the DESIRABILITY angle of your merchandise in the minds of himself, his employees, his customers, his family. If it is a finer article that will arouse the envy of the other fellow, so much the better. Remember to discuss the CONVENIENCE of your product, as regards its operation, its handling, its delivery, its packing and shipping. Above all, don't forget the feature of DISPLAY value in his windows, on his counters and shelves. This feature alone has sold many a product for many a salesman. Thank him for his CONSIDERATION in letting you demonstrate your product. Yes, indeed—applesauce still catches more flies than vinegar; and no matter how big a big-shot or how small a little-shot he may be, COURTESY still makes more friends than nonchalance!

Insinuate Your PERSONAL Value

How can you use your EXPERIENCE to help your prospect? Have you been engaged in his lines of business? Do you know his problems? Can you suggest solutions that will convince him of your value to him? Have you had experience with related lines? Don't be bashful about cashing in on your experience—it is worth money to both of you. How about your personal BACKGROUND? Does your education tie up with your prospect? Did it fit you to give advice on matters that trouble him? Do you come from the same town? Do you know the same people? Have you the same friends? Who knows—perhaps you both graduated from the same school; friendship bonds have been tightened on less than that. What features of HELPFULNESS can you offer? Can you work with his clerks; make suggestions to his organization; advise him on his advertising, or sales promotion, or merchandising? Can you be of help in getting him unusual service from your factory? Can you suggest creative ideas for store or window display? When you get right down to it—what good are you, anyway? That's what he wants to know! Can you sell him on your LOYALTY? How will you prove it? Have you other customers who will talk up for you? Have you the backbone to fight for your customer's rights —even against your factory? Or do you think your factory is entitled to all the breaks? Does your ENTHUSIASM put you across with him? Can you generate the same feeling in him? Why not? Whose fault is it? Are you genuinely enthusiastic about your merchandise, or do you just shout about it because you have to? Think you can get anywhere without enthusiasm? Yeah . . . ?

What kind of SERVICE can you give him on orders, shipments, replacements, emergencies? Do you know what it means to run out of stock unexpectedly and be caught in a jam? Does your factory know? Do they care? What does your prospect think of your DEPENDABILITY? Think he is ready to trust you with all his business in your line? Do you keep your word to him, or do your promises flow too freely? Does he know anything about the bright side of your dealings with other customers? Why not? Don't you think it would make an impression on him? Is he acquainted with any of your other contacts? How about your attitude of FRIENDLINESS? Do you go more than halfway to make friends, or do you expect him to make the advances? Do you understand what real friendliness is, or do you confuse it with familiarity? You know, you might be a friend of his and still not call him by his first name or buy him a drink. Ever think of his family, his secretary, his assistants? Have you any FRATERNITY point of contact with him? What school, what college, what lodge, what club? Do you do anything that he likes to do, and can you talk about it? Or do you think business is just cold-blooded business? How about your HOSPITALITY? Have you ever taken him to lunch, to a ball game, to a show, to a meeting? Have you ever asked him? How do you know he won't go?

Develop the INSPIRATIONAL Angle

Does your merchandise have any characteristics of STIMULATION? Is it exciting or provocative in its use? Does it lead to thoughts of romance? Does it make the customer want to "go places and do things"? Is it ARTISTIC in its make-up or in its eventual surroundings? Has it any aesthetic atmosphere or value? Is it in GOOD TASTE? Is it something that is used by discriminating buyers? Does your prospect have that kind of trade? Is it SMART? Has it any assets of fashionableness or effectiveness? If so, does it have universal appeal? Will the masses buy it, or does it have a restricted market? Is it DECORATIVE in itself, or in its setting? Is it modern or modernistic? Is it sensibly styled, or extreme? Because of this, will it last indefinitely, or just a short while? Is it ORIGINAL in its design, or is it some new application of an old product or principle? Is it widely IMITATED, or is it apt to be? Is there any protection against ruinous imitation, or is it difficult to duplicate? Is it protected by copyright or patent? Has it a special NOVELTY value that lifts it above competition? Is it timely? Does it tie in with some occurrence or notable event?

Has it a BEAUTY that is beyond the ordinary in articles of similar manufacture? Does this give it a greater market value? Is it a LUXURY either in its use or in its manufacture? Is there a good market for that type of luxury? Or is it a NECESSITY that will make a market for itself wherever it goes? What other necessity does it displace or improve upon? Is it a PRACTICAL product, or is it inclined to be tricky in its application or difficult in its use? Has it any SENSATIONAL feature worth talking about? Does it include any new departure or development in its line? Has it the added value of being a DOUBLE-USE product, either in itself or in its container? If so, doesn't that add to its value and to its market? Does it offer the possibility of RELATED selling? Will it help sell any other merchandise in your prospect's business? That's an important item, isn't it? Is it especially EFFICIENT in the things it does or accomplishes? Can its efficiency be traced or quoted in terms of dollars and cents, or time, or pleasure, or convenience?

Feature the PUBLICITY Program

He will be interested in the NEWSPAPER advertising. Will it be in his territory? Will it tie up with his store? Will it carry his name? Also the PUBLICATION advertising. Will there be any schedule in general magazines, women's magazines, class or trade journals? Will there be any reprints or giant blow-ups that he can use? Is any RADIO broadcasting contemplated? What will it be—chain or spot? And will it reach his customers? How will it be merchandised? What about the program of DIRECT-MAIL advertising? Will it be mailed by him or by the manufacturer? Will it carry his imprint? How will it be written —from the standpoint of the manufacturer or of the retailer? How much will it cost him? Will there be any POINT-OF-SALE material available? Posters, easels, hangers, signs, window displays? Will he have to pay for it? What proportion? Have you some samples to show him? Do you expect to use OUTDOOR advertising? What will it consist of—boards, electric spectaculars, building signs, road signs? Where will they be located and will he have a voice in the locations? Will it carry his name? Will it play up his store, or the manufacturer? Will there be any CAR CARDS? And where will they run—in streetcars, busses, trains, subways? And who will pay for that? And what proportion?

How about a SAMPLING campaign? Will there be neighborhood distribution, or will they be handed out in his store? Will you furnish the samples? Who will pay for the distribution? Do you expect to use DEMONSTRATIONS? Are you going to furnish demonstrators for his store, or for some show, or will there be a home demonstration campaign? Will it be a cooperative campaign, or are you going to pay for it? Do you expect to use NOVELTIES of any kind? Will they be inexpensive give-aways, available to the masses, or will they be items for selected prospects? Does your product lend itself to reproduction in miniature? And last, but not least, how about your PACKAGE? Does it lend itself to effective display, either on the shelf, the counter, or as a part of the window display? Is it colorful, or a novelty container, or an odd shape? Does it stand out in a group of assorted products? Has it a distinctive character? Does it stack easily, handle conveniently, store safely and efficiently? Most important of all, is it interesting and does it have a recognizable identification?

TEST QUESTIONS

1. What do we mean by a "double-track brain"?
2. What do we mean by a "canned" sales talk?
3. What do you think is the most important aspect of a good canned sales talk, and how would you use it?
4. What is the most important quality surrounding good talking points?

5. How, where, and from whom would you acquire new talking points?

6. In what way do good talking points stimulate the circle of selling?

7. How could you develop good talking points from your own business?

8. What do you think would be the four most interesting types of talking points?

9. Do you think talking points built around your company or your factory would be as valuable as those built around your merchandise? Why?

10. In what way do you think you could develop talking points that would have the greatest amount of personal interest to your customer?

Study Suggestions

1. State carefully how you could use a "canned" sales talk in your daily work and yet make it seem spontaneous and interesting.

2. What do we mean by "talking points that point the way to the cash register"? List ten of these so-called "cash register" talking points.

3. Explain in what way talking points built around "your personal value" could help you to sell, and list five such talking points.

4. Discuss the inspirational angle of talking points and compare their value to those built around the publicity program.

5. Select ten of the most important talking points in the section on "merchandise" and list them in their order of importance as you see them.

CHAPTER IX

How to Answer Sales Objections

THE one bugbear that constantly stumps many salesmen is the objections that are bound to be raised by his prospect. Every prospect is just a human being; and it is only human to object to being sold anything, no matter how good it may be. There is only one way to lose the fear of the prospect's objections—and that is, to be so thoroughly familiar with all possible objections, and to be so completely equipped to answer them to your own advantage, that you actually *invite* his objections so that you may be able to turn them into selling points.

When a prospect says, "I don't want it"—he may not always mean what he says. There is always a possibility —and frequently a probability—that he merely hopes to get rid of you; he is afraid that if you talk to him much longer, you might sell him something!

The wide-awake salesman endeavors to turn every objection into a selling point; and, as a matter of fact, I don't know of a single objection that cannot be answered constructively. The only sales objections that will stump you are those that you are in doubt about yourself—which is just another way of saying that you probably need to be resold on your line before you can sell your prospect.

In the usual everyday routine of selling any service,

product, or merchandise, there are a certain number of objections that recur again and again. Here are

25 SALES OBJECTIONS AND ANSWERS

that pack a real sales wallop and make it possible to turn prospect excuses into selling points that bring home the bacon!

1. *"Your Price Is Too High"*

Are you sure about that, or is your standard too low? A quality product deserves a quality price. Figured on the basis of durability, satisfaction, and prestige, this is actually the lowest-price product on the market. Figure it out for yourself by the simplest arithmetic. If you pay only ten or twenty per cent more for a product that lasts twice as long and gives twice the service and satisfaction, which is the cheaper? Regardless of what you buy, you get only what you pay for; and if you pay a cheap price, you get a cheap product. The important measuring stick is not price, but value; what is the greatest value you can get for your money?

2. *"Your Quality Is Too Good"*

No quality has *ever* been too good for the American public! Don't forget that there is a "return to quality" today in every type of buying. The better the product, the more it is sought after. The longer it lasts, the cheaper it becomes. A quality product really gives the buyer an extra premium in return for his discriminating selection. I don't care who buys your merchandise—the persuasion of quality will exert a terrific appeal and will frequently draw the few extra pennies out of the customer's pocket without the slightest pressure.

3. *"I'll Wait Until the Price Is Lower"*

You may wait if you wish, but you will be the principal loser. Chances are ten to one that in this rising market prices will go higher instead of lower. Consumption is increasing by leaps and bounds, and the natural law of supply and demand is gradually forcing up the prices of the raw materials that go into this product. In the meantime, you are losing two profits: one that you make in buying at the present market price, and the other that you will make in selling it to your customer. If you haven't got it in stock, you can't sell it; and when you get ready to buy it, you'll probably pay five to ten per cent more and kick yourself around for not having bought at the low.

4. *"I'm Overstocked Right Now"*

You only think you are, because you're looking at it from the wrong angle. As a matter of fact, you are *understocked* right now because you haven't got a product of this quality in your store. When a good customer comes in and is willing to buy a better piece of merchandise, you're out of luck. You not only get a black eye for not keeping better stuff in stock, but you lose an extra profit, too. The advertising and publicity back of this product will go practically halfway in making the sale for you and in increasing your turnover. Your salespeople need only do their regular selling job. If you are worried only about the mass of cheaper merchandise you have in stock, I can show you how to get rid of that. Put a little more advertising and pressure back of it until you have reduced your stock and then you'll have plenty of space for a product like this, with its extra profit for you.

5. "I Can't Get the Boss's Okay"

Why not? What is his principal objection? Or haven't you sold him on it because you are not sold on it yourself? If you're not enthusiastic about it, you certainly cannot arouse the boss's enthusiasm. Have you any objection to my seeing the boss about it? Come along with me and I'll sell you both at the same time! After all, the boss is interested in profit just as much as you are; if he cannot see the profit in this, it is only because it has not been fully demonstrated. Have you told him that So-and-so is handling this line and making money on it? Have you told him what we are willing to do to help you put it over? Have you pointed out the detailed differences between this product and what you are now carrying in stock? If anybody ought to be able to sell the boss, you should; and if you can't, the fault is probably mine in not having been able to sell you on it!

6. "I'll Have to Get Competitive Prices"

What good will that do you? All you can do is possibly get cheaper prices for cheaper merchandise. You cannot get this grade at a lower price. The thing you are mostly interested in is merchandise of this quality—and quality always costs a little more because it is worth the difference. Even your customers know that. Competitive prices will only tell you that you can buy cheaper merchandise, and you knew that a long time ago. Anybody can quote you a cheaper price on any type of product you ask for —but the lower the price, the cheaper the merchandise. You've got all the low-end merchandise you need. What you need is a quality product that will help you to trade up your customers and build up your profit!

7. *"Money Is Too Tight Right Now"*

What do you mean, tight? Do you mean money itself or do you mean your inferiority complex on money? Money is loosening up daily, and there's more money in circulation today than there has been for several years. More people are at work; more wages and salaries are being paid out; more consumption of necessities is occurring; and there is a greater demand for the better and finer things of life than we have seen for many years. Even the bankers are loosening up; and a vast amount of money is available today for credit at reasonable rates. Better times are here right now; and the harder we go after the business the better we make it.

8. *"I Should Get Lower Prices on This Repeat Order"*

On the contrary, one of the things that should make you feel safer with us is the fact that we have only one price for everyone, regardless of how often they repeat. The fact that you give us a repeat order doesn't lower the cost of manufacture for us. It will cost us exactly as much to make up this order for you, as the last one. The thing that governs our price is the quantity you buy; and anyone else who buys the same quantity can get the same price. The one thing we *can* do for our regular customers is to go out of our way to give you the finest kind of service, and you can certainly depend on my doing that. This is a one-price house with the same square deal for all.

9. *"There Is No Demand for Your Product"*

That doesn't mean a thing; and it sounds like the old query: "Which came first, the chicken or the egg?" Demand is a state of mind that is frequently brought on by the aggressiveness and initiative of the retailer. Do you mean to tell me you had a demand for every article in your store before you bought it? Don't forget that credit must be given to the buyer with imagination who can visualize the demand he can develop for any particular product. If you are sold on it, you can sell your customer on it. As a matter of fact, the customer is delighted to see a new product or a better product in your store. All you need to do is present it, demonstrate it and talk about it!

10. "I Won't Deal with Your House"

Well, there must be a reason for that. Won't you tell me what it is? Didn't the other man treat you right; or did the firm fail you in an emergency; or wasn't the last shipment up to specifications; or what? You must have some complaint or reason for feeling the way you do, and I'd like to clear it up. Why cut off your nose to spite your face? And why make a new man suffer for the misdeeds of the old? Be a sport and tell me what the trouble was and you can bet I'll go the limit in straightening it out for you. After all, no one is perfect; we are just as apt to make an occasional mistake as you are; but we try never to make the same mistake twice. I need your business and you ought to have our merchandise; and I'll certainly get a black eye at the factory if I can't make a friend of you. That's what I want to do!

11. "I Must Have a Special Discount for Quantity"

I'm sorry, Mr. Jones; I would certainly like to be able to give you a special discount, but my hands are tied. As I told you before, we are a one-price house and we have exactly the same discount for all. Our regular terms are 2 per cent 10 days, net 30 days, and we have never been known to deviate. That's the very thing that should sell you on the idea of dealing with a house like ours; you can always feel positive that no one can get a better deal than you. The trouble with some manufacturers is that they occasionally have preferential discounts for special customers, with the result that you never know where you are. With us, you can always feel certain of getting just as good a discount as anyone else, no matter how long they have dealt with us.

12. "Your Factory Is Too Far Away"

Yes, I realize that we are a thousand miles away, but that shouldn't have the slightest effect on your desire for our quality merchandise. We can give you as good service as any other manufacturer. We are on the main line of Such-and-such railroad; freight rates are low; fast freight service is available any time; and in case of emergency we can ship by express. Yes, I know that So-and-so's factory is right here in town; but what you are interested in primarily is our quality of merchandise and not the convenience of their factory.

13. "Our Business Is Different"

Yes, sir, I certainly do realize that; and that's exactly why I came in to see you instead of going to So-and-so down the street. For our type of merchandise we require a more constructive type of businessman and a different type of business than the ordinary run of stores. We find that the man who runs the "different" type of business usually has the necessary courage and vision to stock a product of our high quality. Our merchandise is different from ordinary merchandise, and we always try to sell a store that is different from ordinary stores.

14. "You Don't Buy Anything from Us"

That's quite right, Mr. Jones; but it is only because we don't believe in reciprocal buying of the forced kind. We don't attempt to come in here and buy from you just so as to place you under obligation to buy from us. We like to feel that our merchandise is strong enough to stand on its own feet and to make its own way regardless of who the buyer is; and I'm sure you feel that way about your own merchandise, don't you? That doesn't mean we wouldn't be glad to buy from you after we became acquainted. We just don't tie ourselves up with reciprocal buying obligations, and I'm sure you don't want to, either. We want you to feel perfectly free to buy wherever you wish, regardless of whether we buy from you or not.

15. "I Pay So-and-so Less than Your Price"

I am perfectly willing to believe that, but at the same time you get merchandise that is of lesser quality than this. After all, you get only what you pay for in this world. You cannot get high quality at a low price; that is the millennium; but you can pay a fair price and get quality so high that the *eventual* cost of that merchandise is less than the price quoted on cheap merchandise. That is what produces repeat business from your customers and cuts down the expensive returned-goods evil. And that is what will bring us repeat business from you!

16. "This Cheaper Product Is Good Enough"

Nothing is good enough for the American citizen. He is always looking for something better; and when he finds it, that is where he does his shopping. If you will only consider the development of luxury buying in this country you will realize that there is always a market waiting to be developed for something better. If you make a practice of keeping only cheaper merchandise in your store, you run the risk of losing a great number of customers who continually shop around for higher grade merchandise than you can offer them.

17. "Your Company Is Too Small"

That is the very reason we do such a big-capacity business. Most people like to do business with a company our size because we are not too big to lose sight of the personal contacts that are so necessary in developing friendships. And we can give you that necessary personal service that is so important to you in developing special merchandise and special ideas to suit your business. Yes, we may be a smaller company than some you know; but you will notice that we are rated even higher than some of the larger companies. Smallness of size is an asset these days because of the personal touch that is possible with our executives; and knowing you as we do, we can frequently do more for you than a larger company could.

18. "We Cannot Afford to Buy Now"

I'm sorry to disagree with you, but that is a fallacy that is easily disproved. I merely use the old familiar saying that you cannot afford *not* to buy now, for four specific reasons: First, prices will undoubtedly go up in the near future because of natural advances in cost of raw materials; second, you cannot afford to pass up the profits in this grade of merchandise; third, you cannot afford to remain understocked as you are now without merchandise of this character; fourth, you dare not take the risk of losing customers who will go shopping elsewhere for this merchandise.

19. *"We Have Always Done Business with So-and-so"*

Far be it from me to interfere with any relations you may have with a competitor. I merely want to suggest that it is not always advisable to have all your irons in one fire. Some day you may be glad to have an extra source of supply. After all, even your regular supplier cannot furnish you with all the newer developments in your merchandise; and if you are to avoid getting into a rut of having only one type of merchandise, you will want to maintain contact with another reliable organization. The fact that you do so is no disloyalty to your regular supplier; it is merely a necessary safety factor for your own protection.

20. *"You Can't Meet My Budget"*

I'm just wondering, Mr. Jones, if you haven't put the cart before the horse in setting up a budget before knowing what kind of merchandise you were going to buy. Instead of fitting the merchandise to your budget, it might be advisable for you to rearrange your budget to fit merchandise of our quality. You can always change the figures in your budget, but you cannot always sell the wrong kind of merchandise.

21. *"Your Materials Are Not Genuine"*

I'm afraid, Mr. Jones, you have been listening to some of our competitors who have not been altogether ethical. In the first place, we have the reputation of being the highest grade supplier in our industry. In the second place, we have spent about forty years specializing in our type of merchandise, and if anyone knows good materials, we should. In the third place, here is the merchandise in question and I'll be glad to tear it apart just to prove to you how it is made. And finally, if we had ever dared to use substitute materials it would have affected both our reputation and our business; whereas our business figures show a regular and steady increase in volume every year, and our name has become a hallmark of quality everywhere.

22. "Your Styles Are Not Up to Date"

As far as I can see, the only reason for that statement is the fact that we do not have as many faddish novelties as some of our competitors. Ours is a business of great stability because we play up the styles that are preferred by customers of good taste; and it is those customers who buy the better grade of merchandise. Temporary fads and short-lived novelties are relegated to the rear in our scheme of manufacture; and for that very reason, the stores who stock our character of merchandise enjoy the same stability in their business that we do in ours. That doesn't mean we don't produce any novelties at all; but it does mean that we usually keep clear of great extremes.

23. "So-and-so Gets a Better Price Than I do"

Yes, I agree with you, he does; but the only reason for that is that he buys our merchandise in much larger quantities. You know as well as I do that the price of all merchandise is regulated by quantity. In manufacturing larger quantities at one time we can effect certain economies in production, which are passed on to the buyer. Exactly the same prices for similar quantities are available to you, or for that matter to anyone else. That is the advantage of doing business with a firm that has only one schedule of prices.

24. "That's Pretty Expensive Merchandise"

Well, it all depends on what you consider expensive, Mr. Jones. If you compare our prices with our competitor's prices, it is true that we are exactly fifteen per cent above him. But if you place our merchandise and our competitor's merchandise side by side, feel the material, consider the quality, and realize that it will give your customer fifty to one hundred per cent more service, then you see that our competitor's merchandise is much more expensive. In the meantime, the customer has the joy and satisfaction of our finer materials; and the more he enjoys his purchase, the more he thinks of you. It is all in the point of view and how that point of view is presented to the customer.

25. "I Can Beat Your Price, Anyway"

I don't doubt that in the least; but the one thing you cannot do is to equal our quality. So far as price alone is concerned, almost any competitor of ours can beat our price, especially if he knows we are in the running. But after all, price itself is the least important element. One must consider so many more vitally important factors in any merchandise or trading transaction. Prices are constantly subject to mutilation and fluctuation, but that is not the case with long-standing reputations for integrity and fair dealing such as we enjoy.

Test Questions

1. How many different things might a prospect **really** mean when he says: "I don't want it"?

2. How can you turn a sales objection into a selling point?

3. What do you think is the one sales objection most frequently raised?

4. If a prospect objects to buying merchandise of high quality, is he right or wrong—and why?

5. What is wrong with the objection: "Money is too tight right now"?

6. What is the answer to the prospect who says: "There is no demand for your product"?

7. What would you tell the man who insists upon reciprocal buying?

8. What is the right answer to the prospect who says he doesn't want to give up his regular source of supply?

9. What would you tell the man who complains that his competitor gets a better price than you are quoting him?

10. How would you answer the man who says he can beat your price?

Study Suggestions

1. After you have decided which is the most commonly raised sales objection, state why it is so, and give three constructive answers.

2. How many different types of sales objections can you remember; and which do you think is the easiest and which the hardest to answer?

3. Consider the prospect whose objections are all concerned with the subject of price. Mention three different answers designed to take his mind away from price.

4. How would you answer the man who complains that your company is too small; it is too far away; and he doesn't want to deal with your company anyway?

5. Do you think it is a good or bad thing for the prospect to raise objections? Explain in detail why, and how you might be helped in your selling.

CHAPTER X

How to Avoid Lost Sales

It is a well-known fact that none of us is perfect—which is possibly one of the reasons we are still human beings. But if we ever sat down with ourselves to analyze, honestly and confidentially, the reasons for our lost sales, we would be astonished at the findings.

I have known a lot of salesmen during the past fifteen years—including myself—and it has been interesting to catalogue the alibis and to see how many of them sounded the same familiar strain and fell into the same old groove.

I have come to the conclusion that if all the sales lost by salesmen could be laid out end-to-end—and analyzed for their weak links—many of the reasons would be found in the following list:

1. High Hat. This salesman had seen better days and still considered himself far, far above his present status. Instead of using his past experience and knowledge to make his present job bigger and better, he high-hatted the world without realizing that he was only high-hatting himself! In talking with his prospect, his self-important attitude was so obvious and so overbearing that the prospect was smothered—he just naturally didn't have a chance, and gave up in irritation and disgust.

2. Bad Temper. This man couldn't "take it" when it came to price competition. He didn't realize that he couldn't possibly get all the business and that he had to take an occasional price beating, even though his product was better. There are all kinds of buyers in the world—and this one was price-conscious more than quality-conscious. When the salesman lost the order, he also lost control and flew off the handle at his customer. Result—he himself closed the door to a return call later on and lost a valuable customer on whom he had spent a lot of time. Next time he loses an order, this man is going to be a better sport about it.

3. Impatience. Trying to rush a prospect into a quick decision is sometimes equivalent to rushing yourself out of consideration. This salesman had given his prospect the whole story. His merchandise was okay; his prices looked fairly reasonable; and he was well on the way toward getting the order—but he couldn't give the prospect time enough to make up his mind. He didn't notice that his prospect was the slow, careful type of buyer who had to make doubly certain about every little detail before going ahead. Because of his impatience, the salesman lost his poise—the prospect lost his confidence—and the company lost the business!

4. Disagreeable Aggressiveness. There are still some so-called salesmen out in the field who have an idea that salesmanship consists of walking into a prospect's office, engaging him in a verbal battle, and dragging the order out of him. A system like this may work in the squared ring; but in cornering this particular customer, the salesman should have known that an ounce of persuasiveness would have had sixteen times more value than a pound of aggressiveness. Some schools teach salesmanship on the principle that you've got to *force* your prospect to give you the order—but they sometimes forget to add that the moral force of diplomacy beats the big stick forty ways. Nobody likes a salesman who is extreme—least of all a prospect. If you can't be nice, at least be careful—you may want to call on him again!

5. *Procrastination.* Here is a sad, sad story. The salesman had the order signed, sealed, and delivered on that rarest of days—a Saturday morning. Instead of putting it right into the mail so that the factory would have it bright and early Monday morning, he stuck it in his pocket, went out to the ball game—and forgot all about it until he walked into his office on Monday. Result: the factory didn't get the order until Wednesday, by which time the customer was expecting the rush shipment—and getting madder 'n' madder every minute!

6. *Crape-hanging.* Call him a calamity-howler, if you prefer. His middle name was "depression." Business was still pretty bad; Bill Jones had just gone broke and lost his store; the New Deal was all wrong; everybody was out of step but himself. By the time his prospect had started thinking seriously about his line, he had begun worrying seriously about his business and wondering whether it was such a smart thing to buy more goods now. An extreme case? Not at all!

7. *Sorehead.* This salesman thought he lost business only because the world was against him. His failures got his goat and he went around his territory with a chip on his shoulder. Lord help the prospect who questioned his prices, or kidded him about his job, or made a constructive criticism of his merchandise! One day he ran into a prospect who seemed to think that his competitor's line was as good as his—and said so. As a matter of fact, the prospect wasn't so sure about it himself. He wanted to draw out the salesman's arguments and become thoroughly sold on the line before he ordered. But the sales-

man couldn't stand the mention of his competitor. He got huffy and all but insulted the prospect for even presuming to mention any other line.

8. Poor Main Office Support. This man was up against a lack of cooperation at home. The prospect wanted detailed information about the technical aspects of the product. The salesman wrote to the main office; but in the absence of the sales manager on a road trip the letter lay around for a week before it was answered—and then the information given was sketchy and incomplete, as if they resented the prospect's demand for details. Of course, this wouldn't have happened had the sales manager been at home; but cannot things be handled carefully even if the sales manager is away?

9. No Advertising Support. Here was a salesman talking to a prospect about a new product—something the prospect had never heard of before. The factory thought their reputation on other products would carry this one along to rapid acceptance. They not only provided no publication advertising; they didn't even send a circular or a form letter out to the trade. They left it all up to the salesman—and it was impossible for the salesman to break down the prospect's resistance entirely without publicity support. Just a little too much to ask of any salesman!

10. Lack of Follow-up. This man had made several calls on the prospect and had given him up as a bad job. What he didn't know was that the prospect was getting ready to open a branch office in another city in his territory. By that time he had dropped him from his list and had stopped calling on him, with the result that he lost a chance at an opening order that would have repaid him for all the previous calls he had made. How could he have prevented that? Well, an occasional telephone call would cost him only a nickel and would have maintained his contact with the prospect.

11. Nonclicking Personality. It is quite possible that on rare occasions two personalities just will not click, no matter how nice the salesman tries to be. He must either try another point of contact, or turn the prospect over to his assistant (if he has one), or get the home office to maintain the contact by mail. Of course, the man doesn't like to admit such a failure to his sales manager, fearing a possible reflection on himself; but such a case will happen occasionally to the best salesman.

12. Lack of Enthusiasm. This man wasn't in the best of physical condition and never realized that it reflected in his lack of pep. He couldn't get his prospect enthusiastic on something he couldn't get excited about himself. Enthusiasm breeds enthusiasm, just exactly as the opposite holds true. He couldn't just "take" the order—he had to "sell" it; and he was in no condition to do any constructive selling. As a matter of fact, he was out on a party with a customer the night before and hadn't turned in until three in the morning.

13. Lack of Creative Help. This prospect had a particularly complicated problem to solve. The salesman took a chance at it himself instead of calling for help from the factory experts. By the time he figured out his own inadequate solution, he had his prospect thinking he wasn't competent to be entrusted with his business. All because he wanted to be the whole cheese himself and wouldn't "lower" himself to call on his factory for help. After all, that is what his factory was for!

14. Improper Price Analysis. Here was a prospect who was highly ethical; who despised chiseling and price-cutting; who was willing to buy a good product and pay a fair price. But the salesman couldn't wait to get his business in the regular course of events. He went back with an offer of a slightly lower price on the same product, instead of going back at him with a constructive talk on the value of his quality manufacture in increased satisfaction, in greater durability, and in cutting down the returned-goods evil. Before he got through, the prospect had lost confidence and wouldn't consider *any* price he was offered.

15. *High-pressure Selling.* Most salesmen realize that low-pressure constructive selling is the order of the day; but here was a man who thought he could still high-pressure his prospect into giving him an order "right now!" He rushed into his prospect's office all steamed up with a sales talk that sizzled and reached hysteria as he reached his climax; but all he succeeded in doing was making himself appear ridiculous and reducing his prospect's respect for him. High-pressure selling had its day in the seller's market of the past; despite your optimism, this is still a buyer's market—and don't you forget it!

16. *Knocking Competitors.* Here is another selling evil that went out of fashion many years ago. To this salesman, a competitor's sample was like a red rag. The moment he saw it, he sailed in and did a first-class job of destruction with a flood of well-chosen words, instead of ignoring it and concentrating more strongly on the talking points of his own line. He didn't stop to realize that his prospect knew the merchandise as well as he did. In this particular case, the competitor's sample was even a better job than his own product—and in trying to tear his competitor to pieces, he merely cut his own throat!

17. *Improper Contact.* Calling on important execu-

tives these days is a ticklish job and requires all the finesse you can develop. They all have secretaries—and, whether you like it or not, they must be catered to. Sometimes, unfortunately, the secretary is even more important than the executive. Here was a salesman who writhed, ranted, and raved under the secretary's excessive cross-examination, instead of taking it easy. He not only didn't get to the front office, but the secretary got even by telling her boss about him and piling it on thick. He *never did* get to the front office!

18. *Sympathy Racket.* I knew a salesman who had got into the habit of retailing his personal troubles all over his territory. He had to be wet-nursed and sympathized with by all his customers and prospects—and it wasn't long before they got tired of it all. The man who succeeded him heard the most intimate details of his family troubles all over the territory; which may possibly have been one of the reasons for a new man on the job. At least the new man kept his troubles to himself.

19. *Pestiferous Calling.* There was another salesman who worried his prospects as a cat worries a mouse. He pestered them to death with calls every few days, either in person or on the telephone. While it is necessary and desirable to keep in touch with your trade, there is also such a thing as running a good horse to death! After all, your contacts have other things to attend to besides *your* business; and it is easily possible to get a man sick of seeing you. Calling, just like everything else, must be done in moderation and with consideration for the other man's time.

20. *Price Discrimination.* If you've got to give your prospect a special deal to get the business, better be sure it is not one that will get back to another customer and

get you into trouble. I knew a man who lost an actual customer because of a price concession he offered a prospect nearby. The customer heard him boasting about it and called the salesman on the carpet. The safest and fairest thing to do—is not to do it! If one man gets a concession, others are going to hear about it—and you are going to have your hands full of serious complaints.

21. Lack of Knowledge. Do you know all there is to know about your product? Or are you apt to be caught in the embarrassing position of admitting you don't know about some vital detail of manufacture and its suitability for the prospect's definite requirements? You might get away with it once or twice; but if there are things you don't know about your line, you are liable to lose your prospect's confidence and to be left out on a limb when he orders from someone else. When that time comes, are you going to tell your sales manager you didn't know?

22. Reciprocity. Don't make the mistake that another salesman did—insisting that a prospect buy your merchandise just because your factory happens to be buying something from him. He may come back at you and tell you that he sells his merchandise because it is able to stand on its own feet, and that he buys his supplies on the same basis. And he will be perfectly right, too. Of course, if you can insinuate the idea tactfully, well and good; but don't make it an issue of the sale or you'll be headed for trouble.

23. Too Many Collections. It is not always the wisest thing to have a salesman make past-due collections from his customers. This process of collecting money frequently brings on the development of hard feelings; and to get a salesman mixed up in this job is likely to have an unfortunate effect on his future relations with his customer. The customer who begins to look upon the salesman as a collector finds it difficult to think of him as a friend—which is the only thing the salesman should be. Business solicitations and cash collections do not mix!

24. Unsatisfactory Service. The customer blames the salesman for everything and rarely praises him for anything! If the factory is about to fall down on delivery, or on quality, or on price, or on assortments, or on any other factor that may disturb the customer, the salesman should be given the full facts immediately as a protection to himself and to his firm. He must be fortified with the necessary information to placate his customer. He must have authority to make whatever reasonable adjustment is necessary on the spot. He can always get another order after a proper adjustment is made; but he cannot always get another customer after a factory falls down!

25. Out of Town. Have you ever had a customer eager to give you a rush order when you were out of town— and he couldn't reach you? Is there someone in your office to take care of him when you are away; or can you depend on his sending the order direct to your factory? Or will he follow the line of least resistance and call in your competitor? Do you leave a route list with your office; or do you call the office occasionally from the road; or do you telephone your good customers before you leave town and see that they are okay? Don't forget that a live wire on your customer list is worth several names on your prospect list. Keep in touch!

Test Questions

1. Why do you think the various alibis for lost sales all seem to strike such a familiar note?

2. What kind of salesman do you think never loses a sale—and why?

3. Name five personal reasons frequently responsible for lost sales.

4. How would you clear up the troubles resulting from lack of support at your main office?

5. How would you make good on a lack of follow-up with the prospect?

6. What do you think you would do where the prospect and yourself just cannot seem to get along together?

7. How could you get additional creative help in selling a prospect?

8. What do you think would be the effect of criticizing a competitor before the prospect?

9. How do you think more knowledge about your line might help you avoid lost sales?

10. How would you go about curing unsatisfactory service that might result in lost sales?

Study Suggestions

1. Consider the case of the perfect salesman who never loses a sale. What kind of person do you think he is, and how did he get that way?

2. If you found that you were losing too many sales, what would you do? Give the complete steps in your procedure.

3. If you were told that you were about to lose an especially important sale, would you let it go at that and just consider it hard luck, or what would you do?

4. If your sales manager called your attention to the fact that you were losing too many sales, what do you think you could do to square yourself?

5. List the five most important reasons for lost sales, and their remedies.

CHAPTER XI

How to Regain Lost Customers

Every organization has a certain number of customers or clients who somehow or other manage to become lost, strayed or stolen. Getting them back on the books is "something else again"; nevertheless, it is a job that deserves considerable thought and attention because of the rich reward at the end.

Every lost customer brought back into the fold is a tribute to the salesman's vision, hard work and everlasting persistence. Not only that, the customer regained is an actual paying dividend in the form of extra business and extra profits; and he helps to push the sales quota over those last few difficult figures that brings a hearty "well done" from the top executive! In these days the salesman is going to look around for—and welcome—all the extra business he can get; and the forgotten lost customer may well become an unexpected windfall.

The question is, how do customers get away from us in the first place and what can we do to bring them back home? Here are some practical methods of getting back eight different types of lost customers.

1. Credit Troubles

It hasn't been so very long since we were all pretty hard-boiled about extending credit. Some of us are still that way—and probably need to be. But there has certainly been a vast improvement in credit conditions. Money has been loosening up—and so has credit; and if we don't know it now, we may find out later to our sorrow that the other fellow has been getting the business.

Accounts that we formerly considered too small for our attention; credit ratings that bordered on the danger line, or at least the caution zone; new firms that we didn't want to gamble with; accounts that were slow pay or troublesome . . . all these have probably listened to the siren song of our competitors or have moved upward and out of the c. o. d. zone and demand more sympathetic attention—or else!

Yes, it takes a diplomat to call on a man who has previously been turned down for credit; but if salesmen aren't diplomats, are they *salesmen*? Don't forget, the man who calls on one of these lost customers today is a rejuvenated salesman; he is full of pep and enthusiasm; he presents an entirely different psychological front to the customer than he did in "the dim dark days"; he is prepared to storm the fort and take the customer into his own camp; he *knows* that the average lost customer—deep down in his heart— wishes he were back in the company he belongs.

Speaking of the customer—he's not so dumb, either. He knows very well that there were two sides to the old credit story and that he himself was not entirely blameless. Yes, indeed . . . many of these lost customers would probably meet the friendly, constructive type of salesman half way if given half a chance; all they need is a graceful opportunity to admit that they have never been entirely satisfied since they left "the old crowd." Just an occasional call; a friendly letter from headquarters; a pat on the back

. and a glimpse of some new samples, new plans, new faces —and they might be the first ones to say:—"Oh, well, let's call it square and start all over again!"

2. Merchandise Faults

Who can always tell just why one complex human mind didn't like some particular thing? "One man's meat is another man's poison"—the customer who switched over to our competitor may have become piqued at any one of a number of things—little or big. It is possible that he didn't like the way our stuff was packed; maybe we didn't always live up to the letter of our specifications; perhaps our quality in the old days got to be a little spotty; our colors may have been offshade or possibly they didn't match from one lot to another. Regardless of what it was, the fact remains that he thought our competitor had something to offer that we didn't; and whether he was right or wrong is not the principal story.

The important problem is, how to change his frame of mind and get him back on the right track. And to accomplish that objective, what is better than a face-to-face visit and a heart-to-heart talk by a salesman or a sales executive who has the ability, the knowledge and the courage to "speak softly and use the big stick"?

Little faults assume large size in retrospect. But the thing that looms large today is the ability to serve that long lost customer *better* than anyone else in the market —and the ability to *prove* it to him with indisputable evidence! The proof of the pudding lies in the eating; certainly we can get up a special display or exhibit that will prove to the customer in plain facts and figures that it lies in his own interest to reverse his position.

3. Merchandise Adjustments

Well, maybe we were *not* as liberal in the old days as we might have been! Maybe we *did* occasionally bill at the wrong prices and take our own sweet time to make good. Maybe we *were* a little more peevish than we should have been at some unwarranted discount, or at a little extra dating, or at a little slower pay than usual. All right— we had our troubles, too, just the same as the customer did, although *we* needn't have been quite so hot about it. And what's more, the customer knows that he, too, was just as much on the wrong side of the fence as we were —only *he* won't admit it. So what?

This just gives us an opportunity to go more than half way to prove that we can take it—and admit it! We can afford to be bighearted and broadminded about it now; and if we are, the chances are the customer will be, too. Is that too much for us to do to try to get an old friend back? Let's get him to admit that times are different now and that people feel different and work in a better frame of mind. Let's tell him that he can have the shirt off our backs. Let's show him that we mean business by offering now to give him the things we quibbled about so long ago. And let's show him what he has to gain, too. Let's go after him and give him all the attention and solicitation that we would give a brand new prospect. Who knows? A little flattery here, a little wheedling there, a diplomatic showdown with all the cards on the table—and first thing you know, here's an order with the old familiar name on the dotted line!

4. Service Troubles

You know, it doesn't take many of these little service troubles to lose a customer. Just an occasional slip now and then—and finally the "straw that breaks the camel's back"—and bingo! . . . another good name on the ledger hits the dust! The trouble is, most of the time we don't even know what it was; the customer keeps his own counsel and all we know is that his ledger sheet is blank.

Do we check him up carefully and follow through? Do we go out of our way to make a special call, or to write a special letter? Do we discover that it is poor delivery, or slow shipping time, or lack of dealer helps, or insufficient advertising, or lack of promotion plans, or improper newspaper tie-up . . . or what-have-you? And then do we admit our errors and try to remedy them, or do we try to bluff our way through and take the attitude that we are perfect and that the customer hasn't got a kick coming anyway?

Many a customer slip-up results from a service trip-up —and then personal relations go from bad to worse. Unfortunately, sometimes the salesman, too, is given the impression that we are in the clear and that it's up to the customer to go down on his knees—which he never does. Instead of that, it's up to the salesman to make the graceful big-hearted gesture that will save the customer's face for the customer and save his business for us—instead of letting a competitor get in solid. It shouldn't be so difficult for you to give ground and to place the customer up on the pedestal where he likes to be—and where he really belongs! After all, there's many a good supplier in the market, but there's only one customer! Just as there's many a good salesman who can turn the trick . . . !

5. Competition

Competition may be the life of trade, but it is also the principal trade of life. Whether it is competition in price, style, quality makes no difference; competition is still one of the chief causes of lost customers. Not only because the competition was there, but because we didn't recognize it when we saw it; we went on our merry way serene in the conviction that the customer got good merchandise and a good price and that's all that was necessary.

It never occurred to us that the customer had to be sold over and over again on the fact that our merchandise was good, that we were the best house for him to deal with, that we gave him the best service, the best prices, the newest styles, the latest ideas. We don't always realize —until it is too late—that we must recognize our competition in advance; that we must offset the advance flutterings of our competitor's salesmen by everlasting and continual selling of our own.

When the deed is done and the customer has slipped his leash, we are apt to alibi on everything except ourselves. The only thing we can do then is face the music, marshal our reserves before it is much too late and march directly to the customer's door. We must hit—and hit hard—with everything at our command. When the worst comes to the worst, it shouldn't be impossible for us to set up all our facts and figures side by side and compare price with price, style with style, quality with quality and, above all, value with value! Remembering at all times, of course, that a good offensive is usually the best defensive. In other words, why wait until the customer is lost before we bring up our selling reserves?

6. Insufficient Contacts

If there is one thing the average customer does not like —it is to be ignored. He has a deep-seated conviction (and rightly, too) that he is the salesman's staff of life and that he is entitled to all the attention, all the consideration, all the breaks he can possibly get. Stop calling on a customer and the customer stops calling for you! His is usually an attitude of "out of sight, out of mind"; and the salesman who will let him languish from insufficient contact must be out of mind himself.

Still, many a customer gets away because we don't contact him closely enough. When that occurs—and competition slips into the picture—we can only redouble our selling efforts to atone for previous failure. We must bring every bit of pressure to bear; we must use whatever friendship we have; we must present our product again and again in the most attractive light possible, playing up the advantages of our line in quality, value, style, attractiveness, desirability and, last but not least, the familiarity of the customer and his trade with our line and our trademark. We must leave no stone unturned to bring him back; and we can even swallow our pride enough to admit that we were at fault and that it "won't happen again."

Many times the salesmanager himself finds it necessary to step into the picture and perform the feat of magical diplomacy that is necessary; and if the salesmanager thinks it advisable, even the head of the firm may be called upon to use his prestige and his influence to perform the well-nigh impossible. Regardless of who does it, the customer *must* be brought back, because defections of this type are apt to spread and cause serious damage. The impossible *must* be made possible!

7. *Creativeness*

It is sad but true that many a salesman neglects to play up the creative ability of his organization. Sometimes it is the fault of the salesman himself in overlooking the value of this vital talking point. Occasionally, the headquarters staff is at fault, because they don't feed the sales organization enough sales ammunition that stresses the creative ability and helpfulness of the home office organization.

It is necessary *only once* for a customer to get the idea that his supplier is behind the times, that he is slipping in the development of new ideas, new plans, new adaptations, new styles, new colors, new designs. The moment he gets this doubting complex, he becomes fertile ground for the new ideas of a competitor; and when he switches over to his new allegiance, it is a superhuman job to get him back. A new job must be done with brass tacks, down-to-earth selling of the most convincing character. It may be necessary almost to bring the entire factory organization up in review; to lay all the different functions plainly on the table; to stress the comparison of past, present and future plans with the value of his new allegiance; to prove beyond all reasonable doubt that the factory actually *is* on its toes, that it *is* ahead of the parade, that it really *is* the leader in the industry—and that all ideas to the contrary are the unfortunate result of human fallibility and *not* factory failure.

This is one of the toughest jobs on the calendar; but in the last analysis, the best way is to apply the needed ounce of prevention long before the actual catastrophe. It is so easy for a salesman to save the time of calling on a regular customer just because he is a regular customer! It is so easy for many of us even at headquarters to take the regular customer for granted and to save most of our efforts for new prospects! If we can only remember that no matter how long the customer's name has been on the books—our "selling job is never done from early morn to setting sun!"

8. Personalities

One of the most prolific sources of lost customers is the troubles that arise from clashing and conflicting personalities. A customer goes sour on a salesman, or the salesman goes sour on the customer. The human element being what it is, arguments will arise as to adjustments, prices, service, quality, politics—any one of the innumerable things that run the entire gamut of human emotions. The customer refuses to do business with the salesman, or the salesman gets disgusted with the customer and neglects him. Whatever it may be, the customer doesn't worry—he is always sure of a haven of refuge with a competitor.

However, the clash occurs. A major operation is indicated—and a major operation it must be! Personal feelings have no place in the picture, unless it is agreed that these are more important than the customer. Conflicting personalities must be divorced. A new face, a new presentation, a new attitude, a new smile, a new personality works miracles with a disgruntled customer.

After all, this is not one of the hardest troubles in the world to correct, but it is certainly a delicate situation to handle without doing irreparable damage to the feelings of either the customer or the salesman. Most important of all, is the ability to diagnose the condition properly and to apply the remedy promptly. This is one case where certainly "a stitch in time saves nine!"

TEST QUESTIONS

1. Why waste any time on lost customers?
2. How could your Credit Department help you to regain lost customers?
3. What would you do to get back a customer lost on account of shipping poor merchandise?

4. Name three things you could tell a lost customer about faulty merchandise adjustments in an effort to get him back.
5. What do you think real service consists of?
6. What is the best way to avoid most competitive troubles in advance?
7. How many times do you think it is necessary to call on a customer?
8. In what way could the creative ability of your factory help to bring back a lost customer?
9. What would you do if a good customer refused to do business with you because of some personal disagreement or aversion?
10. What do you think are the three most important reasons for lost customers?

STUDY SUGGESTIONS

1. Instead of wasting time and effort in regaining your customers, why not use the same time and effort in going after new customers?
2. How would you go about preventing service dissatisfaction after shipping an order?
3. Let us consider you have taken over a new territory where a number of customers have been lost for many of the reasons mentioned in this chapter. How would you find out just what had happened to cause the loss of customers?
4. Referring to the last question: Just how would you plan to avoid such difficulties in the future?
5. Write down five things that you would do to make certain you have as few lost customers as possible.

CHAPTER XII

How to Avoid Gaps in Selling

THINGS left undone are sometimes more important than the things we do. Very frequently, their omission results in the tragedy of a lost order. Every salesman has an occasional gap in his selling; but having too many of them is like trying to hold your profits in a strainer!

No salesman ever hurt himself or wasted his time by checking into the reasons for postponement of a sale, or by analyzing the where-for and why-for of a lost customer. Some salesmen build up a customer to a satisfactory peak —and then let down—only to be rudely shocked at a later date by the total loss of the customer. All because the salesman began to take the customer too much for granted and got into the habit of leaving important things undone. Show me a salesman who takes his customers for granted and I'll show you a man who is taking it for granted that his competitor is asleep at the switch—and the danger in that attitude should be obvious to any salesman. The trouble with the salesman is that he thinks he has the customer tied up for life because he sold him a bill of goods once or twice. As a matter of fact, the customer's continual life on his books is assured only by the constant attention he gets from the salesman.

15 CHECKING POINTS FOR SALESMEN WHO WANT TO BEAT COMPETITION

Here are some of the gaps in selling that even the best of us occasionally leave as an easy mark for competitive salesmen! In the days ahead, our competitor is going to take the fullest advantage of every opportunity we are kind enough to offer him. And any time you think your competitor is asleep at the switch, just forget your customers for a while and see what happens! In the game of modern selling there is only one way to beat your competitor—and that is, to work at it constantly.

1. No Follow Through

It is pitiful to see how many salesmen work up a prospect almost to the point of closing and then, because they become discouraged too soon, take him off their list.

They not only give up their own chances for business, but they actually turn the prospect over to a competitor on a silver platter. They do all the missionary work; they do all the heartbreaking pioneering; and just because they haven't the patience to follow through and keep their shirts on, the other fellow reaps the benefit.

There is only one really safe rule to remember. If a prospect is worth following up at all, he is usually worth following through to the finish, until he has bought or until he definitely says he will not buy—and even then I wouldn't always believe him! Patience is not only a virtue, it is an absolute necessity in selling. If you have no patience, you will do no selling; and the more patience you have, the more selling you will do.

2. Fear Complex

The timid soul who is afraid to grapple with his customer, is licked before he starts! A certain amount of aggressiveness, tinged with diplomacy, is essential to successful selling. The man with a fear complex must knock that complex out of his system before he can become a successful salesman.

Some men are afraid of prospects who look like "big shots." They don't realize that some so-called "big shots" are no bigger than themselves. The man who is a real "big shot" is usually a great deal more democratic than the runner-up. Truly big men are usually easy to work with if you have real sales ability; while the runners-up are usually false alarms with an exaggerated ego—so why be afraid of either of them?

Another thing that bothers many salesmen is that they are afraid to approach a showdown with the prospect and actually ask for the order. They will do all kinds of preliminary work and bring the prospect almost to the closing point, but when it comes to the crucial point of asking for the order, they go into a coma and never come out! They stutter and stammer and exhibit a first-class case of stage fright; when all they have to say, calmly and quietly, is: "Now, Mr. Jones, let's get this material moving along to you right away so you will have it when you need it; how many cases can I order for you today?" You may talk yourself hoarse and talk rings around your prospect, but if you haven't got the nerve to break out and say: "How many do you want today?" you are wasting your time!

Forget your fear complex and get yourself into a selling complex. Remember that your prospect isn't going to ask you how many you will let him have; it is up to you to *ask him* how many you may ship him! Remember, also, that your prospect *expects* you to ask him for the order every time, so why not live up to his expectations and ask him for plenty? The law of averages will usually give you a good solid portion of what you ask for—but if you don't ask for it you are entirely out of luck and your visit has been just a social call. Are your commissions figured on social calls or on sales?

3. Too Much Temperament

You may be an artist in your selling, but you cannot afford to be artistic in your temperament! Bear in mind that temperament is usually another word for temper— which is what 95 per cent of it is anyway—and any time you acquire the habit of exhibiting temper with your prospects or customers, you may as well realize you are on the way out.

The man with temper lacks what we discussed before— patience; and lacking patience he frequently loses control of his temper and then considers himself temperamental. This is just an alibi that covers his lack of control. I wouldn't blame any human being for having a temper, but I certainly would blame any salesman who cannot control it. The man with an uncontrollable temper is a constant menace not only to himself and to his customer, but also to his company. No company can afford to be represented by a salesman like that, for the plain and simple reason that they are going to lose entirely too much business through his impetuous acts and mannerisms.

No prospect or customer will long put up with so-called temperamental selling. Why? Because there is always another salesman waiting just outside the door who understands the full meaning of the word patience!

4. Failure to Check Up

It may not be so difficult to get an initial order from a customer, but the trick is to give him the kind of service and attention on that order that will result in a repeat order later on.

How many salesmen check up on an order after it goes through? First, to see that it is properly shipped; second, to see that it is received by the customer in good time and in good order; third, to see that the customer likes the merchandise after he receives it; fourth, to see that it is properly sold or efficiently used by the customer; and last but not least, to check up on his stock from time to time to see when he is ready for another order.

Occasionally a salesman will be so shortsighted as to take an order from a customer and then completely forget about him until he gets another inquiry. In other words, the customer is left entirely to his own devices, which means that he is open to constant pressure by competing salesmen to change over and try their line of goods. Eventually, he realizes that the salesman is interested only in getting his order, and that his interest in him comes to an end the moment he gets his name on the dotted line. It is only human nature to resent this, and the customer does so because he is normal and has a notion that he is entitled to a little attention now and then even though he does not always order.

5. Competition Complex

This is a mighty dangerous complex for any salesman to have. It is bad enough for the salesman to let himself think too much of competition; but if and when he reaches the point where his selling is directed to competition rather than to his customer, he is approaching a catastrophe.

We have all seen the salesman, at one time or another, who walks into his prospect's office and proceeds to damn everything his competitor produces. He spends half his selling time tearing down his competitor instead of building up his own merchandise. That is nothing short of manslaughter in the first degree!

Surely no salesman can be stupid enough to imagine that his firm has a monopoly on everything that is worth while. He must realize that even a competitor may possibly have something just as good as he. The important thing he overlooks is that his prospect may think so, too. The prospect resents the salesman's wholesale damnation of everyone else and may consider him so ridiculous and unworthy that he loses confidence in all he says.

The best way to handle a competition complex is to drop it with a dull thud! Stick to your knitting and mind your own business. Your business is to sell *your* merchandise to the prospect and to use every moment of your selling time to impress him with the desirability of *your* proposition. Forget your competitor. Don't even mention him, for you may remind your prospect of some competitive merchandise he never thought of before! You may even arouse his curiosity as to your competitor! Don't forget that your competitor may be just as good a salesman as you, and if you remind your prospect about him and give him a chance to get in, he may push you out of the picture entirely!

6. High Pressure Selling

The familiar old time high-pressure artist has almost entirely vanished from the selling scene, and the modern business man won't stand for his return.

The high-pressure man was a one-call salesman. He prided himself on the fact that he could sweep the prospect off his feet and get his signature on an order blank by the flood-like forcefulness of his sales presentation. He was not too much concerned with the possibility of over-selling, or with the ethics of a proposition, or with the idea of getting any repeat business. His main interest was to get the prospect and to get him good, by hook or crook.

Even in this day and age a salesman may make the mistake of trying to sweep a prospect off his feet with the enthusiasm of his selling. It is always much safer, however, to tone down your sales presentation to a low-pressure level, and let your prospect work himself up to a high-pressure pitch if he can. In other words, low-pressure salesmanship leads to a constructive buymanship on the part of the prospect. Don't forget that any order your prospect gives you must be logical, sensible and in accord with his needs and requirements—or *you* will be the goat, and no one else. You may trick your prospect into buying once, but you will never have a second opportunity. In modern business, it is the second and the successive opportunities that bring in the real profits!

7. Price Complex

More than one salesman has forced the subject of price into his prospect's consciousness simply because he had a price complex himself and talked price instead of quality. More than one prospect has been started thinking about price against his original intentions, when he might just as easily have been sold the highest price merchandise in your line had you confined your remarks to that alone!

Too many salesmen still have their minds filled with a

price complex instead of a quality presentation. Any sales-man can easily prove this to his own satisfaction. If he will agree to delete the word "price" and the corresponding dollars-and-cents figures from every single sales presentation he makes for a month, unless he is positively put to the question by the prospect, he will be amazed at the number of quality sales he will make without any undue discussion of price!

In these days of a return to quality buying, price arguments and discussions are superfluous. Customers are interested in getting good merchandise rather than in worrying about price. The trend is definitely and unwaveringly toward finer quality merchandise in every line.

Forget your price complex and follow the trend of quality to greater profits and increased commissions!

8. Overselling

The principal thing to remember about overselling, is not to do it, regardless of the temptation. Every time you oversell the customer you undersell your chances of friendship and repeat business. To make a permanent customer out of a prospect, you must fill him with confidence in your sincerity, your honesty, and your desire to serve him properly. To the extent that he catches you taking advantage of him, he will lose confidence in you—than which there is nothing more unfortunate.

It is all very praiseworthy to want to sell as much as possible. But it is a grave error to sell one man more than he needs. When he gets stuck with it, he will not blame himself or his sales people—he will blame the man who sold it to him and the company that man represents; and then I defy you to go in there and sell him again and keep him on your list permanently.

Take a tip from the times. Business men buy what they can resell and what they can use within a reasonable time. When they find themselves with more than that amount, they spend considerable time and effort looking for a goat —and you don't want to be it! The thing that counts in your business is not what you sell the dealer, but what the dealer sells off his shelves. Help him on the re-sale end and he will help you on the selling end. That's where the figures will really count in your quota!

9. Poll-parrot Selling

Canned sales talks are valuable because they present a good sales talk in logical sequence; but canned selling is like cooking without salt—the life and the relish are left out. The salesman who can take a canned sales talk to pieces and then inject his own personality and enthusiasm into every line of it, is the man who is bound to make a good sales presentation. But the man who takes a canned sales talk literally and starts doing a lot of canned selling, is just like a poll-parrot who repeats, monotonously and lifelessly, the words he has learned!

Selling of this kind lacks enthusiasm. It lacks the sparkle and magnetism that produce an interesting personality, and it has a deadening effect on the prospect. You might just as well put your sales talk on a Victrola record and mail it to your prospect.

Lack of enthusiasm in selling develops a negative reaction on the part of the prospect. Taking too literally the canned sales talk that is supposed to be taken figuratively, is responsible for a lot of poll-parrot selling that repels rather than attracts the prospect. Every salesman must learn to talk interestingly and convincingly before he can interest and convince his prospect. The surest way to find yourself on the wrong side of the door is to learn your sales talk "by heart" and speak your piece like a parrot! How do you think you would like to listen to a talk like that?

10. Argumentation

An argument takes you everywhere and gets you nowhere! Some people argue on any subject at the drop of a hat; but the salesman who joins the argument not only drops the hat but also the order!

The wise salesman will let an argumentative prospect talk himself out. He will even stretch his conscience to agree with him wherever possible. He will never join the argument; and more important than all, he will certainly never start an argument himself. It is a queer quirk of human nature that most people like to argue; but this is one time the salesman must realize that silence is golden.

When the prospect starts to argue about one point, it is high time for the salesman to start talking about a new point; and he may come back to the original point of contention a little later when the atmosphere has cleared. Volumes have been written about the dangers of argumentation; but it is still a fact that many salesmen are in the class that love to argue, and they hate to be deprived of the pleasure. They are always confident that they can win the argument, and probably they can. The question is, would you rather win the argument or win the sale? In nine cases out of ten you cannot win both!

11. Incomplete Line

A great many sales are lost because of the propensity of the salesman to talk about a single product rather than a complete line. Salesmen occasionally make up their minds in advance that a particular prospect will be interested only in a certain product, and nothing else. They put all their pressure behind that one product and pass over the rest of the line entirely.

As a matter of fact, when a prospect becomes partly sold on a salesman or on his company, he is open to consider anything and everything the salesman has to show him. The salesman cannot always guess what is in the prospect's mind, and he doesn't know what his plans are for the future. When one product is acceptable, the salesman should attempt to carry over that acceptance to the other items in his line. At least, it does no harm to show these other items. It is possible that the prospect will become interested in some other item that he never knew existed. Often you will hear a prospect say: "Oh, I didn't know you made such and such; I thought you specialized on this other product exclusively." Why didn't he know about it? Why does a salesman deliberately pass up the opportunity for extra sales by failing to show the entire line?

When the salesmanager turns a salesman loose in the field, he expects him to talk about everything he has to sell. He knows that the more things the salesman has to show, the more chance he has of interesting a prospect and making a sale. Buyers' minds and tastes are varied; and a varied line is the surest way to make the law of averages produce for you. Variety is not only the spice of life, but also the spice of buying and selling!

12. Profit-less Selling

Did you ever hear of a manufacturer who got so many orders that he lost money? That is not a fairy tale—it is a fact. His salesmen were so intent on grabbing all the volume they could lay their hands on, that they forgot the all-important matter of profit and got into the habit of taking orders at any cut price they could get.

Volume without profit is just as bad as a factory without sales. In both cases there are the usual fixed charges, overhead and sales expense to be covered by profit—but the profit is missing! Because of the size of an order, salesmen are sometimes tricked and deluded into cutting their prices and commissions to an extent where they are working for the customer rather than for the firm. They don't realize that their firm operates on a small profit margin and depends on that margin to cover their expenses. Every cut in that profit reduces the firm's possibility of covering expenses; and every time you let a customer cut your price, you are not only cutting your own commissions but you are also taking chances with your job. No well managed firm will permanently retain a salesman who continually takes orders on a cut price basis. It is safer to lose both the salesman and the business than to operate at a loss. What would you do if you were in business for yourself . . . would you sell your goods at a loss and expect to remain in business?

13. Importance Complex

Yes, I have seen salesmen who acted so important that their overbearing manner actually drove the prospect away. They seemed to say: "I'm a big guy and my time is very valuable; let's get right down to business because I can't afford to waste much time on you." Needless to say, they didn't last long in any one job; because if there is one thing the prospect won't stand for, it is to be treated with disdain.

The prospect is the one to be considered important, not

the salesman. The moment this relationship is reversed, the sales fly out of the window. If you cannot approach a prospect with a reasonable amount of humility and a vast amount of patience, better stay out altogether and avoid a bad reputation.

You will never get a prospect to admit that you are an important man to him, because he expects you to realize that *he* is the only important man around here. Which is quite true! The salesman's importance is only assumed; the prospect's importance is life or death to the salesman. And on more than one unhappy occasion, the prospect's reaction has brought about a sudden and final exit to the salesman!

14. Unkempt Appearance

Strange though it may seem, salesmen still have to be reminded that the first impression on the prospect is tremendously important. They frequently never have an opportunity to make a second impression. And that first impression depends a great deal upon the personal appearance of the salesman!

How many times have you see a salesman walk into a prospect's office looking as if he had slept in his clothes? His hair ruffled, and sometimes even hidden by his hat; his shoes with a second-hand look instead of a bright shine; his fingernails in mourning; his vest unbuttoned; his shirt and collar in need of a laundry; and his socks flopping over his shoe tops! Probably not all these things at one time, of course; but enough of them to present a sloppy appearance.

The prospect himself is probably a spic-and-span business man. What would be his natural reaction to a *salesman* who appears before him with an unsavory personal appearance?

15. Lack of Service

It is true that "service" is a badly abused word; but it also is true that service is sometimes very badly given.

A salesman's importance to his customer increases only to the degree that he can serve him in the way he expects to be served. The final judge of that service is the customer, and his judgment makes or breaks the salesman. Whatever the customer expects in the way of service (even if occasionally unreasonable) is the job that devolves on the salesman; and as he falls down on his service, he falls down in his business.

It is bad enough for a salesman to fail in his service; but not to keep the customer informed is criminal. If the service that the customer expects is not forthcoming—and there is no suitable explanation of its absence—the salesman gets a black mark in the customer's mind that requires a long time to erase. Lack of service may occasionally be excusable; but failure to keep the customer informed of conditions as they arise, is absolutely inexcusable. If you cannot give your customer the service he expects, it is much safer for him to hear about it from you, than to discover it for himself!

Test Questions

1. In what way do you think analysis of your everyday job would help you in selling?
2. Why do you think it is necessary to keep in touch with a man after he becomes your customer?
3. How do you think your personal fear complex could affect your customer?

4. Just how temperamental do you think a good salesman can afford to be?

5. What is the best kind of competition complex to acquire?

6. In what way do you think a price complex is a gap in selling?

7. Discuss the pros and cons of poll-parrot selling.

8. Exactly what is meant by profitless selling, and how does it occur?

9. Don't you think a salesman is just as important as a customer, and that he needn't be afraid to show it?

10. What difference does it make how a salesman looks so long as he gets the business?

Study Suggestions

1. How many important things can you list that a salesman occasionally leaves undone in his selling?

2. Just how far would you go in checking up on your service, or your company's service, after the customer gives you an order?

3. List three of the various personal complexes that a salesman might accidentally acquire; which do you think is the most unfortunate, and why?

4. Select your own choice of product, and give two short examples each of both high pressure and low pressure selling.

5. What do you think is the modern trend in salesmanship as regards these so-called gaps in selling?

CHAPTER XIII

How to Handle the Price Problem

HERE are 28 stimulative questions and answers for price-conscious salesmen; they will be valuable and helpful to you in these days of rising costs.

Human nature being what it is, salesmen will always have the problem of answering price objections; so there's no shame in admitting its existence. The only shame lies in not being properly equipped to dissipate its many alibis, because in most cases price is not a proper subject of argument at all—it is merely an alibi that must be broken down the same as any other.

The average salesman's price troubles depend largely on his own mental attitude *toward* price. For example, if these questions were aimed at you, how would *you* answer them?

1. How do you *look* at price?
2. How much do you *think* of price?
3. How badly has your prospect *scared* you on price?
4. How often do you give way and *cut* your price?
5. How often do you think of your merchandise *without* thinking of price?
6. Do you present your line to your prospect in a way that will *offset* his low-price complex?
7. How do you know he *has* a low-price complex?

8. Who *gave* it to him—you or the other salesmen?
9. How often do you use the word *price* in your sales talk?
10. Have you ever shown him the difference between price and *value*?
11. Have you ever suggested a lower price before he *asked* for it?
12. Are you sure he won't pay more money if you *forget* to talk price?

The first reaction of some buyers is: "I can buy your merchandise for less money—why pay you more?" But *can* he? It is true, he may have some merchandise in mind that *seems* just as good. It may look the same, it may even feel similar—but will it give the same service? Will it wear as well? Will it look as good after it has been in service for a time? Will it give the customer the same feeling of luxurious satisfaction? Will it retain its character and distinction over a long period, or will it break down shortly and require premature replacement?

After all, price is only comparative; it is a measure of value and service. The greatest barrier to selling quality merchandise is the necessity for paying a few cents more initial cost per unit in order to obtain a great deal more value and service. Every product or piece of merchandise holds just so much inherent durability. Part of this includes the qualities of character, distinction, and appearance which have been built into it with unusual care. In a cheaper product, these qualities break down quickly in use, with the result that you have a shabby-looking product long before it is actually useless. In a quality product, these durability factors retain and hold their characteristics far beyond the average and almost to the very end of its usefulness. *Which product is cheaper in the long run?*

During the recent depression shabbiness, cheapness, and false economy were badges of pride. Many buyers lived from hand to mouth and bought from day to day. They fought, bargained, and chiseled their way through the weakened morale of many manufacturers. But we have become "fed up" with cheapness. We are disgusted with shabbiness. We are hungry for quality merchandise —for the exquisite feel of real silk, for the warmth of all wool, for the luxury of genuine leather, for the appearance of craftsmanship in the things we use and live with. There is a definite trend back to quality, and as quickly as we receive wage returns from regular jobs so quickly do we succumb to this quality urge.

However, we are still in the stage of transition from price-buying to quality-buying, so these are the complaints you most commonly hear from people who like to say your price is too high:

13. *"You Want Too Much Money"*

Not at all! On the contrary, I'm asking less money than any other manufacturer you know, quality and value considered. As a matter of fact, I am actually offering you the most inexpensive merchandise of its kind on the market today—and I can prove it by the simplest kind of arithmetic. If you buy an article for $1 that lasts only a year, and I offer you a similar article made so much finer that it lasts two years and yet costs only 15 or 20 cents more, which would you say is cheaper? It's the finer grade merchandise that I'm offering you here; and by any kind of measuring stick you want to set up, **it** is the cheapest merchandise you can possibly buy. You just don't dare to buy anything for less money than this, because what you get will be so much less in quality that your cost in the long run will be much more than I am asking you.

14. "Come Back and See Me When the Market Is Lower"

If that's the way you feel about it, I'm afraid I won't be back for a long, long time. The trend of the market for some time has been sharply upward and it will continue so for a long time to come. Don't forget that the steadily developing law of supply and demand is very much against you. Buying activity becomes more pronounced each day; and with it, prices of raw materials are increasing by leaps and bounds. It doesn't need an economist to figure out that prices are going to be a great deal higher before they ever start to get lower again. And if you're going to hold off on that account, *you* are going to be out of luck, your *customer* will be out of luck, and your *profit* statement is going to be out of luck! I'm not trying to kid you. You can see for yourself from all well-known and reliable indications that present prices are as low as they will be for many a moon; and the smart thing to do is to take advantage of these prices now before they go up.

15. "I Don't Need Such High-grade Stuff"

Maybe *you* think you don't, but I wonder what your associates and your customers think about it. Don't forget that people have been buying cheap junk for so many years that they are sick of it. They are delighted to see good merchandise and tickled to be able to buy it again. Believe it or not, there is a definite swing "back to quality," and the merchant who cannot read the handwriting on the wall is going to lose business to the man who has the vision and the courage to stock the kind of merchandise the American public is hungry to buy. We have always been the world's greatest purchasers of quality merchandise; and now that the recent "economic interlude" is rapidly becoming ancient history, you are going to see a sharp revival of quality-buying in every line. Before very much longer, you are going to be looking around for all the "high-grade stuff" you can locate!

16. "You Ought To See What Your Competitor Quotes!"

Is that so! I'm afraid you've got the cart before the horse. First you ought to see what my competitor *produces*; and then consider his quotations in the light of his quality. After all, you can probably get any one of our competitors to quote you lower prices on any item in our line, especially if they know we are in the running; but what you *cannot* get them to do is to duplicate our quality at our price. That's the only thing that is important to you. Prices alone mean nothing. It is no news to you that you can go out in the market and get lower prices on cheaper merchandise; but what *is* news to you is the fact that our grade of merchandise is the cheapest kind of merchandise you can buy for both yourself and your customers. And just between you and me, which grade of merchandise do you think will do a better job of trading up your customers and building up your profit?

17. "What! No Discount on This Repeat Order?"

Why, no; whatever made you think we could give you a discount just because this happens to be a repeat order? Don't you realize that this is all specially made merchandise, and that the only thing that governs the price is the quantity made up at one time? It costs us just as much to make up one order for you, as another. It makes no difference how many repeat orders you send in, you will still pay the same price for the same quantity. And at the same time that should make you feel pretty safe, too—knowing that because of our one-price policy everyone else pays the same price you do, with no special favors or special prices to anyone. That is the advantage of dealing with a reputable house; and that's why our reputation for fair dealing during the past forty years has placed us at the very top of the industry. No matter when you send us an order, you can always depend upon it that you are getting the lowest price available to any of our customers!

18. "I'll Have to Check Your Prices First"

That's perfectly okay, but why waste time and money? I can tell you now that you can get lower prices, but of course it will be on lower-grade merchandise. You cannot get lower prices on my quality merchandise, and after all, it is my quality that you need to give you the economy you are after. For just a few cents more than the lowest price merchandise, you can get a quality that will give you two or three times as much wear and service. There's true value and real economy for you! Where is the money saving in paying a few cents less now and a great deal more later on? It's just like looking through the wrong end of a telescope; the wrong perspective doesn't get you anywhere, but the right vision will actually save you more money in the long run than you will spend now!

19. "Bill Jones Says He Pays Less Than the Price You Quote Me"

That is quite possible, because he is a big-volume buyer and gives us orders for much larger quantities than you. After all, our price, like everyone else's, is regulated by quantity; and you can get exactly the same price for the same quantities that Bill Jones gets. Naturally, the larger the order that goes through the factory at one time, the greater the economy; and that economy is passed on to you in proportion to the quantity you order. All you have to do to get Bill Jones' price is to give us an order of the same size. If you'll ask him what quantity he usually orders, and compare it with your quantity, you'll soon see where the difference lies!

20. "Do You Think I'm a Millionaire?"

Yes, I'm willing to think that you and all your customers are millionaires so far as your tastes are concerned. That is what the high standard of living has done to us, and that's why none of us is satisfied with cheap junk merchandise. Price is not always the most important factor in a transaction. Sometimes it is worth asking yourself whether you are buying "merchandise" or "price." If the former, then you are not concerned with price except to be assured that it is a fair price, quality considered; if the latter, then I can take it for granted that you don't care what grade of merchandise you get so long as you get a cheap price. Is that true?

Unfair Price Competition

In their fight to sell quality as against price merchandise, salesmen are continually harried by price competitors who are still living in the days of "dog-eat-dog" and who never at any time paid much attention to the principles of fair competition. There are at least eight types of such competitors for whom you must be on the lookout, who are responsible for numerous attempts to wreck the price structure of many industries:

21. There is the *outside manufacturer* trying to "horn in" on another industry, who submits a cutthroat bid and offers to take a job at any price in order to get started in that industry. It should not be difficult to prove to your prospect that this competitor is a rank outsider; that he is neither competent to handle the job because of his limited experience in that line nor worthy of receiving it because of his methods of price attack.

22. There is the *pirate manufacturer* who deliberately offers to cut any and every price the prospect may receive. The only thing to do about him is to talk to your prospect along the lines of mutual self-preservation and decency in order to submerge his possible desire to save a little money regardless of ethics. Most buyers are broadminded enough to realize that pirates are a menace to every business and are not to be encouraged.

23. There is the cutthroat *competitive manufacturer* who offers to make special price cuts only in order to take business away from another manufacturer. Sometimes this competitor will treat your business as a "loss leader"—but he cannot continue to do so indefinitely. Here you can only appeal to your prospect's own sense of justice and fairness, and most of the time your appeal will have good results.

24. There is the *low-end manufacturer* who submits his low-end prices against high-grade merchandise and says it is "just as good"! Don't you think you have enough ammunition in your own samples and in your own sales talk to squash this kind of fake alibi?

25. There is the *big-volume manufacturer* who pits his mass-production prices against the little fellow's quality, merchandise and craftsmanship. Certainly you're not going to have any trouble proving to your prospect that quality merchandise of *your* character is much better and cheaper in the long run for both himself and his customers—and that it is the long run that counts!

26. There is the *deceptive manufacturer* who submits "skeleton" prices (although he doesn't admit it), to which must be added a number of extras to equal the other manufacturer's quality. It should be as simple as A B C and an exquisite pleasure to expose this man's deceptive prices and practices.

27. There is the *fly-by-night manufacturer* who is here today and gone tomorrow. It should not be difficult to convince your prospect that dealings with this type of manufacturer are certain to end in disaster because of his lack of service, the danger of substitution, the prospect of orphanism, and the complete absence of ethics and moral obligation.

28. There is the *three-price manufacturer* who offers his first price as a feeler, his second price as a reduction, and his third price as "the last word"! In cases like this it is a great pleasure to be able to talk to your prospect on the subject of his safety in dealing with a reputable one-price house, that depends for repeat business on its quality manufacturing ability rather than on its haggling and bargaining abilities!

TEST QUESTIONS

1. How is it possible to present a product without discussing the price question? Or is it possible?
2. How can you offset a low price complex on the part of your prospect?
3. In what way do you think that price and value have any common relation?
4. How would you answer the prospect who tells you that you want too much money for your product?
5. What about the prospect who wants to wait until the market is lower?
6. How would you handle the prospect who constantly talks about your competitor's prices?
7. How would you answer the prospect who is always asking for special discounts?
8. What would you say to the prospect who always likes to shop around?
9. Why should one customer get a better price than another?
10. In what way could you use the American standard of living as a talking point on price?

STUDY SUGGESTIONS

1. Select both a price product and a quality product. How would you handle a request for cut prices on each product, and in what way do you think the arguments you use might be interchangeable as between the two products?
2. Write out your own careful definition of the difference between price and value.
3. What do you think might be the country's economic factors in bringing about a quality buying period instead of price buying?
4. Name four different types of manufacturers who might

give you unfair price competition, and indicate briefly your comments to the prospect on each of them.

5. If you were selling a high quality product, what would be your attitude toward the customer who spends all his time talking price, and how would you go about offsetting his price complex?

CHAPTER XIV

How to Handle the Chiseler

WHAT constitutes a chiseler? How can we recognize him? How many different types are there of these diabolic wielders of the business monkey-wrench? What can we do about them?

Just because a prospect or a customer attempts to get a lower price from you does not necessarily stamp him as a chiseler. It is only natural for a man to ask you to lower your price and to accept your reduction if he can get away with it. Any man may properly coax you to lower your quotation. It is entirely a question of whether he *asks* you to do it, or *forces* you to do it, or *tricks* you into doing it.

Any one of your contacts may occasionally urge you to cut the price of a product by qualifying it, possibly with different credit terms, larger volume, reduced packing or shipping charges, lower priced manufacturing processes, or similar differentials or changes which might make it possible to reduce the price, properly and ethically. Or he might figure with you on similar merchandise of slightly lower quality or lesser desirability in order to bring the price down to his normal budget level or to his level of trade. Attempts like these are perfectly proper and legitimate, and no man can be criticized for such action.

There is always a right way and a wrong way to do

everything. The methods indicated above are thoroughly ethical and honorable. They are methods that are used every day in every branch of industry and commerce. However, when one of your contacts resorts to unfair methods and unethical practices, or goes to dishonorable extremes, in a destructive effort to cut your price, or your profit, or your commission, then he deliberately lays himself wide open to a suspicion of chiseling and to the appellation of chiseler.

We all realize that this is by no means a perfect world. There are chiselers of different kinds and degrees in every avenue of activity; and we will always have the chiseler with us in one form or another. Therefore, conditions being what they are in our selling activities, it is advisable to acknowledge this existing evil and to learn how to recognize and deal with these unfortunate practices.

In my experience, I have discovered at least a dozen different types of chiselers who are prevalent in all branches of business. It may be that my methods of dealing with this species, outlined in the following pages, will present suggestions and helps to you in your own daily problems of selling.

ANATOMY OF A CHISELER

1. The Supercilious Chiseler

Here is the gentleman who (figuratively speaking) wears a monocle in one eye and a look of disdain in the other. He lets you understand that the privilege of doing business with him is not to be taken lightly. The least you can do in return is to give him an extra cut for the business. Think of the pleasure of bragging about the order you got from Mr. Supercilious Chiseler!

RESULT:—Frequently his loftiness is all too effective. It takes a strong will to stand fast against the prestige lure of some of the big names in business. Pop!—There goes your profit!

REMEDY:—When he starts elaborating about the "glory of the name," don't forget that his name got that way because he made a profit on his business. Go thou and do likewise!

2. The Sardonic Chiseler

He wields the bitter weapon of sarcasm. In your presence he compares your offerings with your competitor's —and with the greatest of ease he detects unsuspected and often nonexistent defects in your merchandise. Like the well-known leech, he sucks your blood drop by drop, until in desperation you deprive him of your presence before he deprives you of your profit.

RESULT:—Frequently you throw up the sponge because of the odor of his methods. In any event, you'll probably slide out of his office with your spirits dragging and go out of your way to avoid calling on him again.

REMEDY:—Know your merchandise, your prices, your limits—and stick to them! Open up both barrels and give him the works! More often than not, he'll take it and like it. And if he doesn't, it's mighty good riddance.

3. The Reciprocal Chiseler

His principal philosophy of life is: "Scratch my back and I'll scratch yours." He never gave anyone an order without trying to get one for himself. He never did anyone a favor without looking for an immediate return.

To him, business is just an act of barter, a continual feeling of obligation. "If I do something for you, you must do something for me, regardless." "I cannot stand on my own feet; you must help support me."

RESULT:—If you do attempt to get your firm in line, you will waste more time and acquire more ill favor than the order is worth. But most important of all, you place yourself in the same weakling category.

REMEDY:—I recently said to a man of this type: "I'm sorry I can't do anything for you. We sell our merchandise on its own merits—on the basis of its quality, its service, and its price. We never tie ourselves up with obligations of this kind and I'm sure you wouldn't want to, either. After all, if what I am trying to sell you isn't strong enough to stand on its own legs, you certainly don't want it on any basis."

4. The Nonchalant Chiseler

He is an exquisite poseur. "Poker face" is his middle name. Quiet, soft-spoken, thoroughly indifferent to your most attractive offers—apparently. He is not interested in your merchandise—much! He is not enthusiastic about your prices—much! He is not concerned about the standing of your firm—much! But indicate the slightest willingness to give ground and you will find him the smoothest poker player that ever bluffed a pair of jacks. He wears you down with his indifference, drives you to desperate bidding—and then doubles you with a snap when you overbid yourself. He has a mind like a steel trap; and he can usually detect a possible price cut around a blind corner with periscope eyes.

RESULT:—If you are not his equal at bluffing, you are liable to find yourself squeezed into an inadvertent price reduction. And you'll be explaining to the boss later how he outsmarted you.

REMEDY:—Beat him at his own game by playing his own brand of poker. But you've got to be sport enough to lose occasionally, too. Analyze your man—set your price objective accurately—and stick to your guns!

5. The Cheerful Chiseler

Deceptive because of his amiability and highly dangerous in his deceptiveness. Is usually recognized by the effusiveness of his greeting and by his constantly repeated promises to repay you in the future for the chiseling he does today. He is a first-name hound and a congenital backslapper. Anything to dope you into appreciation of his friendliness—which usually lasts exactly long enough to cut your price. He is a difficult man to refuse, because you dislike terribly to disappoint his childlike faith in you.

RESULT:—You hurry back to your boss with an enthusiastic recital of the vast future benefits to be received from So-and-so if you can help him out "just this time."

REMEDY:—Laugh him out of countenance. Tell him you have been kidded by experts and that you have long since learned that every order you take must pay a profit today—not tomorrow!

6. The Unethical Chiseler

While all chiseling may be more or less unethical, there is one particular type of chiseler who is most unscrupulous. He is the man who lays your samples, your prices, your proposition on the table before your competitor and says, in effect: "Beat it—and the job is yours." When he gets a better price he comes back to you and repeats his performance. And so on, ad infinitum. Here is the most dastardly type of chiseler in existence today. Fortunately, he is becoming increasingly rare, because this type of nausea is really more than the average stomach can stand.

RESULT:—If you ever permit yourself to become a party to this type of chiseling, you are forever lost. You will never have the buyer's respect in the slightest degree and you will never make so much as a postage stamp out of his business. Most important, you will forfeit your soul, your decency, and your self-respect.

REMEDY:—When approached with a deal of this character, tell your man plainly and firmly that your house does not tolerate such operations. Stand up for your ethics, or you will lie down with the devil!

7. The Unamiable Chiseler

After all, if I have to be chiseled, I prefer to have it done cheerfully. Deliver me from the chiseler with the hard glassy stare who bores you through with the eyes of a brass monkey. He is a past master at the art of making you uncomfortable; and even after he has beaten you down on your price—and chiseled a section of your soul along with it—you are to feel that he has done you a favor in accepting your proposition.

RESULT:—Whatever you give him, you give him with gloom and bitterness; and it takes a combination of fresh air, sunshine, and a cheerful call or two to wash your spirit clean.

REMEDY:—Grit your teeth and be as sweet as syrup— even though it hurts. In many cases, unamiability is a defense mechanism. The buyer has a weird idea that if he becomes too friendly, you might take advantage of his good nature. He overlooks the little things you can do *for* him if he is decent—and the things you can do *to* him if he is not!

8. *The Mendacious Chiseler*

There is a saying that "figures will lie and liars will figure." The truest compliment that could be applied to this type of chiseler! He shows you the competitive figures but doesn't tell you the qualifying conditions. He figures the price you should quote him, but never the price he should pay. His mathematics are doubtful; his veracity is terrible; and he places his chief reliance on his ability to befuddle you with figures.

RESULT:—He figures you deaf, dumb, and blind—and then attempts to stampede you into acceptance. If he is successful, you are usually out of luck!

REMEDY:—Never let this man rush you into taking his word for anything. Check the figures and specifications yourself very carefully, either right then and there or in the quiet of your own office. That's the only way to catch the nigger in the woodpile—and to save yourself a lot of grief.

9. *The Discontented Chiseler*

There is more than one way of killing a cat. This type of chiseler waits until your merchandise arrives. Then he goes over it with a powerful magnifying glass and expands the most imperceptible defect into mountainous proportions. Ever since his childhood days, making a mountain out of a molehill has been his favorite pastime. No merchandise is ever so perfect that this man cannot find something on which to base a claim for adjustment. With this man, a profitable taking price doesn't mean a thing until you have received his final check. Frequently, his claims for fancied damages eat up not only your profit, but also part of your cost.

RESULT:—If you don't stick to the letter of your specifications and keep a careful check on your shipments, you are going to run into unfair and unjust claims that are just another type of chiseling. Of course, if you want to let him get away with something, that's up to you.

REMEDY:—There are only two things to do with a buyer like this. Back yourself up with the facts and have a hard-boiled showdown with him, or blacklist him for future business. Profitless business is the most thankless thing in the world. You are not in business either for your health or for the sole benefit of your customer.

10. The Blustering Chiseler

Here is the original Don Quixote of the business world —constantly tilting at the price windmills of the business structure. Only there is nothing chivalrous about him. If he cannot scare you to death with his empty thunder, he is likely to sneak around behind your back and chisel you out of your commission by working on your main office. It is not safe to believe that this "barking dog never bites." He occasionally gives you an unexpected nip in the rear, and—wham! there goes a healthy piece of your commission!

RESULT:—You're liable to mistake noise for importance and give him much more than he deserves. Or, your home office is apt to get the wrong impression if they hear from him direct.

REMEDY:—Remember that two can usually play at the same game. Try a little noise yourself, if this is all he understands; and keep your home office fully informed of the facts for your own protection.

11. *The Two-per-cent Chiseler*

To this man, a cash discount date is just another day to duck. If he cannot cut your price any other way, he will take an extra thirty days to settle your bill and still have the audacity to take the cash discount, too. It seems that for some persons, nothing is too small or too mean. Naming a cash discount date to him is like waving a red rag in front of a bull. "The 10th of the month, huh? Is zat so! He'll take it when he gets it—and like it."

RESULT:—Let this type of chiseler get away with it once and you'll never get him in line. The fact that you may have to pay your bank to carry his account is of no interest to him. His principal pleasure in life is seeing how many weak-kneed suppliers let him get away with murder.

REMEDY:—Immediately your two-per-cent chiseler starts operating, send him a bill for the cash discount— and keep it up until you get it. If you let up, you're lost. Of course, if you are afraid to collect from him, that is something else again.

12. *The Extra-service Chiseler*

Here's the man who is always looking for a handout. Something for nothing is the most attractive thing in the world. He cannot break down your price, but there's nothing to prevent his asking you "a little favor." It might be a matter of shipping in small lots, packing in special cartons, billing him a month later than usual, adding a do-jigger here or there. Whatever it is, it costs you real money. Because you want the business, he figures he can get a little extra service out of you for nothing—and half the time you don't dare refuse.

RESULT:—You frequently let yourself in for added expense that cuts deeply into your profit. In fact, you might have come out better if you had let him chisel your price down in the first place.

REMEDY:—Stand up for your rights. You've come through so far with colors flying. Chances are, he is just making a final effort to get something out of you that he can show to his boss and say: "See, I got this for nothing!" Is he going to get away with it? It's up to you.

TEST QUESTIONS

1. What do you understand by the term chiseler?
2. Do you think it is possible to reduce a price quotation without chiseling? How?
3. In what way do you think chiseling might affect an entire industry?
4. What is the difference between a "Supercilious" and a "Sardonic" chiseler?
5. What would be your most important reply to the "Reciprocal" chiseler?
6. Which type of chiseler would you rather work with, and why?
7. Which do you think is the most frequent type of chiseler today, and how would you handle him?
8. What is the "Unethical" chiseler's method of operation?
9. How does the "Discontented" type of chiseler operate, and how would you forestall him?
10. How does the "Extra Service" chiseler operate, and how would you handle him?

STUDY SUGGESTIONS

1. How many different types of chiselers can you list right now?
2. What effect do you think chiseling has on business in general?

3. In what way do you think industrial trade associations might have any effect upon chiselers?
4. Do you think chiseling and price-cutting are identical? If not, why not, and how do they differ?
5. What effects do you think chiseling has upon the profits of yourself, your company, and your company's selling program?

CHAPTER XV

How to Beat Friendship Competition

MANY A TIME a salesmanager gets the report that his sales-man is stymied by the buyer who says: "Sorry, old fellow, but So-and-so is a good friend of mine and he supplies all my requirements."

I'll admit that may be a tough nut to crack without the right nutcracker. We have to step on eggshells to try to sell that buyer, because it just isn't so easy to say anything against a friend. But isn't there some twist—some "reverse English"—by which this very "friendship" competition can be turned to one's own advantage? Truly, there are two sides to every objection. This being so, even the "friendship" objection offers an angle or two that can be presented in our own favor; but we've got to be mighty careful about our comeback—our answers must be presented so tactfully and so smoothly that no friendly toes will be stepped on.

Here are fifteen sensible answers to the man who says he must buy from his friend. They are answers that will hold water against even the tightest form of "friendship" competition, simply because they are reasonable, logical, truthful and practical:

1. Keep an Open Mind

No matter how good your friend may be, he cannot have everything. Some of the things he doesn't have, may

179

be just the things you need. Why close your mind to everything else developing around you just because one man supplies all your requirements? The broadminded buyer today listens to everyone's story and is ready to take advantage of any new idea that presents definite promise of betterment. While his friend may get most of the breaks, the modern buyer doesn't permit his friendships to replace his judgment or to interfere with his openminded perspective of the market. If he did, he would soon find himself in a state of splendid isolation—which, while it might be splendid, might not be most beneficial to a well-rounded business!

2. Don't Dry Up Your Sources of Supply

This is an easy thing to do, but a dangerous one. While your friend may be taking care of you now, he may not take care of you forever; and when you and he come to the parting of the ways you may find yourself out on a limb. While he was serving you, you gave everyone else the cold shoulder. Other suppliers may have given you up as hopeless, and if you suddenly have to turn to them after a long period of "frozen consideration" you may find yourself faced with the same cold shoulder! An occasional order here and there outside your regular friendly supplier helps to keep the chill off the atmosphere and is good insurance for you later on.

3. Lazy Buying

Friendship buying leads to lazy buying! And lazy buying is literally what it means—the type of buying that makes a man too lazy to look around the market, to check up on prices and terms, to examine qualities and styles, to consider packaging, shipping and general service, etc.,

etc. It is so easy to say to Bill Jones:—"Ship me fifty each of the same models I got a couple of months ago." But it is *not* so easy to alibi yourself out of a jam when the boss discovers that his competitor is featuring a brand new model that you never even heard of, let alone looked at when the salesman came around! By the time you've talked yourself out of that impasse you may have acquired a different viewpoint on this subject of friendship buying.

4. Don't Keep All Your Eggs in One Basket

It may be all right, if you can spend all your time watching that one basket, but you probably have other things to do, too. Safer to have several salesmen watching your problems, than to have all your eggs in the basket of one man who is mortal enough to pick up just as many troubles as your eggs. In the final analysis, it is much more efficient to divide your problems among different salesmen who have the inclination—and who can spare more time than you can—to specialize on each individual problem. In this way you can be assured of not only uninterrupted service regardless of what may happen to one man, but you also have the advantage of choosing from several different solutions and from several different minds.

5. Friendship Bias

No matter how good your friend is, he cannot help but be prejudiced in favor of his own line and against every other line. Wouldn't you act the same if you were in his boots? Of course you would! Consequently, when you ask for his suggestions and recommendations, do you honestly expect to receive an unbiased opinion? If you have new ideas that conflict with his line, he is certainly going to talk you out of them if he can. After all, that's what he gets paid for. Yes, he can do that and still feel that he is loyal in his friendship for you, because *he* honestly believes that his line is better for you than any other. It is you who should be in an untrammeled position to act as umpire between several *different* lines, to avoid the very certain danger and narrowness that stem from friendship bias.

6. Two Heads Are Better Than One

Whether you are buying or selling, the old adage still holds true. To get an impartial, unbiased viewpoint of any problem in a particular industry, you sometimes have to go out of the industry. But to get it within the industry —and to get the technical aspect of the industry with it—the best way is to get the opinions of several different salesmen and then to orient their combined opinions to your particular problem. Do you think you can get anywhere along that line with just one friendly salesman? Have you ever tried it—and do you know how rare is the salesman who can give you a broad picture of his entire industry without tying it down to his own individual line?

7. Labor Turnover of Salesmen

This presents just as much of a problem with salesmen as with any other type of employee. About the time you have put all your eggs in one basket and turned that basket over to one friendly salesman, he may find himself out of a job and out of that industry,—and you may find yourself with an empty basket! Nothing to do but do the same job all over again, with similar prospects of the same problem recurring later. How much safer to divide your requirements among two or more different sources of supply and thus insure a regular, steady flow of everything that your one exclusive friend can give you!

8. Friendship Covers a Multitude of Sins

The things you won't stand for with the average salesman, you take without complaint from your regular salesman-friend. The sins that are covered by a halo of friendship include practically everything in the category of selling; but never a murmur from you until someone higher up takes a hand and decides that good selling is better than good friendship. A penchant for extreme friendship regardless of anything else has placed more than one buyer on the block by affecting his efficiency and his buying judgment. Friendship is splendid; but friendship carried to unpractical extremes can occasionally involve a buyer in a net of obligations that he finds it impossible to break through.

9. You Cannot Fight a Friend

Friendship sometimes ties a buyer's hands and stills his wrath, to his own misfortune. It is uncomfortable and embarrassing to criticize or argue with a friend. No matter what his mistakes or his misadventures, the softening shadow of friendship frequently prevents the criticism that you could direct at the average salesman to remedy a bad situation. With any other salesman who walks into your office, you can lay down the law and correct any attitude or mishap that might have caused trouble. But you always find it difficult to fight with a friend; so the grievance is allowed to slide.

10. Friendship Brings False Security

A man who buys constantly from one salesman-friend is likely to develop a false sense of security, in that he gets in the habit of depending on his friend for more than he should. He loads more and more of his problems on the salesman's shoulders; and as the load increases he may get less and less in return. He sometimes forgets that the salesman has other customers to take care of, also, and that no salesman can have the same vital interest in a problem as the buyer himself. Consequently, a buyer is frequently disappointed in the results he gets from his friendship. If he had several salesmen at hand to take care of the load he would have a series of fresh, new, differing viewpoints to solve his problems.

11. New Minds Mean New Ideas

Whatever your business, whatever your problems, whatever your requirements—there is greater safety in numbers. A new mind presents a new aspect of an old problem, an entirely new idea for a new clientele, a constructive presentation of modern selling, a new product to replace a staple, a new bit of window dressing for an old front —all these things and more are available to you when you have different minds and different suppliers to draw from. No one mind can supply everything, but everything that you need can be had from different minds in the same industry. New minds mean not only new ideas, but also immensely greater possibilities for your own business!

12. Competition Tests Your Friends

Even your friend will be put on his mettle by competition. True, he may not like it; but after all, are you concerned with what he may like or with what you should have? Competition is the life of trade and salesmen are the life of competition. Your friend cannot compete with himself; you need one or two other salesmen in the picture; and when you have finally obtained this competition in quality, in styles, in prices, in everything that enters into the picture, then you can feel assured that you are getting all you should get either from your friend or from other salesmen.

13. Friends Take All for Granted

The average salesman-friend who supplies all of your requirements is sometimes apt to take too much for granted. He knows he handles all your business; he knows you look to him for all your needs; and as a result, he feels that he doesn't have to exert himself too much to keep on getting your business. He may unconsciously let down in his selling and take your business entirely too much for granted. With this let-down, you lose the value of his flow of creative ideas and suggestions, and eventually your business gets into a rut with him and stays there. First thing you know, someone else comes along and puts you in the shade by telling you and showing you how much you have missed; and if you are the smart buyer you're supposed to be you make additions to your salesmen's list that will insure the free flow of new ideas and suggestions that you require!

14. I Don't "Go After" Competitive Business

I never deliberately go after another man's business and try to take an account away from him. Why give him a good excuse to do the same to me? But if I am called in by you and asked to solve some specific problem, then I can forget the other salesman entirely and go right to work for you with a will. I lay all my cards on the table; I offer you everything I've got; I present myself, my factory and my merchandise in the best light I possibly can; I do everything I legitimately can to interest you (except talk about my competitor) ; and then, if you give me an order, I do everything I can to make good. But I never deliberately attempt to displace another salesman. There is only one man who can do that—and that is the buyer!

15. Business Experience

Frequently a buyer will overlook one of the most important details of a salesman's ability—his personal background and business experience. He may think that the only thing of value is the merchandise he sells him. He overlooks the pertinent fact that with the merchandise itself the salesman should have the knowledge and ability to present some advertising and sales promotion ideas, some display and demonstration ideas, some information about the manufacture and use of the merchandise, or other ideas that will help to build up the merchandise in the eyes of the buyer and his customers. Only a salesman with the right background and experience can do these things, and only such a salesman is entitled to the precedence and preference that a friendly buyer is inclined to give him. It is all very well to desire such preference from a buyer; but when you get right down to brass tacks, how many salesmen have the background that entitles them to such preference?

Test Questions

1. How does openmindedness benefit the average buyer?
2. Why should a buyer bother with more than one source of supply?
3. What do we mean by lazy buying?
4. Is it a good idea for a buyer to keep all his eggs in one basket?

5. In what way would you say that friendship covers a multitude of sins?

6. In what way does friendship buying sometimes tie a customer's hands?

7. If new minds bring new ideas, how can they have any effect on the customer's business?

8. How can a buyer use competition to test his friend's ability as a good salesman for him?

9. What do you think of the salesman who takes a customer's business for granted?

10. In what way can the business experience and background of different salesmen help the buyer?

STUDY SUGGESTIONS

1. Of the fifteen ways listed to beat friendship competition, which do you think would be the three most effective, and why?

2. Select any product you wish and show how a customer might suffer from too much friendship bias.

3. Can you think of any one product in which it would be possible to beat friendship competition?

4. Discuss in detail the advantages of two heads over one, and show how the labor turnover of salesmen might have an unfortunate effect on the buyer.

5. In what way do you think friendship buying might prove to be embarrassing for the buyer, and what is the best way for him to avoid it?

CHAPTER XVI

How to Build Repeat Sales

ONE sale makes friends—repeat sales make profits! Admitting this truism, anything that properly helps to build repeat sales goes a long way toward increasing profits.

Repeat business is built entirely on a keystone of Confidence—confidence in the firm, the product, the salesman. All selling being a matter of confidence, anything and everything that contributes to the customer's confidence, increases the salesman's business.

The factors that develop confidence of the customer in the salesman are so simple as to be elementary—so elementary as to be overlooked—but so important that they bear constant repetition. One salesman says he has a customer "all sewed up"—and yet a wiser salesman crashes through his defenses and takes the customer away! Not because he has an "in" or because he is lucky, but because he has been able to instil greater *confidence* in the mind of the customer.

These 10 "confidence factors" streamline their way into the customer's consciousness, smoothly and persuasively, and build the repeat habit! There is no short cut about them. It is a case of the longest way 'round being the shortest way to the business! But it is the only way that customer relationship can be built—brick by brick—on a basis of enduring permanence. Let us, then, consider these confidence factors briefly and see how we can apply them to our own job of building repeat sales.

1. A Reliable Firm

The mere statement that my firm is reliable, no matter how emphatically I may repeat it, doesn't mean a thing. To bridge the gap between my tonsils and the mind of the customer, I must dramatize my firm's reliability with interesting facts and comparative figures and with concrete examples drawn from everyday experience.

For instance, I might say that my firm has been in business 40 years. So what? Age alone means nothing. But if I say that during their entire 40 years of experience they have been so progressive that they have led the industry in new developments, new ideas, new improvements of their products; that they have always been looked up to as the quality leader; that they have always been known to bend over backwards in making necessary adjustments; that they have never been known to let down or fall down on a customer; that they always put themselves in the position of the customer and consider his angle first; that other manufacturers in the industry hold them in high respect because of their supreme position; and if I supplement these statements with actual facts and figures and names, showing credit ratings, financial standing, names of customers, friends, etc.—then I have said something that appeals directly to my customer's questioning attitude and that helps to break down his skepticism!

I might even go further and tell him how we handled a recent shipment to a man he knows; how it was badly damaged in transit and that, even though we were not responsible, we duplicated the shipment *first* and argued with the transportation company about it later, even though it cost *us* money; that in another case where there was an alleged shortage, even though our count was as good as the customer's, we made good immediately without argument; that in still another case, where there could have been an honest difference of opinion as to which way a job should have been made, we took it back promptly and made it the other way to satisfy the customer; and I could add that we do this sort of thing constantly because it is the only way we know how to do business! Is there any question of how close to the customer I can get with such practical examples of reliability?

2. A Good Product

Repeat sales can only be made with a good product; but I must dramatize and build up a comparison picture of the goodness of the product before I can build up repeat sales on it. Merely to tell the customer that this is the best product on the market only makes him more blasé. I must be able to tear down my product, piece by piece, and prove to the customer how and why and where it is a good product; why it is better than some other product; why it will sell better or give better service; wherein its improvement or betterment lies; why we know it to be a good product and why other people will consider it the same; what makes a product good and what is responsible for its repeat sales; and I must be able to quote actual names of other customers who consider this a good product and who constantly give us repeat business on it. In this way I can present my product to the customer with a background of specific fact and actual proof that are convincing in themselves and that do not require supplementary statements of generalities. Nothing proves like good proof! And a good product requires just as much proof as a poor one—sometimes more—because it may have the additional handicap of a little higher price!

3. An Unusual Salesman

A salesman is unusual in so far as he can do the usual thing in an unusual manner. He may have a personality that is beyond the ordinary in its dynamic attraction and pleasantness. He may have an address and a manner of approach that betoken authority and bespeak attention. In his presentation, he may have a style of sparkling interest or an attitude of convincing dignity. His background of experience and his consequent knowledge of the customer's problems may have equipped him with a sureness and a confidence that begets a like confidence in the mind of the customer. At any rate, he is not apt to be flippant, or ridiculous, or belittling in his contacts.

The salesman who seizes every opportunity to instil more confidence in the mind of his customer is the man who continues to make more money as he grows along! He is entitled to be called "unusual" because he guards against doing the usual things that ordinary salesmen do. He always manages to add some plus value to his acts; and in doing so, he builds respect, appeal and confidence at the same time that he is building repeat sales!

4. Indisputable Value

Price is one thing, value is another—but the two are frequently confused, one with the other. The true method of estimating the cost of an article is in its value; and value is represented by the equation: Price divided by the amount of Satisfactory Service!

Most people ask for the price of an article when they

are really concerned about its value, which is its true cost. Strange how few salesmen are prepared to discuss cost in terms of value rather than price! In building for repeat sales, this is particularly important, because we can open the eyes of many a buyer and many a customer by stressing the *value* of our product in terms of the equation given above. And they will listen, too, if the equation is dramatized by specific examples proving how long the particular product (or a similar product) has given satisfactory service.

We are rapidly coming out of the price era of buying and entering the value stage. All that is necessary is for us to keep pounding away on the exigency of value, which, in the long run, is what everyone is really interested in anyway. If we will bear in mind that price is a commonly used misnomer, and steer clear of it as much as possible, we will eventually prove our claims to indisputable value and go a long way toward convincing the customer and keeping him sold!

5. *Constructive Contacting*

Strange as it may seem, contacting as a fine art is not too well understood among salesmen. Making regular contacts on a customer and developing a rising curve of interest is one of the most delicate problems in selling— particularly in building repeat sales.

An occasional call to say: "Hello, how's business" is many a salesman's idea of making a contact and is his method of keeping himself in the mind of his customer. He overlooks the fact that it is one thing to make "just a contact"—but another thing to make a contact that *sticks*!

Yes, the customer may remember you; but will it be

just a casual, passive remembrance, or will *your* company, *your* personality, *your* product strike a spark in his memory as something out of the ordinary? What have you done to increase his interest, to build up his desire, to retain his confidence? Have you added another solid brick to the foundation you laid in previous calls? Have you added another tiny bit of *favorable* impression that will stick with him until your next call or until he needs another shipment of your merchandise?

I don't believe it is *ever* advisable to make an ordinary "hello" call on a customer. I believe my customer likes me to remember that his time is just as valuable as mine—probably more so—and if I want to keep myself constantly welcome I must keep myself constantly interesting. And to accomplish this, I *never* make a goodwill call without having some little thing of interest with me—whether it is a new sample, a new specification, a new plan, a new advertisement, a new model, or even just a brain flash—so long as it is up the customer's alley! I like to feel that he can see the door open on my presence with a feeling of anticipation rather than with a sinking feeling of boredom.

Whether I call on that customer ten times or twenty times, I believe that I must add a little more interest at every call in order to compound my personal value in his mind and to build up my desirability as his regular supplier. Every salesman has his own idea about making a call; but every call-back had better be built on an idea or it is liable to result in a call-down!

6. Uncommon Service

More than one buyer has been known to place his repeat business with a certain salesman because he could be

counted on for uncommonly fine service. While the word
service has been badly abused and exploited, its true definition is still the "act or occupation of serving"—and he
serves best who serves first! When the customer wants
service, he doesn't want to argue about it or wait for it.
And that applies whether it is a delivery, an adjustment,
a repair job, or some act of personal service required from
the salesman. He expects the salesman to keep him advised
of price changes or opportunities, model or product
changes, changes in delivery or manufacturing schedules,
style or fashion changes, new trends and developments in
the line—in short, anything of interest to the buyer in his
use or re-sale of the company's products. And the ratio of
his respect for the salesman will rise or fall in direct proportion to the amount and character of this service as, if
and when he receives it! Uncommon service is the nearest
thing I know of to a short cut on the road to repeat sales!

7. Creative Helpfulness

As a supplement to service, nothing is more outstanding than the help a salesman can give his customer in the
marketing or merchandising of his line. It is not always
possible, of course; but where circumstances will permit,
the salesman does a good turn for himself as well as for his
customer by tactfully passing along all possible information of practical value from his personal experience or
from his contacts in the territory.

In addition to information of a general nature, the
salesman may also be able to work with the salespeople
who sell the line for the retailer, dealer or wholesaler, or
with the employees who use the product in the offices of
the customer. If the product is of a technical nature, a
few words of explanation to the employees who use it will

go a long way towards building acceptance. If it has new and unusual features, they can be presented to the salespeople as strong selling points. The wide-awake salesman will locate many points in his customers' organizations where this strategy of creative helpfulness will earn him the appreciation of his customer and his continued patronage.

8. Complete Knowledge

Certainly the salesman who knows his line fully and completely is best equipped to develop the confidence of his customer. Not only is it desirable to know the line itself, but the application of the various items in the line to similar or allied items used or sold by the customer.

This is an age of cooperative specialization. The specialist who knows his line from A to Z, and who is well grounded in the most efficient methods of putting his various products to satisfactory use or in line for effective distribution, is the man who endears himself to the customer. He is the salesman who never needs to worry about the repeat sales from that customer. He is the man whom the customer speaks about as "my regular salesman." Just let a competitor try to break into *that* business!

9. Sparkling Enthusiasm

Not the kind that bubbles over vociferously with neither rhyme nor reason, but the constructive type that has a point and is tied to an ultimate objective. A lot of men blare forth that "this is the greatest thing of its kind" instead of tying down their enthusiasm to some specific proof or practical comparison.

A salesman who is enthusiastic about his product can overcome a multitude of other sins, and he has a right to be optimistic about the customer's acceptance; but he does *not* have a right to take the customer's acceptance for granted just because he is enthusiastic. If he does, he is due for many a dull thud of disappointment. In his contacts, he must carry on his enthusiasm from one call to another. He must still do a first-class job of constructive selling. But it can be said without fear of contradiction that a spirit of sparkling enthusiasm will help him over many a rough spot and bring back many a repeat order again and again!

10. Constant Dependability

There is no substitute for dependability. Whether the customer is contacted over a period of six months or six years, he must always be made to feel and given to understand that the salesman is constantly dependable no matter what stress or what circumstances may develop. With the loss of that confidence in the salesman, the customer loses everything—interest, desire, appetite—and repeat sales are transformed into initial orders for a competitor.

The most dangerous situation arises when a salesman reaches the point where he takes a customer for granted! He unconsciously lets down and eventually passes out of the picture. Moral: Never take a customer for granted! Take him as an opportunity and as a constant challenge to your spirit of constructive salesmanship. Only on this basis can repeat sales be built on a bedrock foundation of everlasting confidence!

Test Questions

1. How many of the Ten Confidence Factors can you remember?
2. What value is there in building repeat sales?

3. What is the best way to build permanent customer relationship?

4. As between a reliable firm and a good product, which factor do you think would carry the greater weight in building repeat sales and a permanent customer relationship?

5. What would you consider the essential characteristic of a good salesman in building repeat sales?

6. State what we mean by "contacting as a fine art."

7. What is the most effective way to make good-will calls?

8. In what way can the "creative helpfulness" of a salesman build repeat sales?

9. If we say a salesman's enthusiasm is constructive, how does it compare with that which is non-constructive, or destructive?

10. Why is dependability important in a salesman, particularly one trying to build repeat sales?

Study Suggestions

1. Consider yourself the salesman of an intial order to a prospect. What are several things you would do to attempt to build repeat sales and to make a permanent customer of the buyer?

2. List the Ten Confidence Factors; and next to each Factor write down its opposite. Does a chart like this emphasize the constructive importance of the Ten Confidence Factors as shown?

3. If you had to justify your firm's position in an industry and prove its supreme reliability, how many things could you say about it?

4. Likewise, how many constructive things do you think you could say about one good product?

5. What is the advantage of discussing price in terms of Value?

CHAPTER XVII

How to Use Advertising

ADVERTISING is to selling what voice is to telling! Advertising does a splendid job of reducing sales resistance, building up sales acceptance, and increasing sales turnover. Then why not tie it down to our individual selling and focus it sharply on every one of our prospects and customers in our daily contacts? Here are a dozen ways for salesmen to capitalize on the firm's advertising investment.

Advertising and selling are the Siamese twins of modern distribution! The salesman who plays up his advertising is just as smart as the advertising man who plays up his selling. The salesman is really in a better position—he can capitalize immediately on the advertising by using it in his selling directly to cut down the sales resistance of the prospect and to get the order.

It is both interesting and valuable to see how many different ways there are of using advertising in helping us to make sales. It is of secondary importance whether we use it as a direct selling help, or as indirect suggestion, or as an atmospheric back-drop in the stage setting of our daily effort. The important thing is that we *use* it *regularly* in one form or another; that we create new ways to tie up with, and to capitalize on, the thousands upon thousands of dollars invested in advertising the products we sell.

How we use advertising in daily selling may be largely up to our own initiative; so here are a few suggestions to act as practical stimuli to our salesmanship:

1. Used as Prestige

Advertising that builds prestige and reputation for a manufacturer builds the same qualities for the dealer that handles his line. And that same prestige has cast a shower of glory over many a doubting dealer and contributed definitely to his material success, whether he admits it or not!

Nothing succeeds like success; and nothing makes for success so surely as prestige and reputation. Every prospect and every customer is perfectly willing to ride along to success on the prestige of a reputable manufacturer, particularly if that prestige is sold to him in the wake of an impressive advertising campaign.

Advertising that builds prestige is one of the strongest weapons known to salesmen in persuading dealer acceptance and dealer continuance. It would be a shortsighted or short-tempered customer, indeed, who would fly in the face of providence and turn down or discontinue a line that has been built up to a prestige peak by continuous advertising. Advertising campaigns are used successfully to bring dealers into the fold—and keep them there—because they know the manufacturer won't fold up so long as he continues advertising properly. The salesman who uses every piece of his firm's advertising to persuade his dealers to tie in with this known prestige and reputation is cashing in on one of the most valuable selling helps he could lay his hands on! He is doing his customers a favor, because he is offering them a plus value that is nothing less than added profit insurance on the line!

2. Increasing Turnover

Every one of the firm's advertisements that creates a continued demand for their products is a definite help to your customer in increasing his rate of turnover. Profits increase as turnover increases; and turnover increases largely because it is built up incessantly by the firm's advertising! This is not only a logical talking point with your regular customer, but it is also a helpful big stick in breaking down the sales resistance of the hesitant prospect.

Each advertisement that appears on a particular product has a definite cash value to the customer. Show it to him in your advertising portfolio, or in its actual magazine or newspaper setting, and let him see for himself how it helps to increase his rate of turnover by building up demand.

Never overlook an opportunity to stress the advertising in its relation to the customer's business and the customer's profits! It is important to remember, too, that advertising not only increases the rate of turnover for the customer—it also increases the rate of confidence in his mind. But when it comes to a discussion of profit possibilities in handling the line, there is no single point more valuable than the advertising that helps to increase the customer's turnover!

3. Personal Publicity

Every customer is human enough to enjoy seeing his name in print; and one of the most potent pieces of sales leverage is the advertisement that allows the customer to tie in with his own name. Whether it is newspaper, magazine, outdoor, direct mail, radio broadcasting or any other kind of advertising—if it carries the name of the customer, it carries a handle that the salesman can grasp and use to good advantage.

With an implication of subtle flattery and personal prestige, a customer can be induced to feel a pleasure and satisfaction out of all proportion to the cost of the effort. And, of course, there is a real merchandising value to this tie-in. It ties the advertisement down to a specific place of distribution and ties the dealer up with a well-known manufacturer. The salesman who is eager to get every bit of help that the advertising can give him will play up this merchandising value in a big way and get the customer to realize that it is of even more advantage to him to be tied up with the manufacturer in this way, than the reverse; because in the majority of cases, the average customer will benefit materially from association with a great big manufacturer who is well and favorably known.

4. Reliability Assured

One of the most common come-backs of the average prospect in a sales discussion is that he doesn't know anything about the manufacturer's reliability. And he is not to be sneered at for this attitude, because it is only natural.

Aside from credit ratings and financial standing, one of the strongest possible indications of a manufacturer's reliability is a continuous program of advertising. An unreliable firm would hardly be expected to make the substantial investment necessary for good advertising. Thus, the salesman who represents a regular advertiser has at his hand another valuable bit of sales ammunition in answering objections of this kind. He can even anticipate the objection by bringing the reliability of his firm to the foreground with the advertising.

5. *Quality Guaranteed*

The same thing can be said of quality as was said of reliability. No manufacturer can afford to continue advertising a product of inferior or deceptive quality. No manufacturer who advertises regularly can afford to take chances with his quality and thus take a chance of losing out on a big advertising investment.

In this way, advertising in itself is an additional guarantee of a quality product; and every customer on the salesman's list must be continually sold on the fact that this additional quality guarantee is ever present in the firm's advertising! Here is just another effective weapon for the salesman who is smart enough to tie up the advertising to his selling.

6. *Sales Promotion Helps*

Advertising is the backbone of sales promotion, and sales promotion is the backbone of selling! Everything that comes under the head of advertising can be used in modern sales promotion. However, many times the sales promotion man doesn't know about all the helps available from the manufacturer and it is up to the salesman to keep him informed. *This* is the salesman's opportunity!

Every manufacturer uses a number of different kinds of advertising and sales promotion helps designed to develop desire and to stimulate demand from the dealer. The publication advertising—newspaper, magazines and trade journals—does the first line job. Proofs and reprints can be used by the salesman in personal contacts or in the mails. Then there are radio broadcasting, outdoor advertising, cooperative advertising campaigns, and commercial movies—all of which present possibilities for merchandising to the customer. In addition, there are dealer helps, samples and novelties, point-of-sale material, and home and store demonstrations. Last but not least, there are direct mail campaigns that include a host of folders, leaflets, broadsides and letters.

It is important for the salesman to keep in touch with all this advertising material, and to see that his customer is kept in touch and supplied with his needs. The customer knows that his sales promotion man cannot begin to keep advised on all this material; and it is a narrow-minded customer who would not appreciate the salesman's help in this respect. To say nothing of his being a mighty short-sighted salesman who couldn't see the value of going the whole way in extending this helpful service to his customer!

7. Style Authority

When a manufacturer "tells the world" that the style of his particular garment is right up to the minute, his statement is pretty apt to be authentic. After all, the larger the audience, the greater his need for authenticity and the greater his position of authority. We certainly should be able to capitalize and depend upon the style flashes of a large advertiser; not just because he is an advertiser, but because, by virtue of his tremendous investment in the advertising, he must make doubly sure that his style really is authentic so as not to jeopardize his investment.

Therefore, the customer who rides along on this manufacturer's advertising investment can depend upon a style authority that is the last word in assurance. And the salesman's job is just that much easier as he brings these facts to the attention of his customer!

8. Business Testimonials

Many a smart advertiser uses the names of well-known customers in his advertising; and many a smart salesman capitalizes on these advertised names and uses them as sales leverage in cutting down the resistance of new prospects. It is a well-known trait of human nature that one man pays more attention to an item that another man uses; and if this customer's name is played up in the advertising, it results in the finest kind of testimonial—the kind that can actually be used to get new business! Testimonials of this nature carry an authority and conviction that can never be equaled by reams of so-called testimonial letters.

9. Technical Information

Frequently advertising is used to play up certain technical details and specifications that are new to the trade or not too well understood. The same thing applies to the various uses of a product, or to the discovery of new uses of old familiar products.

It also happens occasionally (and unfortunately) that the salesman himself is not fully informed by his factory and sometimes gets this information directly from the advertising. In such cases, the salesman has a double duty—first, to familiarize himself with the details; second, to pass the story on to his customers. Much of this type of material appears in trade journal advertising; some of it in catalog supplements or direct mail folders; occasionally, a technical improvement of outstanding importance will appear in magazine or newspaper advertising.

All of this material is made to order for the salesman. It is convenient to use, helpful, interesting, valuable—and it is usually appreciated by the customer. Particularly convenient for the salesman are the reprints he receives from his factory; and if he doesn't receive them, he can probably get them for the asking and put them to good use. The principal problem is for the salesman to know what to ask for, to know what he can use and how he can use it!

10. Helping the Product Family

When a manufacturer makes a long line of products, and advertises a new product in the line, the advertising should tie up with the entire family of products; and then the salesman can use this advertising to acquaint his customer still further with the other items in the line.

Customers don't always buy a manufacturer's entire family of products. If they did, the salesman's life would be a bed of roses. But because they don't, it is the salesman's job constantly to remind his customer of every other item in the line. Advertising that ties up with the entire line is a great help to the salesman. It turns the trick painlessly, easily and effectively; and it should earn the undying gratitude of the thinking salesman because it simplifies his job and helps to build up his business. All he needs to do with advertising of this kind is to *use* it!

11. Publicity Stories

Every now and then we see a straight publicity story break on some new product; or on some new invention that brings about changes in an industry; or about some manufacturer or group of manufacturers; or about some well-known personality with whom we, or our customer, may have a connection; or some national development with which our line may be connected.

News of this type is the most interesting kind of advertising for us; and there is no reason why we cannot capitalize on such newspaper or magazine stories just as we do on our advertising. The customer may be interested in anything that concerns the line being handled by him—and we are certainly interested in the same thing. Regardless of what kind of publicity it is, so long as it is favorable, so long as it has some bearing on the line or on the customer or on ourselves, let's take hold of it and use it for all it is worth!

12. Direct Mail Helps

Not every man likes to write letters, but every salesman can write an occasional note to a prospect or a customer that ties up with the advertising and helps to put it across.

I am a great believer in every salesman being supplied with a sufficient quantity of proofs, reprints, folders, leaflets, catalogs, samples, etc., etc., so that he may be able to pass them out properly, either in person or through the mails, and thus be the direct means of tying up the advertising with the product through his own salesmanship. When I acknowledge a customer's order, I like to be able to enclose with my letter a reprint of one of our latest advertisements. When I write to a prospect, I want to enclose a folder that tells an interesting story and supports my salesmanship. When I write to check up on a customer's re-orders, I might enclose a proof of a new advertisement that has some special message for him. When I answer a complaint by mail, I want to be able to enclose an insert of some kind that will add a soothing, interesting touch to my letter. And when I acknowledge an inquiry by mail, I certainly want to be able to enclose some prestige-building advertising material as well as the necessary technical specifications!

Direct mail helps are extremely useful to the salesman because they do a practical bit of work all by themselves, and at the same time they help to carry on the salesman's job of contracting. And last, but not least important, the type of direct mail that is developed into a substantial campaign—with letters, folders, broadsides, etc.—is one of the most effective things in the world for salesmen's tie-ups and one of the most resultful methods of using advertising in selling!

Test Questions

1. What is the position occupied by advertising in modern business?
2. What is the relationship between advertising and selling?
3. In what way can advertising be of value to us in our selling?
4. How can advertising build prestige for a manufacturer?
5. What do you think is the difference between advertising and publicity?
6. What do you think is the difference between advertising and merchandising?
7. What do you think is the difference between advertising and sales promotion?
8. How many specific advertising helps can you recall?
9. What are business testimonials, and what do you think of them as compared to general testimonials?
10. What do we mean by the "product family"?

Study Suggestions

1. Consider the subject of turnover; and tell us exactly how turnover can be aided by advertising, and how the entire subject can help us in our selling.
2. List all the different ways you can recall of using

advertising to help in your selling; then tell us which you think are the three most valuable, and why.

3. How many different advertising mediums do you know of, and which do you think could be used as a selling help?

4. What do you understand by the term "sales promotion helps"? List five such helps that could be of value to you in your selling.

5. Tell us exactly what you understand by the term "direct mail helps." List five such helps that could be tied in to your selling efforts.

CHAPTER XVIII

How to Dramatize Your Selling

Long passed into ancient history are the days when a salesman walked into a customer's office, threw a sample on his desk, and intimated by his manner and by his tone that if he didn't get the order right then and there, it would be the customer's own hard luck. The old-time high-pressure seller's market of "take it or leave it" has been transformed into a low-pressure buyer's market of "leave it and talk it over."

In the present era of salesmanship there is a great deal more to selling than just throwing down a sample, casually and nonchalantly, and picking up the order. Highly intensified and increasing competition for the buyer's dollar is forcing the individual salesman to a much higher plane of constructive effort; and one of his most vitally important tools in today's selling is the quality of Dramatization!

Dramatization is the highest degree of showmanship—and showmanship is the highest type of salesmanship! Dramatization is not confined to the theater—not by any means. It is the showmanship learned and lifted from the theater that makes dramatized selling so effective and so productive. The more intelligently we develop the vital elements of dramatization—action, suspense, mystery, curiosity—and the more directly we focus our dramatized selling, the more easily do we weaken the resistance of the prospect and get his name on the dotted line.

Have you ever noticed how many of the better salesmen are skilled actors, with a highly developed flair for the dramatic? Their entrance, their tone of voice, their approach, their dominant personality, their methods of arousing interest and suspense, their dramatic attitude—every detail of their presentation indicates an instinct for showmanship that pays big dividends.

If you would see a splendid example of such showmanship, watch a group of children at play. Keep your eyes on the one who has the imagination to suggest spectacular games and stunts. Notice how that one child is unconsciously respected as the leader of the group. Think ahead twenty years and visualize what that rare quality will mean to that child's career. Then stop to think how many salesmen you have met who have that same quality of showmanship, and how effective or ineffective they have seemed to you!

While the true dramatic flair is instinctive, showmanship can be developed by anyone who will take the trouble to analyze its make-up and to project his imagination accordingly. Only a comparatively few salesmen ever think of the possibilities of dramatic effect in making an entrance, in discussing a product, in showing a sample or demonstrating a process. Many of our so-called "business ambassadors" go through the routine of their jobs with a lack of animation and enthusiasm—with an attitude of laissez faire—that is appalling in its economic waste!

But watch the showman! When he goes to work on a prospect, it is with the sure-fire touch of a thorough trouper. When *he* offers a sample to a prospect, he takes it out of his case with loving care; he presents it with an air of distinction; he builds up a background of appreciation. He knows that admiration breeds admiration;

that the prospect thinks a great deal more of it if he builds it up adroitly with little tricks of stagecraft. This is no common merchandise, the salesman infers, no ordinary product, no run-of-the-mine idea. It is something extraordinarily fine, something uncommon—just as this salesman himself is decidedly out of the ordinary.

Every star producer has his own method of operation, but his operating methods are usually founded on some form of showmanship. One man might throw a brick at an automobile door to prove it has nonshatter glass. Another man might take a sharp knife and deliberately cut open a leather bag to prove its superior construction. One man walks into a prospect's office and lays one or two samples on his desk; while another man walks in and spreads out a *dozen* similar samples, impressing the prospect just that much more. Still another man lays a specially interesting sample to one side and says nothing at all about it, merely to pique the prospect's curiosity and force him to ask for it. The salesman who understands the stimulating value of *handling* fine merchandise insists on the prospect's taking the product in his own hands and feeling it, operating it or trying it out in some way.

Not long ago a shirt manufacturer demonstrated his nonwilt collars by immersing two shirts in a glass water tank in the window; one collar was all wet and soggy while the other looked perfectly fresh and new. One advertiser takes a double-spread in a magazine and leaves the left-hand page entirely blank and white. Another advertiser takes a half page space in a newspaper and sets all his copy in a small island in the center with a dramatic circle of white space around it.

One salesman throws a composition doll up to the ceiling to prove it is nonbreakable; while another salesman hands you a piece of indestructible material and dares you to tear it. Still another salesman lays his watch on top of his product and impresses you with the fact that "it is manufactured and finished as exquisitely as a piece of jewelry."

There is the salesman who deliberately leaves an important argumentative point out of his sales talk, just so as to force a prospect to ask about it and thus give him a chance to make a more impressive statement. There is the salesman who builds up respect for himself by saying, in reply to a request for criticism: "No, I never discuss a competitor's product; I stick to my own merchandise because I find that I have plenty to say about that."

P.S.—And then there is the supershowman, who takes a tip from the letter-writer with his perky postscript climax; *he* intentionally leaves one of his most important points until the end, saying: "Oh, I almost neglected to show you one of the most important features of all!"

Some time ago, in response to specific requests, I received several letters from some of my good customer friends who discussed the subject of dramatization as applied to their own particular business. It is interesting to look at a few excerpts from these letters to see how accurately they reflect the modern sales urge for dramatization and showmanship:

(Bakelite Corporation)

If a man is concerned with strength, we endeavor to demonstrate just how strong Bakelite is by giving him a few samples of various types to break as he may see fit. If he is concerned with odor, we prepare a display of molded parts along with other well-known materials that are ordinarily considered to be odorless, and then ask him to smell each display. We generally emphasize *one particular property*[1] of our product, depending on our customers' needs. For example, it is possible to mold accurate inside and outside threads in Bakelite. Samples prove this point far better than any other method. In turn, inserts can be molded in Bakelite. Again samples tell the story. Photographs and advertising reprints giving a picture of such parts are used. They are effective, but not as effective as the *actual samples* that a man can *take in his hands* and examine closely.

C. W. Blount,
Assistant Manager of Sales.

Notice how thoroughly the Bakelite Corporation are sold on the idea of placing their product actually in the hands of the prospect. Every one of us prefers to see and feel the thing we are going to buy; and the opportunity to do this easily, makes it just that much easier for us to buy.

(General Electric Company)

A good advertisement can be as dramatic and forceful as any method of selling of which I know. For, in the advertisement there are opportunities for *drama of usefulness*. After all, nothing is so forceful to the prospect as *his own application*. Advertisements putting the product in this light really pull. This advertising, to gather real results, must have the backing of salesmen. After the "ad" has opened the door, the salesman has his opportunity. Then, if his strong point is drama, he has the stage well set. The salesman must choose his properties to fit the product and the prospect. For, after all, the real acceptance—the success or failure of a dramatic sales talk—depends on Mr. Prospect. He is the audience—and the play is written for him.

Fred A. Parnell,
Manager, Construction Material Advertising.

[1] All italics by the author.

If advertising is truly salesmanship-in-print, then the type of advertising that accurately portrays the "drama of usefulness" is an effective form of dramatized selling!

(A large Insurance Company)

Life insurance is so intangible that our best salesmen agree that it is usually best sold by the use of *motivating influences* and human interest stories. Our salesmen today are not so much interested in educating the prospect as to what life insurance is; they are more concerned with demonstrating to him what life insurance will do for him if he lives—otherwise, what it will do for his family. It is in this phase of life insurance selling that motivating influences and human interest stories play their greatest part. One of our consistent million dollar producers likes to picture to a prospect first the situation of his family and himself *with* the life insurance service; and then if this does not close the sale, he shows the prospect a similar picture of his family *without* the insurance service. These word pictures are often best illustrated by showing the prospect what *actually happened* to other people in a situation similar to his own.

The motivating influences and human interest stories used in the selling of life insurance are frequently the highest type of dramatization. The outstanding success of the experienced life insurance salesman is sufficient proof of the value of this form of dramatized selling.

(Seagram-Distillers Corporation)

I would say that the drama in selling the Seagram line lies in a few well established facts: 1. Our vast stocks of fine old whiskies which assure uniform quality in a business where uniform quality is a virtue. 2. Our unusual, unique and original packaging. 3. The definite assurance of steady profits through the Seagram price protection policy. 4. The above, coupled with forceful consumer and point-of-sale advertising, which create a large demand. To my knowledge, no other company or line in the distilling industry has all these advantages and very few have even a single one. I think that is drama. Aside from these, we do much of our selling through sales talks, *manuals, charts and photographs*. Please note also that we are the leaders in the distilling industry today and daily strive to maintain that position. An example of how this is done is our good will advertising, along the lines of our "Drink Moderately" advertisement, which appeared in over three hundred newspapers.

William Guyer,
Sales Promotion Manager.

A splendid example of modern visual selling (which in itself is dramatic) supported by spectacular advertising.

(Wickwire Spencer Steel Co.)

When Gold Strand proposed the introduction of the revolutionary measuring tape in each roll of its quality screen wire, some method had to be found for effectively presenting this innovation to both the jobbing and retail hardware trade. Turning movie producer was a distinct departure from the accepted merchandising practice in this industry, as well as in the market to be covered, but its possibilities for a dramatic presentation of a new sales story were so great as to warrant a try. Like the 4-star productions of today—except in cast only—a regulation *all-talking motion picture* was produced. Its title:—"Get on the GOLD STRANDARD" was catchy; and when presented to an accumulative audience of some ten thousand or more at the various hardware expositions, it met with an enthusiastic reception. Many dealers were impressed with the new way in which they had been told of something different in screen wire cloth. This initial attempt was followed with another talking advertising slide film, that served as a follow-up to the first release and has done much to develop dealer acceptance.

K. A. Zollner,
Advertising Manager.

One of the many manufacturing organizations that

has deliberately gone to the theater itself for its dramatized selling.

(A large Wire and Cable Company)

Salesmanship is part showmanship. A percolator sample shown against a background of purple velvet looks richer, brighter, more attractive and more saleable. Copper wire, bare or insulated, is a prosaic thing in itself; but an effective demonstration of a short piece in the making, a little piece of raw rubber, a cut-back sample of the finished product showing the successive layers of material in its construction, presents it as an *interest-compelling object*. That's what I call "Dramatized Selling."

Another splendid example of an industry that offers effective illustrations, demonstrations, and exhibits in a successful attempt to dramatize its products!

Test Questions

1. What is dramatization, and how can it affect our selling?
2. What is the relationship between salesmen and actors?
3. How can we dramatize a sample?
4. What do you think the stage can teach us in dramatizing our selling?
5. How can we dramatize a sales talk?
6. How would you dramatize the strength of a product?
7. What do you think are the stage properties available to the average salesman?
8. What do you think is meant by the term "motivating influence" and how does it become dramatic?
9. How would you dramatize the usefulness of a product?
10. In what way do you think dramatization is allied to visual selling?

STUDY SUGGESTIONS

1. Select a specific product, and list all the points of dramatic interest you could develop for use in your selling.
2. What elements of stage showmanship do you think could be of value to a good salesman?
3. If you had the job of selling a rather drab, ordinary, staple product, what would you do to develop a dramatic background for your sales presentation?
4. Tell us a human interest story with a motivating influence as used by a good insurance salesman, and point out how the same principle could be used in the selling of any product.
5. Select any product you wish, and build up an effective background of showmanship in its presentation.

CHAPTER XIX

How to Make More Sales

UNDER the above heading and under the title of this book, the present chapter shows you how to apply all that has been set forth in previous chapters. You have been shown how to find *prospects*, how to handle them and how to sell them. In this chapter you are given the final word in selling—a 10-point plan with 55 practical suggestions to help intensify your selling to *customers*!

By all means continue to make your regular calls and find all the prospects you can, but *don't forget* that one good customer in the hand is worth a dozen prospects in the bush!

These are days of intensified selling and growing competition. When it comes to developing your sales there is no more profitable method than developing the customers you already have.

It is easier to build a casual buyer into a regular customer than to turn a casual prospect into a buyer. One has already taken your selling to heart, while the other may take the heart out of your selling. The salesman who concentrates on his current customer list has a seven-league advantage against the scattergood who skips all over the territory in the hope of lighting on a good break!

Divide your list of *customers* into the following classes: Casual, medium, good. Bear in mind that if you can devise ways and means to step up each customer only one classification, you will step up your total sales to a sensational degree. Take one customer at a time. Put on your thinking cap and analyze him and his entire business against a check list of possibilities that contains something like the following factors:

1. The Customer Himself

The *special deals* that your factory gives you from time to time will always have an appeal to your customer, particularly if they are attractive and timely—and if they were not, your factory wouldn't promote them! To be doubly appealing, don't fail to stress the practical promotion tie-up. *Special prices* and *job-lot* offers give you an effective advantage, especially when there is such a good reason for them as end-of-season clearances, old models, hurt goods, overstocks, etc. *Special discounts* that you can offer for quantity buying are a prolific source of increased business; many a customer can see his way clear to put more sales pressure behind greater quantities if it is made worth his while. Your *price quotations* for any quantity requested should always include prices for the next two or three higher quantities; you never can tell when a customer may become enthused over a much better price for the next higher quantity.

If you will play up your *cash discounts* properly, you can exert an additional leverage. When you realize that terms of 2 per cent for cash in 10 days means 72 per cent a year, it is worth remembering and featuring at all times. When you walk into a store, do you look over new *counter displays* with a thoughtful eye? And when you walk down the street, either on Main Street or on Broadway, do attractive *window displays* stop you and stimulate your thoughts? **Many a** display in one line of merchandise has offered constructive ideas for another. The same possibility applies to the *special sales* that you might know about, particularly those of a novel character. One of your customers might greet you with open arms and greatly increased business if you gave him a practicable idea for his own business!

The growing practice of *ensemble selling* in many departments and businesses gives you some practical talking points on which you can build more sales per individual customer; and the same is true in the selling of *allied products* all over the store. The idea of selling a pair of shoes to match a dress, or a pair of draperies to match a couch, has been carried forward to a degree where suggestive and allied selling ties up umbrellas with rubbers, electric refrigerators with wedding rings, radios with automobiles, roofing shingles with weather reports, etc. A field of selling that is frequently overlooked is that of *premium selling*. This has tremendous possibilities if your product is at all suited to it—and if you keep your eyes open and make constructive suggestions. The same is true of articles suited for *sales contests* or other types of contests. These are constantly growing in popularity and in possibilities. And don't forget that price is not always an important factor in the better type of contests!

Have you ever sounded out your customer on the possibility of trading up his selling? A small amount of research and observation on your part may develop some striking talking points in favor of better grades of merchandise! In getting up *new samples* for one customer (that are not exclusive), do you ever show them to another? If they are worth making up and showing to the first customer, who can tell how much interest and desire they might arouse in the minds of others?

Incidentally, do you sell your *entire line* to your customer, or only one item? And why? Shouldn't your present customer be your most logical prospect for almost everything you have to sell? Sometimes the customers with one-track buying minds get that way from salesmen with one-track selling minds. Are you in the *double-track* class?

2. The Customer's Employees

How well do you know them—or do you know any of them? Some of the most valuable *tips and ideas* you can get come from friendly employees who are well disposed toward you. A *good* salesman sells everyone he contacts; he never knows where lightning will strike or where favor will arise. Most frequently, your customers depend upon recommendations from their employees or assistants, regardless of what you have for sale. Moral: Your selling job is never done! More than one good salesman has built up his sales with his customer by building up his *contacts* with his employees through strictly legitimate across-the-table selling, by courtesy and consideration, and by friendship! Too many salesmen high-hat the subordinate employee in favor of the superior officer, only to find themselves eventually high-hatted by both!

3. The Customer's Potentialities

In these days of radio, direct-mail, and telephone selling, *territorial lines* are not so tightly drawn around any business. Occasionally, you can introduce your customer to potentialities for your merchandise in neighborhoods and territories he never thought of before, or through channels he never dared consider. You may have heard of *customer preferences* for his store and you may be able to suggest ways and means for him to reach out for more business. It is not impossible that this may result in his opening a *new department* for your merchandise, or *new branches* in new neighborhoods, or *new offices* in other territories. All these things have possibilities at one time or another, and they all mean new business for you!

4. New Campaigns

A common form of increasing sales with your customers is in the effective presentation of your factory's *advertising campaigns*. Certainly a good advertising appropriation by your factory, that will sell the goods off your customers' shelves, merits increased purchases from you! Do you carry your advertising portfolio with you at all times? New *sales promotion* plans likewise provide a potent sales leverage for you. The same arguments hold good with plans for *radio* broadcasting, *direct-mail* campaigns, *telephone* selling, *sampling* campaigns, and plans for home or store *demonstrations*. A new campaign is a new idea; a new idea is a new selling point; and a new selling point should mean new business—all depending on the way you present it to your customer!

5. New Trends

The world today presents to your customer and to you a constantly shifting scene of *fashion* changes. It is a panorama of *new styles* and *new developments* in wearing apparel, in house furnishings, in office appliances, in building construction, in transportation, in industry and commerce, in the arts and sciences—in everything that we live by and live with. The latest novelties and fads soon make way for still newer trends. Off with the old and on with the new! Each succeeding cycle of change results in discarded and outmoded merchandise and products of every kind and character. The salesman who keeps his *eyes open* and his wits at his fingertips senses the possibilities for new business from one change to another. He is at his customer's door almost before the transition occurs and is prepared to take orders for his latest requirements. Such is the profit of watchfulness and preparedness!

6. New Uses

Another prolific source of new business is in taking the fullest advantage of your factory's research work in discovering *new uses* for old products. By means of personal contact in the field and through academic research work, and by contacting store employees who continually feel the pulse of the public, new uses are discovered almost daily. The advertising campaigns and radio broadcasting programs presented by your factory, seeking for new uses, stress the truism that there really *is* something new under the sun, even though it be but an adaptation, modification, or variation of something old. *Keep in touch* with your advertising and sales promotion departments for new ideas under this heading; you never know when a *new suggestion* will provide you with a powerful leverage for greater volume in the item your customer is now buying, or for the acceptance of an additional item or two in your line.

7. New Age Groups

Every twenty-four hours a vast number of men, women, and children enter new age groups. They encounter new conditions of life and build up *new habits* of living.

New habits develop into new *needs* and new *wants*; and new *desires* develop into new *demands* for the things you have to sell your customers. Shakespeare's "seven ages of mankind" thus feed the everlasting cycle of supply and demand. If you can sense the changing needs and desires of the multitudes as they move from one age group to another, you will more often than not discover new reasons for demanding increased volume from your customers!

8. New Wage Groups

Beating their way back to prosperity, we see greater numbers of *wage earners* returning to store, desk, and factory. *Additional* wage groups and increasing *levels* of wages bring the masses of people closer to the *buying line*, with a constantly rising curve of *buying power*. Your factory's research work in checking employment conditions in various localities and neighborhoods will supply you with additional sales ammunition to use on your customer. How many more plants are working full time? How many more men and women are back at their old jobs? How many more dollars are going into pay envelopes and finding their way eventually to stores, dealers, amusements, and services? Do you keep your head up and your eyes open when you travel your territory?

9. New Markets

A greater faith in the stability of better business conditions forces your customers to act on long-delayed plans for expansion, and involves the opening of *new territories*. This results in orders for new *stocks* and *supplies* from you. Changes in *buying habits*, due to a gradual but steady return to *quality* and *luxury* buying, are responsible for the quickening of *sales activities*. Population *shifts* and *changes* affect both old markets and new, and present possibilities that you can follow up and turn into good selling points!

10. Psychological Factors

There are many sides to a sale and many facets to a solicitation. Have you ever considered the effect of *outside influences* on your customer—such as his reputation and yours—among *competitors*, among other *customers* and *friends*? A favorable word passed here and there is of immeasurable service to you, while the opposite is just as destructive. Gossip, rumor, and small talk—if not certain to be favorable to you—must be anticipated and offset in constructive fashion. *Prestige* among different groups is a decided asset to be seized upon and used as a selling point in your favor at every proper opening. Whether he admits it or not, the customer is always interested in the prestige of a product or service as it affects *his* possibilities for profitable use or resale!

But of all the qualities that make it possible for you to increase your customer sales, there is none more important nor more desirable than *personal friendship!* Other things being equal—and they frequently are—the salesman with the more friendly *personality* and with the greater capacity for *helpfulness* is absolutely certain to get the bulk of the business! In calling on your customer you have the contact, you have the entree, you have the personal touch that is bound to react favorably upon the customer's humanness and friendliness *if* you will go more than halfway in extending the same qualities!

It is just the old, old story that "friendliness pays the world's biggest dividends." Whether in commerce or industry, out in the field or behind the bench, no one has ever yet devised a worthy substitute for friendship! Do you know of any?

Test Questions

1. How would you value a customer as against a prospect?
2. What would be the simplest and most effective way of developing your sales?
3. How would you analyze your customers in order to make more sales?
4. Mention six different things you could mention with "a customer himself" that might help you to make more sales.
5. In what way can the customer's employees be of help to you?
6. What new campaigns could you mention that might interest your customer?
7. What is the difference between "new trends" and "new uses"?
8. How could the arguments about new age groups help you in your selling?
9. What do "new wage groups" and "new markets" imply?
10. Can you name three different psychological factors that might help your selling?

Study Suggestions

1. You have a customer whom you have sold two items out of a long line of products. How would you build him up to make more sales?
2. Define in your own words each of the following classes of customers: casual, medium, good. Tell us how you would build one into the other, and how you would keep him as a permanent customer.
3. What do we mean by "the customer's potentialities"— and how would we analyze his potentialities so as to help us make more sales?
4. Tell us in detail how the subject of "new trends" could be developed to make more sales for you?

5. Tell us exactly what value you think friendship has in making more sales, and just how you could capitalize on your friendships in developing customers into the classes of casual, medium, and good.

CHAPTER XX

How to Handle Your Job

AFTER all, the problem of handling your job really reduces itself to the problem of handling yourself! A salesman always handles his job exactly the way he handles himself. If he is timid or pessimistic, he approaches his prospect or customer with an inferiority complex. If he is cynical or sarcastic, he is apt to present a disagreeable front. If he is overly aggressive and full of high pressure, he may go around with a "chip on his shoulder" and find himself frequently in hot water.

On the other hand, if the salesman is in an optimistic, enthusiastic frame of mind; if he is naturally cheerful, friendly, and constructive in his attitude, he is apt to find that expected difficulties have an inspiring habit of vanishing into thin air; and that prospects and customers literally cling to him because of his optimism and enthusiasm. Businessmen like to do business with a constructive type of salesman. There are so many calamity-howlers and crape-hangers in the world that it is a positive relief to encounter a salesman with a cheerful disposition who may be a natural-born optimist, who knows what he is talking about, and who doesn't really think the world is about to come to an end.

The efficient, effective handling of your job as a better-than-average salesman involves so many important personal virtues that to set them all down here would result in a chapter reading like a schoolboy's copybook. Therefore, to tie up these virtues with the specific problems encountered by salesmen everywhere, I have taken the liberty of evolving a new set of Ten Commandments—for salesmen out in the field—hoping they may serve as practical inspiration and present a widely discussed subject in helpful form.

TEN SELLING COMMANDMENTS

1. Sell the "Service Trinity"—Your Firm, Your Product, Your Self!

The ability to dramatize your subject and pull it out of the rut of routine is one of the greatest selling helps known to salesmen. Whether you are selling pins or potatoes, animal crackers or advertising, your prospect *must* be made interested in the Service Trinity.

Believe it or not, the most important member of the Trinity is the Firm you represent. What is their position and prestige in the industry? What is their reputation—for integrity, for quality, for knowledge of their market and merchandise, for progressiveness, for treatment of their customers, for price dependability—for any little thing the prospect might be interested in?

Take the Product you are trying to sell. Is it a staple or a novelty? Is it a service, a necessity, or a luxury? Is it an advance or an improvement over an old model? Has it a quality appeal that lifts it above the head of your competitor, or has it a price advantage that makes it especially desirable? Is it a long-profit item that moves slowly or a short-profit item that sells in volume; or is it that rare combination of long profit and good volume that occasionally appears on the business horizon?

What about your Self? Can you offer your prospect exceptional service? Is there any outstanding interest or value in your personal background or experience? Can you be of any help to your prospect in his business? Do you know his methods, his trade, his problems—and can you prove it? Are you just a casual visitor and order-taker, or do you make a definitely favorable impression that your prospect cannot overlook? Are you just a good mixer, or are you the vital element in the cocktail of selling?

Be proud of your business and you'll have a business to be proud of! Select all the advantages of the Service Trinity—and *dramatize* them. Lift them up, one by one, on your own exclusive little stage, with every bit of showmanship you can develop. Remember that you are only one of a number of salesmen your prospect sees every day. The vital question is, how many does he remember—and *why*?

2. *Keep Your Chin UP!*

No matter how well you know me, don't walk into my office and start crying on my shoulder. The order you lost yesterday or the troubles you had this morning don't interest me—I have my own. If you cannot walk in with a snap in your step and a smile in your voice, for the love of heaven stay out!

Talk optimistic merchandising instead of pessimistic depressionizing. Talk success . . . of men who are doing business—good business . . . of ideas that will develop business . . . of new deals, new prices, new styles, new merchandise . . . of the public that is merchandise-hungry . . . of constructive reorganizing and planning for the good times that are coming. Don't start today by remembering yesterday's defeats. Remember that enthusiasm is contagious—dead-pan selling is negative. If you cannot cheer me up, I can certainly cheer you out!

To sell me a bill of goods today you've *got* to make me believe what I would like to believe, and make me feel the way I would like to feel. I'll do my own gloom-dispensing; but I can certainly soak up a vast amount of hopeful enthusiasm if you can feed it to me properly. I may even forget my troubles and sign on the dotted line.

It is your continual job to generate your own optimism and to recharge your own storage battery when it runs down. If you can do it, you're a self-starter. If your sales manager must do it for you, you're just "one of the salesmen." But whatever you do, don't forget—when you walk into *my* office, keep your chin up!

3. *Know Your Story and Stick to It*

I don't care whether you use a canned sales talk or make an extemporaneous speech—if you cannot talk *interestingly* and *convincingly*, you are out of luck. Present your sales story in logical form—and make it sparkle! Make your prospect feel that you know your subject, or you'll lose both his interest and your audience. The man who walks into my office and starts talking about the weather or telling stories is on a par with the salesman (?) who asks: "You don't want any books today, do you?" Life is too short and fast and furious these days to waste time on salesmen who waste your time.

The great advantage of canned sales talks lies in their logical development of your sales arguments. The smart man is the one who can take this material and present it in his own interesting manner, so that the prospect actually gets a glimmer of what it is all about before he loses patience. The man who jumps from pillar to post is apt to be left at the post before he gets well started.

Stick to the facts of your sales story. Be specific about its adaptations to my particular problems and I'll listen if you don't take too long to get to first base. If you don't know the full story of your product, I'll find it out before long—and *you'll* be out before long!

4. *Play the Three "Tees"—Loyalty, Honesty, Activity*

In the game of business there is only one stance you can take. Both feet on the ground, solid and firm, with no droop to right or left. Take a good healthy swing at the ball and shoot onto the fairway—*straight!* No slicing permitted.

Deliver me from the salesman who complains about his firm doing this, that, or the other. If you cannot be loyal, at least be honest—honest enough to get out. Loyalty breeds respect. Honesty develops confidence. Activity compels admiration. Loyalty is due to the customer who supports you just as much as to the firm who hires you. The first time you fail me, you begin to lose caste. The second time, you'll probably lose out with me. I cannot afford to take too many chances with you. Too many good men are constantly knocking at my door.

The value of honesty with yourself, your customer, and your firm is surely self-evident. Evaluations are academic and superfluous. The first time I catch you, there won't be any second time.

Activity is a quality I admire but don't often get. When I ask you to do something for me, I unconsciously expect it done at once. I am not concerned about your other customers. When I give you an order, I want it delivered yesterday afternoon. Whatever you may do for me, I admire above everything else your evidence of activity in doing it. Even though I am occasionally unreasonable, I expect your compliance with my requests. After all, the thing that makes a hit with me, is the thing you want to play up to in order to continue making a hit.

5. Sell Merchandising—Not Merchandise

It is a well-known fact that I am not interested in your merchandise as such—only in the opportunities for profit in its resale. Then why not concentrate your sales talk and your sales effort on the possibilities for profit in selling your merchandise and on the best methods of selling it?

I am always open-minded to constructive suggestions. The more you know about my business, the more I like your business. You may think I am just a hick storekeeper or a small-town businessman, but show me a really worth-while idea and I'll throw my arms around you. The more simple you can make my merchandising problems, the more merchandise I will simply buy from you. I would be dumb to do otherwise—and regardless of what you may think, I am usually not so dumb. I have become ultra-conservative because I have listened to so many of you salesmen.

Too many men walk in to offer me a gross of this or a hundred of that, at a special price or on a new deal; but too few of you come in with a practical plan to resell the things you would like me to buy. Remember—it is not how much I buy, but how much I sell, that counts in your quota. What a tremendous hit a real merchandiser would make—regardless of what he wanted to sell me, or how much!

6. *Keep Your Territory and Your Territory Will Keep You*

This is a truism as old as selling itself. You get out of a territory only what you put into it. How do you develop *your* territory? Do you actually cover it—or do you hop, skip, and jump through it? Many a man in many a territory calls on a prospect here and there—and hopes for a miracle to bring the rest into the fold. Have you a regular calling plan of campaign? Why not?

Every territory contains an average number of Expects, Suspects, and Prospects. How many of these do you transform into customers? And how many casual customers do you develop into good customers? The test of a good salesman always has been—and always will be —the number of casual inquiries he can develop into good customers.

Too many men worry about getting more territory, rather than concentrating on what they have. The grass on the other side always seems a bit greener, but it is just an optical illusion. Men overlook the fact that a larger territory involves more time, more overhead, more expense. To scatter your effort over too much territory is like firing a load of buckshot at the stars and expecting a flock of customers to drop down. These are days of intensive selling and concentrated attack. Intensive concentration on a limited territory is apt to bring home the bacon much easier and with less expense than spreading your wings over more than you can cover efficiently.

The salesman with genuine vision will take a limited territory and build up a personal following that will do credit to his methods and win a cheer from the home office. One good customer-friend is worth half a dozen prospects.

Why not use your gray matter to build up what you have rather than take a chance on an unknown quantity?

7. Follow Through on Your Follow-up

Despite the number of times your golf pro has pounded this in, a good follow-through is still one of the rarest virtues in business today. How easily are you discouraged? When you fall down, do you go Boom—or do you bounce right up again? Do you call on a prospect once or twice and then call it quits? Or do you keep a prospect list and keep him alive as long as there is the slightest chance of his being alive?

Don't be afraid to make repeat calls on your prospects. The good old Law of Average still favors the man who wears out the most shoe leather. You may have called on your prospect six times—and he is all ready to buy on the seventh call, but you gave him up—isn't it just too bad? If your prospect is worth calling on at all, he is usually worth following up. The only touch of genius in selling is the man who keeps in touch with his prospect and keeps his prospect in touch with his business. The only way to break down sales resistance is to build up sales persistence. And you can never tell just when your prospect's will power has reached the breaking point and he is ready to give you an order that will more than make up for all your time and effort. Don't forget that the "hard-to-get" prospect is the "hard-to-lose" customer! Treasure every contact you make and he may develop into a treasure for you.

Never dare to assume that a thorough sales talk is wasted. Into every garden you must plant some seed; and the only way to make your job bigger is to plant constructively for the future. The thought you implanted in your prospect's mind a year ago may blossom this year into an order that will place you at the head of the class. And don't forget this: In spite of hell and high water, keep your shirt on! Never close the path to a return call on your prospect; you may regret it like nobody's business. Remember, the customer can raise the very dickens with you—and get away with it; but the moment you try to reverse the process, he will probably do away with you. This is his one privilege and he is apt to be jealous of it. Anyway, there is an old saying that "New salesmen are easier to find than new customers." Isn't it the truth?

8. *Keep the Courage of Your Convictions*

Your customer will respect you for your backbone and forget you for your wishbone. Develop a mind of your own and mind your own business. Your business is that of developing business for your customer; and the more development work you can do, the more business you will get for your firm. Don't let your sociability sidetrack your objective; and don't let your customer dissipate your convictions. Shakespeare developed the character of Polonius as a foil of ridicule for Hamlet. A "yes-man" is a dead man in any language, and you will "yes" your customer to death at your own peril. Some day a salesman with courage is going to show you up—and you're through!

The respect of your customer is a precious possession, but you cannot acquire it through brute strength. You've got to *deserve* it by unusual service, intelligence, courage, and helpfulness. And with only an occasional rare exception, the business of selling is one in which you usually get your just deserts. "As ye sow . . ."

While discussing respect, don't forget that the respect of your competitor is an extremely valuable asset. What a competing salesman thinks of you is almost as important as what a prospect thinks of you. If your competitor thinks you are a better man than he is, it will unconsciously affect his selling. If he knows he is a better man than you are, it will help his selling. Why conduct yourself so as to help your competitor?

9. Don't Be Afraid to Ask for the Order!

It is strange how many salesmen have this fear complex. He may give his prospect the finest sales talk in the world, but when it comes right down to the point of asking for the order, he becomes as timid as a gazelle.

The average salesman is actually *afraid* to ask for the order. He has been depressionized to death; and when he calls on a customer he just *knows* in advance that he is not going to buy. And he doesn't! Consequently, the salesman never actually gets to the point of *asking for the order*. He hems and haws and beats about the bush, but never once does he actually dare to say: "How many cases do you want today?" Well, I won't say never. Occasionally he *will* ask the customer if he wants a case of goods— but he will never ask him if he wants *five* cases. You may get only half as much as you ask for, but if you ask for only half as much, you will get only half of that! Audacity is the greatest attention-getter in the world. Ask for one case, and he may say no. Ask for five cases and he may laugh at you. But ask for *ten* cases—and he will either have heart failure or sit up and take notice. And the chances are in your favor that he will sit up and take notice . . . *particularly* if you have a good merchandising plan to go with it!

Did you ever stop to think that every prospect you call on is being sold by somebody? Why not you? After all, it is only good business to ask for the order. That is what your prospect expects you to do—and he respects you for it. Fail to do it—and he unconsciously loses regard for you. You cannot kid him. He knows you have called on him to try to sell him a bill of goods. Did you sell *him* or did he sell *you*? What are you afraid of? Don't be halfhearted about asking for business, or you may find your boss wholehearted about losing you. Sell, brother, *sell!*

10. *Remember Your Terminal Facilities*

Any man can start a conversation. It takes a smart man to know when to stop. I have seen a lot of smart-aleck salesmen talk themselves *out* before they got *in*. I have even seen salesmen talk themselves *out* of the order after they got in and got the business.

Get yourself some first-class terminal facilities and you've got something worth while. If you must talk . . . say something! If you have nothing to say . . . listen! Let the other fellow do some of the talking . . . it is his privilege. He may talk himself into a corner—and first thing you know . . . bingo! you've got the order. You can learn more by thinking while listening than you ever will by talking while the other fellow is listening!

When in doubt, remember your terminal facilities. Very often, they will bring you home with the bacon.

TEST QUESTIONS

1. Do you think a man with an inferiority complex would make a good salesman? Why?

2. Do you think a man overly aggressive would make a good salesman? Why?

3. Why do you think the proper handling of yourself is essential to good selling?

4. Describe the "constructive" type of salesman.

5. How many of the Ten Selling Commandments can you remember?

6. Which do you think are the three most important Selling Commandments, and why?

7. What is the difference between merchandising and selling?

8. What do you think is the best way to build up a given territory?

9. In what way can the "law of averages" affect your selling?

10. What is the tenth Selling Commandment, and how is it important in your selling?

STUDY SUGGESTIONS

1. How does this list of Ten Selling Commandments affect you? Do you think it is sacrilegious? Why, or why not? Do you think it is a practical or theoretical list? How would it affect your outlook on life as a salesman?

2. Discuss in detail the first Selling Commandment—the "Service Trinity"—and show how it might affect the handling of your job as a good salesman.

3. In the same way, discuss the fourth Selling Commandment—the "Three Tees."

4. How would you handle your territory so as to handle your job properly?

5. Discuss in detail the ninth Selling Commandment—"Ask For The Order"—and tell us how vitally this affects your selling one way or the other.

CHAPTER XXI

How to Open the Sale

THE road to a sale is never clear until the prospect's mind is opened. Then—and only then—can we drive home our sales-compelling talking points and beat our way to the dotted line!

There are two ways to open a prospect's mind. First, by dynamiting—which is nothing less than high pressure aggressiveness. Second, by persuasion—which is nothing more than low pressure salesmanship. In the dynamiting method, we first force the prospect into the picture with us and later—if at all—we put ourselves into the picture with him. In the persuasion method, we reverse the process by first putting ourselves into the picture with the prospect and then drawing him into the picture with us. In other words, we first put ourselves into his shoes and then lead him into our own camp!

The method we use depends largely on the type of our business. If it is a one-call (or hit-and-run) business, we might use the dynamiting method and get away with it once. But if it is a multiple-call (or repeat type) of business (as most business is), we would most certainly use the persuasion method—which, after all, is the modern method of selling.

A good first impression is half the sale; the other half is good common sense! And by "good first impression" I certainly don't mean good looks! If a salesman presents a friendly personality, an air of alertness and enthusiasm, plus a full and complete knowledge of his job, he is bound to make a favorable impression even on a confirmed grouch. The rest of the sale, then, depends largely on his ability to present his talking points in a constructive, interesting and convincing manner—and to capitalize on them!

There are four necessary steps, taken in logical sequence, that pick the salesman up and lead him to the order.

First Step: Preparing for the Call

Too many salesmen walk into a prospect's office with a prayer on their lips instead of a plan in their minds! They put their dependence on Dame Fortune and Lady Luck, rather than on a specific line of strategy or plan of attack.

The real preparation for the interview begins long before the interview takes place. Before the sale can be completed in the prospect's office, it must first be settled in the salesman's mind. He must consider the problems that may arise. He must analyze the prospect and his business. He must be fully prepared to answer the objections that will be brought up, and to turn them into selling points. He must have his entire procedure mapped out from A to Izzard, and be prepared for any eventuality so that he cannot be caught napping. "The man who knows— and *knows* that he knows—has the prospect in the palm of his hand!"

A devil-may-care nonchalance in the presence of the prospect may result in the same attitude on the part of the prospect; while an air of business-like preparedness arouses his confidence and stimulates his mentality. Dropping in casually on a prospect on a gambling chance of making a sale, not only kills the sale but in many cases also kills the salesman. The prospect likes to be made to feel that he is at least worth proper preparation and actual effort.

I believe in the mental exercise of selling my prospect in my own mind before I call on him. Long before I step into his office I have his business, his position, his potentialities and his probable requirements clearly catalogued in my mind, and against these I make a mental check and review of the type of selling I am going to do and the kind of sales openers and arguments I am going to use. As a result, when I reach his office and enter his presence I am neither stage struck nor stymied; I don't have to hem and haw and talk about the weather—I am ready to proceed naturally, fluently and effectively with my opening and my sales presentation. In other words, I am prepared for the second logical step in opening the sale.

Second Step: Making the Entrance

Bearding the lion in his den seems to be no more terrifying to some salesmen than entering a prospect's office. But why the fear complex? The prospect is a simple human being, regardless of his title or position. He may not be the slightest bit better than we are, except in position and opportunity. We may be just as big as he is, either mentally or physically, or both. It is only his title and his position as a prospect that commands our respect and regard. As a matter of fact, we are here to do him just as much of a service as he can do us, and we can rightfully expect a certain amount of courtesy and consideration. We may not always receive it—but that is where our sales diplomacy enters the picture and tries to correct the situation.

It may be taken for granted that in our personal appearance we will never permit ourselves to be otherwise than thoroughly presentable. In our manner there will be an alertness and friendliness that will be self-evident on approach and that will spark in making contact with the prospect.

There have been many ideas on the amount of dignity and reserve with which we ought to approach a prospect. There have even been arguments on whether a salesman may offer to shake hands with a prospect. I don't believe the subject is open to argument or quibbling! I believe there is only one way to approach a prospect—and that is, to approach him as a human being and to shake hands with him just as we would with a friend or a prospective friend. It is the only way to inject the warmth of human contact into an otherwise cold business proposition. I believe that salesmen worthy of the name can be trusted to have sufficient judgment to maintain the right amount of dignity and reserve, especially in calling on a new prospect. If they haven't, they should not be permitted to make any calls.

The same question holds true in the prospect's office—whether to sit or not to sit down. And my attitude is the same. I believe the salesman should do the natural and logical thing. When one gentleman calls on another, it is only natural and logical for him to be seated. Of course, if the salesman feels that he can work better on his feet and control the situation more effectively, he may stand if he wishes. But when he does so, he does the unnatural thing and calls attention to his actions; and at the same time he sets up a certain amount of resistance in the prospect's mind and prepares him for an out-and-out sales canvass, rather than a friendly discussion.

Another reason why I firmly believe in the natural sequence of shaking hands and sitting down at a prospect's desk, is that it tends to place both prospect and salesman on a plane of apparent equality, at least for the time being. I don't believe in either one dominating the other, any more than I believe in either one taking an unfair advantage of the other. I do believe that a sales presentation can be made just as effectively and just as enthusiastically on a friendly plane of courtesy, cordiality and mutual respect. If it cannot, then the fault is with the salesman in the majority of instances; and it is time for him to call a halt and analyze himself and his methods! Until the salesman can operate along the lines suggested above, he is not in position to take the third logical step in opening the sale.

Third Step: Taking the Initiative

While I do not believe in a salesman being either dominating or domineering, I certainly do believe in his taking the initiative and getting down to business from the moment of his entrance. If he will take this initiative properly and diplomatically, he will dominate the situation naturally without appearing either brazen or hard-boiled.

If there is anything worse than a salesman sitting around and waiting for the prospect to open the conversation, I don't know what it is. The moment the salesman gives the prospect an opportunity to ask: "What can I do for *you*?"—he loses the tactical advantage of first being able to tell the prospect what he would like to do for *him*!

The only way to open a sale is to go right ahead and open it! Beating about the bush only weakens the salesman's position and transfers the offensive to the prospect. In preparing for the call, the salesman has already decided in his own mind on his line of attack; and he is prepared not only to follow it up, but he is also prepared to switch to another line if the prospect's personality or attitude indicates the necessity.

As soon as the formalities are over, he gets right down to business and makes his opening statement. It may be in the form of a statement of fact about his product; or a pertinent question with a punch; or a statement about the prospect's business; or a tie-up between a business or industrial trend and the prospect's present methods; or an immediate offer to be of help in solving an existing problem; or an attitude of eager service in answering an inquiry.

Whatever else it may be, certainly the statement will be positive, it will be interesting, it will be thought-provoking, it will be specific, it will reflect intelligence and enthusiasm, it will indicate knowledge and ability, and, above all, it will be permeated with friendliness and anxiety to serve!

The principal question for the salesman to decide is the appeal that will carry the most weight with the prospect and make the most favorable first impression. For example:

If the appeal is to be PRICE:—"Here is a product you can buy at the lowest possible discount basis, that you can sell at a satisfactory markup, and that will give you a rapid rate of turnover." Or . . . "Is it a fact that you can sell only low price goods, or can you handle any line that is a good seller?" Or . . . "If you are looking for a good low price leader, as everyone is, here is a natural salesgetter that will double the traffic in your department."

If the appeal is VALUE:—"It is said that value is the most economical point between cost price and obsolescence." Or . . . "The value of a product is represented by the equation:—Cost Price divided by the amount of Satisfactory Service." Or . . . "The proven value in this product is exactly 75 per cent greater than any other similar product on the market, and here's the reason." Or . . . "If unusual values are what you like to feature, here's a value that Frank & Goodwin over in Dayton used as a successful keystone for their entire sale."

If the prospect is the logical type for a QUALITY appeal: —"Here is the highest price product of its kind on the market, *but* it is actually the cheapest in the long run— and you know it's the long run that counts." Or . . . "Here is a product we first thought we couldn't sell because it was too good; now it sells so rapidly we can hardly keep it in stock." Or . . . "Do you think any product can be too good for the American public?" Or . . . "Which does your trade like better, high quality at a fair price or low quality at a cheap price?"

The appeal of CONVENIENCE is frequently effective as against a hard-to-use product:—"Here is a product that is exactly twice as easy to use as so-and-so because there are two less gadgets to manipulate." Or . . . "It is a well-known fact that people follow the line of least resistance, and a product that is easier to use, is easier to sell." Or . . . "Every man, woman and child is interested in convenience, so because of its new easy-to-use design this product will appeal to every one of your customers."

If EFFICIENCY is to be the appeal:—"This new model will handle almost twice as many units as the old model, and yet it costs only a few cents more." Or . . . "This appliance has a device that uses about 25% less electricity and actually does 50% more work than the old model." Or . . . "You know that an increase in working efficiency means a saving in operating costs; because of the newly designed carburetor, this motor does about 25% more work on the same amount of fuel as the old model."

For an appeal to NOVELTY:—"The novelty that catches the eye is the thing that opens the customer's purse, and here's the newest novelty that does the trick." Or . . . "Here is a novelty bag that is made on an entirely different principle from every other bag." Or . . . "Even you and I are frequently attracted and sold by a novel design, and here's one that we just imported from London."

Where the appeal must be based on STYLE:—"Of course, we all know that most feminine style originates in Paris; but here's a new style that originated in our own factory and I want to see if you don't agree that it has that exclusive Parisian look." Or . . . "I can show you how to cash in on a brand new trend in men's styles that will sweep the country and find you in on the ground floor." Or . . . "We have all seen that style isn't confined to wearing apparel; here is a newly styled office machine that lifts it entirely out of the rut of conservatism." Or . . . "There are new streamline styles in many of the things we use today; why not new styles in some of the old staples that are covered with cobwebs?"

For the prospect who is interested in DURABILITY:—"Here is a product that is much lighter in weight than our old model, and yet, because of the modern materials used, it is even more durable." Or . . . "Most far-seeing business men are interested in durability, not only as an end in itself, but as a means of cutting down replacement costs later on; that is why this product must be presented as a good investment for you rather than as an extra expense." Or . . . "If you will consider this product on the basis of $5 a year service charge for the ten years' service, you will see that it is much cheaper than the smaller

$30 unit you are thinking of buying." Or . . . "Don't you believe that the low priced units are really quite expensive in view of their light construction; and that much greater durability can be had for a very small increase in price? I can give you a splendid example of that right here."

Statements of this kind offer many opportunities for the wide-awake salesman to present *visual proof* of his facts, and this leads him logically into the fourth step in opening the sale.

Fourth Step: Getting Attention

There is nothing like good visual display to focus a prospect's attention! Every salesman probably has something with him that he can show to the prospect to tie up with his opening statements; and the more smoothly he works it into his opening argument and the more effectively he displays it, the more interest he arouses in the prospect's mind. The salesmen's chances of holding the prospect's attention are many times greater with this visual display than without it.

The most valuable piece of visual display, of course, is an actual sample of the product; or a miniature sample or a sample of the material of which it is made. These samples provide so many interesting openings for a salesman, that it would seem almost criminal for him to be without them.

He may have a portfolio showing proofs of the proposed advertising campaign; or plans for a merchandising or sales promotion idea; or blueprints for some constructional process. He may have photographs of individual products or of complete installations; or charts showing interesting data about facts brought out; or letters of a testimonial nature from other customers or users of similar products. And last, but not least, he may have with him a well-organized and interesting sales manual, which he can use to punctuate his remarks with occasional reference to some of the things mentioned above, and to many others. If he has such a sales manual, he is fortunate, indeed!

The real problem, as a rule, is not the material itself, but the method of using it. Every salesman has a certain amount of mental equipment and visual display material available for use. If he can only be induced to bring it out into the light of day and be shown how to use it with freedom and facility, he can be given a highly effective push along the road to the sale!

Test Questions

1. What are the four steps in opening the sale?
2. Discuss briefly the difference between high pressure and low pressure selling.
3. Just how does "impression" affect the sale?
4. What do we mean by "first impression" and how does it affect the sale?
5. What mental preparation is desirable in preparing for the call, and why?
6. What do you think is the proper way to approach a prospect in his office?
7. What do you think is the natural result of taking the initiative?
8. Name four different types of appeals that will carry weight with the prospect.
9. What do we mean by "visual display" in getting attention?
10. What do you think would be the most valuable form of visual display, and why?

Study Suggestions

1. Discuss in detail the first step in opening the sale—preparing for the call.
2. Discuss in detail the second step—making the entrance.
3. Discuss in detail the third step—taking the initiative.
4. Discuss in detail the fourth step—getting attention.
5. Consider that you are in the prospect's office ready to go to work on him. Give one talking point you would use for each of the six different types of appeals.

CHAPTER XXII

How to Control the Interview

WHEN a salesman can keep his prospect at attention long enough to hear his sales message intelligently, he has covered much of the distance to the selling point! The problem is, how to keep the prospect in one spot until we sell him.

The man who develops the most successful technique for controlling his sales interviews, is the man who turns most of his interviews into orders. We never realize how important this matter of control is until we analyze our failures and discover the lack of it. Control in a sales interview is just as vital as in an airplane. If the salesman doesn't have it, or cannot develop it, the interview may blow up in the air and crash to failure.

What can we do to get the prospect's attention—and hold it? What can we do to develop his interest—and keep it? How can we compete with other things that are clamoring for his attention? How can we divorce him from the reverie of his other thoughts, from the necessary and unnecessary interruptions that are apt to occur during an interview? What are we going to do when an interruption does occur—possibly one after another? And how are we going to bring him back to our side of the desk?

There is only one sure-fire way to keep the prospect under control, so that he will not think of anything else or permit anyone else to interrupt him. That is, to excite his interest so intensely that he is oblivious to everything else! Obviously that goal is the 100% bull's-eye. Being only human, we cannot always attain that state of perfection; but the least we can do is to aim at that target constantly and get as close to the center as we can.

What Kind of an Interview Is It?

Is it just a casual call with the hope of finding the prospect in, or is it a definite appointment? And if the latter, is it an appointment urged by us, or one requested by the prospect? These things affect the receptiveness of the prospect's attitude and the intensity of his interest.

If the interview is just a casual call on our own initiative, we usually have to work harder to get the prospect interested and to retain his attention than if we have a definite appointment. If the appointment is one requested or suggested by the prospect, it presupposes a certain amount of interest on his part, and our principal job is to develop and hold his attention. If the appointment is one urged by us and grudgingly acceded to by the prospect, we are "on the spot" in making the interview worth while to him in return for his courtesy. Also, if the interview is one of a series, we must see to it that it is connected and tied up to every other interview in the series, so as to build up to a successful climax—which is nothing less than the order!

Where Is the Interview Held?

Of course, the ideal spot for the interview, as a rule, is the salesman's office, or his hotel room, or his factory, or some other spot of his own choosing. With such good fortune he almost has the prospect at his mercy! The opposite is true, however, when the prospect has the salesman in his own office, or factory, or some spot that he himself chooses. Then he has a little the advantage of the salesman because he has him in his own territory, so to speak, and the salesman must act accordingly.

There may be occasional calls when the prospect will intentionally come out to see the salesman in the reception room, in order to avoid taking him into his office. This is certainly far from being an ideal spot for an interview. It is the very opposite. In many cases, the prospect knows this and he does it deliberately so as to make it difficult for the salesman to follow through and make his interview successful. In such cases, we must exercise our ingenuity and develop a line of strategy to coax the prospect to take us into his office. We explain the difficulty of displaying samples; the impossibility of speaking confidentially; the necessity for giving a subject calm and careful attention; and sometimes we even have to be aggressive enough to appeal diplomatically to his sense of fairness in not handicapping our sales presentation.

Frequently we can move the prospect to a consideration of his personal interest or a sense of justice and change the locale of the interview to a more suitable spot. But there will be times when the prospect is adamant and cannot be moved or persuaded. Then we must either make the best of it and expect to work twice as hard to control the interview properly, or we can decline to make our intended presentation under such unfavorable conditions and offer to return at a more convenient time for a more favorable reception. Naturally, we will be guided in our decision and our action by the attitude of the prospect and the possibilities for the future.

With Whom Is the Interview Had?

Occasionally we have an interview with one man—and (1) he substitutes a subordinate; or (2) he calls in another man and tries to turn us over to him; or (3) he permits other people to remain in his office during our interview who might either heckle or embarrass us in our presentation.

In the first case, it is up to us to do a good selling job on the subordinate instead of the principal, or to sell him on the idea of either taking us or referring us back to the principal. It is a situation that cannot always be avoided and must be handled with caution and diplomacy.

In the second case, we must try to impress on the principal that the subject is of sufficient importance or interest to justify his presence. Failing in this, we may try to have him agree to see us again after we have gone into the matter with the subordinate.

In the third case, if we feel that the presence of others will not hinder us in our presentation, we can go ahead and try to capitalize on their opinions and sell the entire group. Or, if the presence of other persons is a definite hindrance to freedom of presentation or to the complete attention of the principal, we can attempt to have him set a time for another interview at his convenience when we may have his undivided attention. Needless to say, we must be extremely careful in our manner of requesting such another interview, so as not to reflect on or injure the feelings of those present. It is necessary for the salesman to judge whether the others have a legitimate reason for sharing in the interview; if they do, we will make a virtue of necessity and do a complete selling job on the entire group. If we feel the others are present merely because the principal refuses to give us the necessary attention and consideration, then we must decide whether to go ahead and force his attention by the high caliber of our presentation or to attempt to arrange a more satisfactory interview.

How to Control the Interview

Every salesman has his own manner and method of controlling an interview. At least, it is to be hoped that he has some method for accomplishing this, or he will frequently find himself floundering about in a sea of despair when the prospect picks up the reins and proceeds to drive the interview to his own ends.

It is valuable for the average salesman to have, as part of his stock in trade, several effective methods of holding or taking control of the interview when occasion demands. From his own experience he will develop a number of such methods and ideas and have them available for quick action. Here are several more ideas along the same line that can be added to his mental equipment:

1. Dramatizing Samples

Almost every salesman has at hand the finest implement it is possible to have for arousing the prospect's interest and holding his attention. It makes no difference what form his samples may take—proofs, reprints, charts, photographs, films, swatches, drawings, cut-away sections, or complete products or miniatures—he has at his finger tips the most perfect possibilities for dramatizing his samples.

As was said in a previous book by this writer, "How to Make More Sales":—"Dramatization is the highest degree of showmanship—and showmanship is the highest type of salesmanship! . . . The more intelligently we develop the vital elements of dramatization—action, suspense, mystery, curiosity—and the more directly we focus our dramatized selling, the more easily do we weaken the resistance of the prospect and get his name on the dotted line.

"Have you ever noticed how many of the better salesmen are skilled actors, with a highly developed flair for the dramatic? Their entrance, their tone of voice, their approach, their dominant personality, their methods of arousing interest and suspense, their dramatic attitude—every detail of their presentation indicates an instinct for showmanship that pays big dividends.

"While the true dramatic flair is instinctive, showmanship can be developed by anyone who will take the trouble to analyze its make-up and to project his imagination accordingly. Only a comparatively few salesmen ever think of the possibilities of dramatic effect in making an entrance, in discussing a product, in showing a sample or demonstrating a process. . . .

"But watch the showman! When he goes to work on a prospect, it is with the sure-fire touch of a thorough trouper. When he offers a sample to a prospect, he takes it out of his case with loving care; he presents it with an air of distinction; he builds up a background of appreciation. He knows that admiration breeds admiration; that the prospect thinks a great deal more of it if he builds it up adroitly with little tricks of stage craft. This is no common merchandise, the salesman infers, no ordinary product, no run-of-the-mine idea. It is something extraordinarily fine, something uncommon—just as this salesman himself is decidedly out of the ordinary."

In bringing a prospect's attention back from a necessary interruption by a visitor or a telephone call, there is nothing like an interesting sample to do the trick. Even in preventing an impending interruption, this same sample cunningly presented at the psychological moment will accomplish wonders in holding the prospect. It is all a question of how the salesman handles his samples and how he uses them at different times to bridge a dangerous lapse in interest or attention.

In connection with samples, some salesmen are frequently guilty of an extremely important omission. They hold the sample in their hands and show it off properly, but they neglect to actually place it *in the hands of the prospect*! Get the prospect's own hands on the sample and a substantial part of your selling job is done for you! Let him touch it, let him feel it, let him play with its mechanism, let him operate it himself—and the chances are highly in your favor that he will help to sell himself on it!

2. *Presenting an Unfinished Idea*

In getting a prospect to concentrate on a specific problem, it is a splendid thing to have some sort of an unfinished plan or idea on which his final advice or opinion is needed. It provides a good point to tie him down if he gets restless:—"Here's an idea I've worked out for you, but I've got to have your help on it before I can finish it up." Or, "Here's a rough sketch of a pretty good idea that needs to be filled in with your further suggestions." Or, "What do you think of an idea worked out along this line?"

3. *Asking for Final Okay*

In presenting a new campaign to a prospect on which it is necessary to have final okays, it is sometimes a good idea to present only one piece at a time. In this way, if you haven't the prospect's complete attention, or if he is about to turn to something else, you can always renew his interest and hold him for another period by pulling out another part of it, with the statement:—"Oh, here's another angle on this job that I'd like to have you look over." Or, "Here's another proof that requires your okay."

4. Featuring a Special Sample

An unfailing stunt that always holds the prospect's attention, is to have with you something special that you might have made up for his own requirements. You are pretty certain to get to first base with him when you can say:—"Oh, by the way, here's a special sample I just had made up for you, built exactly to your own dimensions." Or, "Here's what I'd like to do—I'd be glad to make up a special sample of this job for you, if you'll just be good enough to give me the necessary specifications."

5. Competing with the Secretary

When the prospect's secretary tries to remind him of other things to do, it is a great help to be able to start off on a new tack and say:—"Mr. Jones, I brought along with me a suggested 5-point program that I believe will do the job you have in mind. Now is a good time to go over these points and see what you think of the plan." Any number of points can be used, the main idea being to tie the prospect's mind down to something specific that you and he can both concentrate on right then and there.

6. Taking the Initiative

Don't wait for the prospect to have a chance to get restless—and don't give him a chance to get out if he does. It is up to you to take the initiative in bringing up new approaches, new points of attack, new conditions of interest. Remember, it is *your* interview, *you* are controlling it, *you* are running the show. Hang on to your prospect like grim death—but remember that if you cannot continue to interest him, if you cannot devise new ways to hold his attention, it *will* be a case of grim death—for you!

7. Keep Something in Reserve

Certainly, all this proves one of the most important points in the entire category of salesmanship:—Don't shoot all your ammunition at one time. Keep something in reserve, something ready for the emergency that is always bound to come up. There is always a possibility that your prospect may become bored, and the only way you can bring him back to life is by digging down into your bag of tricks and bringing up a new one. The salesman who talks himself out of breath and shoots his entire wad at one gulp is even worse off than the man who doesn't get the interview at all—he is all through and has lost all his possibilities for control; and then the chances are ten to one in favor of the prospect taking control and easing the salesman out gracefully. All of which adds up to just one simple important problem—To control—or not to control. . . . To sell—or not to sell . . . that is the question!

TEST QUESTIONS

1. What relation does the control of interviews bear to the closing of sales?
2. What could be the effect of proper or improper control?
3. What can we do to get the prospect's attention?
4. What can we do to develop the prospect's interest?
5. What can we do to compete with the outside interests of the prospect?

6. What can we do when an interruption occurs, or possibly to prevent an interruption?

7. How can we dramatize our samples?

8. Why is it advisable to place a sample in the hands of the prospect?

9. What do you think is the one most valuable way of controlling an interview? Why?

10. What is the advantage of keeping a good talking point in reserve?

STUDY SUGGESTIONS

1. What would you do if a prospect's secretary walked into the office while you were making a sales presentation and tried to take him away to some other call?

2. If a prospect attempted to hold an interview with you out in the reception room, or out in the hall, instead of his office, what would you do, and why?

3. Suppose you have an appointment for an interview with the prospect and he carelessly hands you over to some subordinate. What would you do, and how would you do it?

4. Discuss in detail three effective methods for controlling an interview.

5. Show how it might help you to control an interview by presenting an unfinished idea or by asking for a final okay on something.

CHAPTER XXIII

How to Close the Sale

ALMOST any cub can *open* a sale—but it takes a smart salesman to *close* it! Why not combine the two qualities in one man and make a *complete* salesman?

Selling is a good deal like baseball. Many a man can produce a single or a double, but lacks the extra punch needed to get him around to home plate. Many a salesman can get into the prospect's office and carry on his contact to a certain point; but when it comes to that extra little punch needed to get him around to the closing of the sale, he falls short, gives up the ghost, and blames it on the prospect or on a "tough break."

It has been said that a good sales opener is not necessarily a good closer—and vice versa. A few sales managers even have "closing specialists" on their staff, who devote most of their time to closing the sales opened by other men. That may be good practice in some cases; but I cannot conceive of any self-respecting salesman being satisfied with that kind of incomplete selling!

A salesman who cannot follow through all the way and do his own job of opening and closing a sale, can hardly be called a *complete* salesman. To qualify for that title he must be not only a self-starter, but most certainly a self-closer. He must be able to stand on his own feet and do his own job of developing attention, battering down resistance, and building desire and acceptance all the way through to the very last period on the dotted line. Then, and only then, can he truly rejoice in the glory and satisfaction of a thorough job well done. Then, and only then, is he entitled to his diploma as a complete salesman!

18 Practical Suggestions for Avoiding Pitfalls and Using Sales Clinchers to Get the Order

In presenting a few suggested clinchers for closing the sale, it is also important to look at the opposite side of the picture and mention some of the things that are sometimes called "order killers." Many sales managers are inclined to feel (and rightly so) that the latter are even more important than the former—on the premise that if we can avoid doing the things that may kill the sale, we have much more chance of closing it with our regular sales canvass. Therefore, I list a few of these order killers as being of prime importance:

9 COMMON ORDER KILLERS
1. Talking Too Much

Many a man has talked himself out of the possibility of ever doing business; and has even talked himself out of the order after it was signed. Keeping quiet at the psychological moment is still as important as anything else in closing the sale. There is a time to talk and a time to stop talking—but some salesmen still talk on past the saturation point, past the psychological moment, and past the danger point—without paying any attention to red lights!

2. Too Eager to Sell

Too much evidence of eagerness is a dangerous thing in every single case, without exception, because it inevitably makes the prospect halt, think and become suspicious. It is laudable to be anxious and willing to sell; but to display eagerness in our attempt to close a sale, carries us far beyond the bounds of safety and prudence. How would *you* feel if a salesman acted as though he could hardly wait to get your name on the dotted line?

3. Incomplete Knowledge

The salesman who has to talk *around* his subject in order to keep away from details that he is not familiar with, is bound to have a hard time in closing the sale. He just doesn't have the ring of conviction in his tone; he doesn't impress his prospect with his knowledge of the merchandise; he leaves the prospect with the feeling that something is lacking; and he naturally finds it impossible to sell a prospect who has not the fullest degree of confidence in the salesman and in the merchandise.

4. High Pressure Selling

Trying to *force* a sale on a customer is just about as sensible as facing him with a baseball bat. It reminds us of the old saying about leading a horse to water, etc. And yet there are still people—some of them salesmen—who have an idea that good salesmanship and high pressure selling are identical. Occasionally we still run across the salesman with the stentorian voice and wind-mill arms who is prepared to sweep his prospect off his feet with the urgency of his proposition—and he cannot understand why prospects are "so dumb." No one will buy from a salesman who is too aggressive. His aggressiveness must be tempered with the qualities of persuasion, good taste and diplomacy.

5. The Fear Complex

This is one of the biggest order killers of all! A man gets a good start on a sale, goes all through his presentation, answers all objections and creates a certain amount of desire—and when he approaches the climax, presto! he suddenly acquires a first-class case of stage fright. He hesitates, stutters, does everything but fall over himself, all for want of a little more self-control and will power. It is a sad fact that a great many salesmen are actually afraid to ask for an order. And if they do not *ask* for orders, how can they expect to get them?

6. Criticizing Competitors

"Of all sad words of tongue or pen . . . !" The man who knocks a competitor or criticizes his competitor's merchandise is on a par with the salesman who still doesn't know that high pressure selling is out of date. The less said about a competitor, the better; for you never know when you are going to cut your own throat, when a wisecrack about a competitor will boomerang into unfavorable reaction against yourself. And what is more to the point, if you want to get your prospect curious about your competitor's merchandise, just keep on talking about it! It would be interesting and revealing to be able to chart the percentage of sales in each man's quota that has been lost to competitors, mainly because of his pointed suggestions and criticisms.

7. Getting Away from the Subject

Every now and then a salesman gets wrapped up in a sociable conversation with his prospect and forgets all about the purpose of his visit. It is so easy to bring in a discussion of outside topics that take the prospect's mind entirely off the merchandise. It is up to the salesman to watch the prospect's conversational meanderings, and to bring him tactfully back onto the main line. If he doesn't, the prospect is likely to become interested in everything *but* the salesman's proposition.

8. Negative Selling Attitude

It doesn't seem possible that a salesman of the modern school would carry a negative selling attitude; and yet he sometimes has it without realizing it. Witness the man who stumbles through his sales talk and then winds up by asking weakly:—"Would you like some of these?" Or . . . "Don't you think you ought to have some of these in your stock?" Or . . . "Can't you use half a dozen of them anyway?" Or . . . "Why not try a few of them and see how they work out?" Is any further comment necessary? Isn't it plainly evident that the only attitude to have in selling is the *positive* attitude?

9. Argumentative Attitude

Another common order killer is the salesman who just loves to argue! An argument is an easy thing to get into, but a very difficult thing to get out of without leaving behind at least a trace of ill-feeling. A trace of that is just as fatal as a trace of poison; and it is frequently all that is necessary to kill the sale. If we get into an argument, we have enough spunk to want to win; and if we win it, the chances are we will create just enough ill-feeling to lose the sale. Which is more important—the argument or the sale?

9 SALES CLINCHERS

1. Press Forward to a Close

Remember, the climax of the canvass is the time to close the sale! All that you have told the prospect, all the questions you have answered, all the objections you have killed, all the admissions you have forced, have made it just that much harder for the prospect to turn backward and say "No" than to move forward and say "Yes." Keep pressing forward to a favorable decision . . . the odds are with you! If he balks, go back to your sales talk and then try again. Don't accept a permanent refusal without attempting to leave an opening for a return call either in the near future or later. Whatever you do, keep pressing forward to a favorable decision!

2. Closing by Suggestion

It is seldom wise to ask for the order point blank. Rather lay the order in front of the prospect, and using your pen as a pointer, show him where to sign. You might even sign your own name on the order as a suggestion for him to do likewise. Ask him where the goods should be shipped, and how soon he will need them. Paint an attractive picture of what the product will do for him as soon as it arrives—how it will work, how it will look, how it will help him. Present some final suggestions on where it should be placed or how it should be operated or used. Don't overlook the suggestive power of "pride of possession"; when you obtain his assenting nod or statement, you have him close to the goal.

3. Automatic Closing

The simpler you can make the closing process for the prospect, the easier it is to leave with the order. It is not so difficult to build up automatically to a successful close by the cumulative power of favorable smaller decisions.

On the way through your sales canvass, qualify him for the close with leading questions:—"Which color do you like better?" Or . . . "Don't you think this is the best style?" Or . . . "How many do you need for your entire organization?" Or . . . "What proportion of each model will you need?" Or . . . "What is the best time of the month to make shipments?" Or . . . "In what quantities do you think these should be broken down?" A sufficient number of these decisions will automatically give you the order when you are finished! And most important of all, automatic closing of this kind avoids the danger of a showdown at the end of the sales canvass.

4. Take the Sale for Granted

There is a good deal of virtue in the quiet supreme confidence with which some men put over a sale. They don't appear to be assailed by any doubts about closing the sale. They go after the sale in full stride, expecting a favorable decision as a matter of course, and acting as if it were the only natural thing that could possibly happen. They show no evidence of timidity or hesitation or fear. As a result, the prospect is more often than not impressed by this positive attitude of confidence and himself becomes impregnated with the naturalness of the decision.

5. "Do It Now" Stimulators

Despite the constant use of this urgency attack, it still works and is capable of infinite variations. Its most important use is with procrastinators; and it does a world of good when tied up to current conditions with which the prospect is familiar. To keep it within the bounds of credibility, however, it must be logical and truthful. Such things as incomplete stocks at the factory, length of manufacturing time, job-lot opportunities, advancing costs of labor and raw materials, diminishing opportunities in certain markets, seasonal limitations, re-sale opportunities tying up with special campaigns or with civic occasions—all these, and many more, are good logical stimulators to prompt action and a favorable decision.

6. Price Clinchers

As a special sales clincher, the question of prices and discounts can be used in many ways to make the sale even more attractive in the eyes of the prospect. Lower prices through quantity buying; special prices for clearance of old models or job lots; varying schedules of cash discounts or term discounts; price reductions through trade-ins; etc. etc. While the question of price should not be considered too important by the salesman, it naturally occupies an important niche in the prospect's mind; hence the value of certain elements of price as a clincher in closing sales.

7. Special Concessions

Occasionally a salesman has something up his sleeve that can be used as a final inducement to the prospect. When everything else is apparently satisfactory, and the prospect still hesitates and seems doubtful, some kind of a special concession will turn the trick. It might be a matter of handling or freight charges; packing in special cartons;

a free deal of some kind, such as a certain amount of free goods with each unit of quantity; a plentiful supply of available premiums; or some special factory service or personal service that will be of definite help in his re-sale problems.

8. Sales Promotion Clinchers

A promise of a demonstration campaign with the use of company demonstrators; or some plan for cooperative demonstrations within a trading area; the use of trial offers for quick orders; the development of consignment selling, with its argument of everything to gain and nothing to lose; special advertising and sales campaigns with or without individual tie-ups—all these things have been known to do wonders in closing a sale.

9. Bookkeeping Clinchers

Another thing that has considerable closing value is the offer of deferred billing or special payments. More than one prospect has been held back by temporary financial stringency, and has still been pushed over by the diplomatic proffer of special terms. Split billing and extra dating have done yeoman service in many similar cases, and will continue to help if used with discretion.

Needless to add, discretion will be necessary not only with the prospect, but also with your firm. After all, one cannot go too far in liberality even in getting an order. There is still such a thing as unprofitable volume and profitless prosperity; but all things being equal, the salesman who can close the most sales will always receive the greatest amount of leeway and the highest degree of recognition from his firm! Isn't that only natural?

Test Questions

1. What do you understand by the phrase, "A complete salesman"?

2. There are nine order killers listed. State the three most common, and tell why they are so dangerous.

3. Why should "eagerness to sell" be considered an order killer?

4. What relation does a fear complex have to the loss of sales?

5. What is the difference between a negative and a positive selling attitude?

6. There are nine sales clinchers listed. Which do you think are the three most valuable, and why?

7. What do you think is the psychological value of "closing by suggestion"?

8. Demonstrate what is meant by "automatic closing."

9. What is the difference between "price clinchers" and "special concessions"?

10. What do we mean by "bookkeeping clinchers"?

Study Suggestions

1. Why do you think some salesmen cannot close a sale, even though they open it and control the interview satisfactorily? Is this an efficient way of working?

2. List all the order killers you can remember, in the order of their importance.

3. List all the sales clinchers you can remember, in their order of value.

4. How do you think you could develop new sales clinchers and discover new order killers?

5. What do you think you could do to make yourself more efficient in closing sales?

CHAPTER XXIV

How to Multiply Your Effectiveness

EVERY salesman in charge of a regular territory is faced with the same problem—how to keep in constant touch with his contacts. When a period of time elapses between visits, it is sometimes difficult to keep a prospect sufficiently warmed up. Even in the case of customers, it is highly desirable to keep them regularly contacted and continually sold on your line and on yourself.

You cannot be in more than one place at one time or make more than one call at a time; and yet there are occasions when you realize that there are not enough hours in the day to do all the things you would like to do and not enough duplicates of yourself to make all the calls that are necessary! The problem is how to overcome the natural barriers of time and space; how to multiply your effectiveness without doing the impossible; how to keep your prospects frequently contacted without the dangerous extremes of either pestiferous calling or insufficient calling.

Contacts are the essence of business and the stepping-stones to friendship and profit. In every avenue of commerce there are four classes of contacts:

Suspects
Prospects
Customers
Friends

As they advance progressively from one class to another they become increasingly valuable. You must hold them, treasure them, and build them!

Both the sales manager and the salesman are vitally interested in contacts. They realize that as they build their contacts, so will they build their business. It is urgent, therefore, that every sales-minded individual be thoroughly conversant with all possible methods of holding and developing original contacts. As a result of my own experience in the field, I have noted and used these

Fifteen Ways to Tie Up the Sales Contact

1. **Write a letter acknowledging the courtesy extended on your first call.**

    Never make an original call on a suspect without following it up quickly with a "thank you" letter. Even in some cases where I have been received not too cordially, this letter goes out; and I believe it results in a favorable reaction that helps to keep that man's door open to me on my next visit. In most cases this is a standard letter, but it is addressed and written separately to each man under first-class postage.

2. **Write a follow-up goodwill letter about your firm and its merchandise.**

    In my case, I represent a firm that manufactures higher quality merchandise. I call attention to this fact, as well as to the number of years my firm has been specializing, to the character of craftsmen in our factory, to the type and names of organizations that prefer our products, to our unusual ability to develop new ideas, etc.

3. Pass along an idea on your next visit or by letter.

   No businessman has ever thrown out a salesman with an idea! If this one does not happen to be suitable, the next idea may be worth a small fortune. If the businessman has any vision at all (and he usually has at least a little) he will welcome with open arms the man who occasionally offers pertinent ideas and suggestions.

4. Write an occasional letter suggesting the adaptability of one of your products to a specific problem.

   If your letter is short, practical, and interesting, it may strike a receptive note in the prospect's mind. I believe that sometimes an executive gets an idea in a letter more easily than by word of mouth, because when he opens your letter he is usually in a letter-reading mood, while when you call on him his mind may be occupied or disturbed.

5. Pass along an occasional idea or news item on the prospect's personal hobby.

   When you come to learn something of the personal interests of your prospects and customers, you will run across many things he would like to see or to know. These are the thoughtful attentions that develop friendliness.

6. Never forget to write seasonal greetings to the man or woman you wish to cultivate.

   Several such occasions arise during the year— Christmas, New Year's, Valentine's Day, Easter, Thanksgiving, birthdays, business or formal anniversaries, celebrations, opening of new offices, stores or branches, etc.

7. Pass along timely news about a customer's competition.

Not in the unethical form of a detective's report, but general points of interest on service, promotional stunts, advertising, merchandising, window display ideas, etc.

8. Don't forget an occasional invitation to something he enjoys.

It may be a sales conference or convention in his industry or yours. It may be a luncheon, a ball game, a lecture, a show, or any one of a number of things that you think would be welcomed by a prospect or by a friend. Sometimes they are not much, but in his mind they may assume an importance that is frequently translated into increased friendliness toward you.

9. Never let an order come into your office without an acknowledgment!

No matter how small the order may be, or whom it is from, it is worth a letter of genuine thanks or a telephone acknowledgment. Courtesy begets courtesy.

10. An occasional friendly telephone call lessens sales resistance.

Never give a man a chance to think he is being neglected. When within local telephone range, there is absolutely no excuse for failing to keep frequently in touch with all your contacts. And even on long distance, within reasonable limits. Nothing warms the cockles of the heart more easily than a cheerful voice saying, "Hello, how you doin'?"

11. Send an occasional novelty or special item of your firm's manufacture.

It need not be a gift; it may be just a loan; but

> if it is something new your own brain will tell you whom it will interest most.

12. Point out interesting developments and trends in his industry or yours.

> Help your prospect, or customer, to keep acquainted with what is going on in his world. There may be developments even in his own industry of which he may not be aware and which may react to your mutual benefit. You can sometimes see more from the outside looking in than he can from the inside looking out.

13. Send him occasional sales helps, direct-mail folders, point-of-sale circulars, display material, etc.

> However, this should be done with discretion. I believe that frequently too much material is forwarded at one time, with the result that the recipient is swamped, his appreciation is dulled, and he uses none of it. I believe material of this kind should be fed in small doses at regular intervals, rather than in indigestible gobs.

14. Don't forget to offer your factory's creative assistance on specific problems.

> Never let your prospect or customer forget that you are the fountainhead of creative ideas in your particular line of business. Get him into the profitable habit of coming to you when he needs help.

15. Offer to work with his salesmen or to address his sales force on occasions.

> If your personal experience and background warrant the assumption of this capacity, don't be backward about offering your services. "Thar's gold in them thar hills!"

In my experience, I have constantly used eight avenues of communication:

1. Personal Visits
2. First-class Mail
3. Air Mail
4. Special Delivery Mail
5. Third-class Mail
6. Fourth-class Mail
7. Telephone
8. Telegraph

The personal visit is, of course, the ideal method of communication. Nevertheless, there is such a thing (and a dangerous thing) as making too many calls on a man. It is possible to make a pest of yourself instead of a welcome visitor.

To supplement my personal visits and to keep my welcome warm with all my contacts, I use Uncle Sam's mail carriers in every way that I can conceive or afford. To my mind here is at once the most effective and the most valuable method in existence today of keeping open the selling lanes of communication. There is nothing to equal the efficiency and the flexibility of the mails.

Pick your prospect, insinuate your idea, and send it *direct* to him with riflelike accuracy! If your stuff is any good at all, it is certain to get some results. If you get no results, you have only yourself to blame and to analyze. Whether you use first-class letters, or postcards, or form letters in postage-saver envelopes, or parcel post—you have a tremendous opportunity that is all too frequently overlooked.

The telephone—local and distance—is one of the salesman's handiest aids in annihilating time and space and keeping alive the warmth and cheer of the human voice. It has only one great danger. Transmitting, as it does, each and every inflection of the salesman's voice *without* showing the accompanying smile that may be on his face, it is vital that he show a smile in his voice—or he is lost!

The great value of the telegraph, as I use it, is its indication of urgency and its demand for immediate attention. The nearest competitor to a telegram (but, of course, no competitor in point of time) is the special delivery letter, either regular or air mail.

It is entirely probable that some salesman will say: "That's too much to do; it would take all my time."

But is this too much to do? I admit that it would be, if it were all done at one time. This is a plan of operation and follow-up for the entire year, to be put into effect only a little at a time.

It is a plan that has been tried and tested and proven to pay thrilling dividends. It is a method of personal follow-up that will *help* to make star salesmen out of cubs. It is limited only by the personality of the individual and by the continuity of his effort. On this basis, it is not too much for anyone!

Try it out yourself. You'll be surprised how many lukewarm suspects you can transform into interested prospects. Human nature is identical the world over. People love to be catered to. They react the same way to these little attentions. And the average businessman or executive is no exception to the rule. Try out this plan on your own contacts and prove the results yourself!

Test Questions

1. What is the value of contacts in building a business?
2. Name four effective ways to use the mails.
3. Name three types of invitations you might extend to a prospect or customer.
4. Why should an order be acknowledged?
5. Name three different ways to use the telephone effectively.
6. What sort of gift do you think it would be most proper to send your prospect or customer? Why?
7. How could interesting trade developments be of help to you in maintaining the contact?
8. How could direct mail be of help to you?
9. In what way could your factory's assistance be capitalized?
10. How often do you think all these things should be done?

Study Suggestions

1. Show what advantages you might have in contacting a prospect in your own city as against one out of town.
2. If your prospect was out of town, how would you attempt to equalize your efficiency in contacting him, as against the prospect in town?
3. What do you think might be the attention value and sales advantage of air mail as against special delivery mail?
4. Discuss how you could use the telegraph to advantage in building up an initial sale.
5. Considering all the suggestions made in this chapter, how many of these things do you think you could do at one time? Why, and how?

CHAPTER XXV

The Futility of Price Appeal

IN ROLLING up our sleeves to do a real selling job for today and tomorrow, let us first of all lay the ghost of Price back among the moth balls of the late depression!

The salesman who sells—or the customer who buys—by price alone is very much in the position of the ruler who lives by the sword alone . . . he usually perishes the same way. The weapon of price is as dangerous as an Australian boomerang. It is an unstable keystone on which to base any selling or buying effort. Any buyer who can buy at a price from you today, may some day buy at a better price from someone else; and when price alone is concerned, the buyer knows no loyalty!

The salesman who sells on a price basis is bound to be an in-and-outer . . . he is in today and out tomorrow. The question of price is the most futile argument that a salesman can possibly use; and yet we still see men who permit their own price complex to drive them into a corner and beat them down.

Price arguments are just as outmoded as high pressure selling. But it is surprising how often the question of price is injected into a discussion by the salesman himself—as if he were afraid the customer might forget about it! More than one salesman has *talked* his customer into a state of price-mindedness when there was no idea of considering price at all.

Why solicit a customer on a price basis and build up trouble for yourself, when you can probably just as well develop him into a quality buyer and build up a good business of mutual profit? The answer is, of course, that the average salesman is still *afraid* to get away from the subject of price; and he hasn't the *courage* to concentrate on the subject of quality. He does not realize that the price market is passing out of the picture and that the quality market is the one to be mainly concerned about. The man who isn't shrewd enough to see that quality buying is on the way up is traveling down a blind alley in a fog with his eyes closed!

The modern salesman who wastes his time talking price, when he has so many more desirable talking points, is about as modern as the old-fashioned "drummer" type of traveling salesman! As a matter of fact, price is logically such a minor element in the average business transaction that it actually belongs in last place in the process of selling. Any article can be made to look interesting and competitive on a price basis by "talking up" the many important quality advantages that a so-called "cheap price" article does not have.

Here are the half dozen vital steps in modern selling, set down in the order of their importance to the man who is building today's foundation for tomorrow's sales:—1. Friendliness; 2. Creative Service; 3. A Quality Product; 4. Product Prestige; 5. Desirability; 6. Price. I defy any salesman of modern merchandise to reverse the order of this procedure and to build up a permanent profitable business for himself, for his firm, and for his customer!

Common Price Fallacies

A fallacy is a false or misleading idea. The mental equipment of every salesman, no matter how good he may be, is apt to be encumbered with one or more of these price fallacies. And it is not necessarily a discredit to him; for these ideas develop unconsciously through imitation and association with customers, competitors and fellow salesmen. The only discredit lies in his refusal to recognize them and to reconsider them in the light of the newer concepts of selling.

I should like to explode at least a dozen of these commonly accepted price fallacies that are misleading and discouraging to business ambassadors everywhere; and show salesmen how to replace the bogey of price with the modern appeal of quality!

1. *It Is a Fallacy to Think That Price Is Everything.* It is but an infinitesimal part of the sale. The only man who thinks that price is everything is the salesman who has a price complex so deeply imbedded in his mind that he cannot talk or think of anything else. The best and strongest method of attack on this price fallacy is to ignore price to the very last ditch, and to substitute all the qualities that are far more important to the buyer—as itemized above. Keep away from statements that automatically lead into price discussions and price comparisons; and everything that remains is constructive quality selling! There are so many things that the buyer is more interested in, that in many cases price need never be mentioned at all except as a matter of record at the end of the sale.

2. *It Is a Fallacy to Think That Price Is a Good Sales Argument.* In many cases it is the poorest argument you can use! It merely indicates that your merchandise is manufactured and offered on a price basis, and that it hasn't the better quality now demanded by buyers. Almost every buyer has become satiated with the price arguments and price limitations he has been forced to recognize dur-

ing the past few years. He is anxious to buy better merchandise; and he knows that quality merchandise and cheap prices just do not go together. Price is no argument at all! It is merely a state of mind; and as such, it can be entirely surrounded and beaten by the proper approach on the part of the salesman.

3. *It Is a Fallacy to Think That Cut Prices Always Hold a Buyer.* Price cutting is a vicious circle that helps no one and hurts everyone. The buyer who continually shops around for cut prices knows no loyalty to any salesman, and can hardly expect to receive it in return. You may sell him this time; but the chances are that the man who cuts your price a little deeper will sell him next time . . . and then where are you? Sell the buyer on your quality merchandise, on your reliability, on your creative service . . . then price will take care of itself. Let the other fellow take the profitless volume. Go out and build yourself some volume with profit! Your buyers will respect ᴊ ᴜ; your firm will appreciate you; and your commission account will look you in the eye with gratitude!

4. *It Is a Fallacy to Think That Low Prices Can Replace Advertising and Salesmanship.* Every now and then some salesman gets the idea that he doesn't have to do any more selling because he has a very low price, and that the price will do the selling job. He doesn't realize that he must sell just as hard, because his low price only spurs on his competitor to greater effort; and before he is through, the competitor may even be able to cut his low price . . . and then he has to start all over again! Why waste all your selling effort on the price end of your line? With practically the same effort, you can talk quality and sell good merchandise at a profit. Price never replaces advertising and salesmanship—it only lowers its standards.

Good advertising develops good leads and reduces sales resistance; good selling builds good business and brings good prices. The American standard of living is moving upward, not downward!

5. *It Is a Fallacy to Think That Low Price Merchandise Is "Just as Good."* The "just-as-good" alibi has been exploded long ago. You only get what you pay for—and if you pay very little, you will get very little. But there is still an occasional buyer who has the idea that cheap junk will serve his purpose as well as good merchandise. He completely overlooks the law of diminishing returns on cheap merchandise, and must be sold on the law of increasing returns with the acceptance of better merchandise. The latter is economically cheaper for him in the long run. If he can only be shown an effective comparison picture of the different grades in your line, he can often be shown that it is to the interest of his own firm and his own personal reputation to stand up for increasingly better grades even though they cost a little more. If he will pay only a little more in dollars and cents, he will get a great deal more in quality. The spread between the ordinary level and the quality level is sometimes very small. That's another law of manufacturing economics that some people don't think about!

6. *It Is a Fallacy to Think That Price Buyers Are in the Majority.* There is a surprising number of buyers who are broadminded and quality-minded. Price-minded buyers are far in the minority these days; and it is an actual fact that some of them got that way only because of a continual run of price-minded salesmen. When you call on a buyer nowadays, take it for granted that he is one of the majority who is sick unto death of the old depression conditions and is delighted that the approaching prosperity

is putting him back in the quality group. You will make no mistake if you concentrate on the better side of your line. The question is, have you the courage to stick to it? If you have, good old human nature and the well-known law of average will bring you out on top and place you at the head of the parade!

7. *It Is a Fallacy to Think That a Manufacturer's Size Affects the Quality of His Merchandise.* There are small manufacturers who are more noted than larger ones, because of the quality for which they are famous; just as there are large manufacturers who are famous for cutting corners on price merchandise. Each manufacturer has his own niche and builds his own reputation for good or cheap merchandise. To say that a manufacturer can make a quality line just because he has a big plant is as misleading as to say that a manufacturer makes cheap merchandise because he has a small plant. Size has nothing to do with quality, but quality very often increases a manufacturer's size and reputation!

8. *It Is a Fallacy to Think That the Cheap Manufacturer Has Everything His Own Way.* That may have been partly true during the recent low tide of business; but in this new day and age the cheap manufacturer is running into surprisingly keen competition from the quality group! His days are numbered, and he is being forced back into the lower end of the merchandising picture. If he is smart enough to sense the trend of the times, he will start trading up; if he doesn't, he will keep on slipping. He cannot stand still while the mounting forces of recovery rush onward. Neither can the salesman! He, too, must decide in which direction to move; and if he "knows his stuff" he will lead the crowd to quality!

9. *It Is a Fallacy to Think That Price Is the First Thing the Buyer Considers.* Many buyers now consider the questions of suitability, quality and durability before they think of price. In other words, they no longer place the cart before the horse. Their attitude toward price has done a right-about-face, and salesmanship has changed along with them. Salesmen have become more cheerful, more active, more quality-minded. They find it easier to persuade buyers to consider the more important things that count in a buying transaction. The question of price is being put in its proper place; which means that constructive salesmanship is once again assuming its rightful place at the head of the business procession.

10. *It Is a Fallacy to Think That the Average Buyer Has No Preference for Quality.* The buyer has his own troubles and his own problems. The fact that he may not always agree with the salesman's ideas doesn't mean that he is not able to. His actions are frequently restricted by organization difficulties or limitations. His choice of merchandise may be prescribed for him by other executives, without regard to his personal preferences. His hands may be tied by budget restrictions. He may not always buy what he likes, but what he can afford. The salesman must consider all these possibilities, but he must not allow them to cancel his salesmanship. After all is said and done, he still has an opportunity to do a job of creative selling with the buyer and his associates. Sell him on the desirability of your quality anyway, and some day he may be able to afford it. It is conceivable that you may do such a good selling job that the buyer, in his preference for your quality, will try to change his specifications or correct his restrictions so as to make a place for it. The buyer may even feel impelled to go back to his executives and

do a selling job for you. When you can get him to do that, you're a salesman!

11. *It Is a Fallacy to Think That There Are Not Enough Buyers for High Grade Merchandise.* There are always buyers for *every* level of merchandise. It is just up to you to find your man—and when you have found him, to build him up to your own level if he is not already ahead of you! In practically every American community you will find every level of buying; but buyers are not always familiar with every level. They *have* been known to become rutted in one track. That is where your creative selling enters the picture and "makes big ones out of little ones." There's your opportunity to attract, to interest, to convince, and to sell!

12. *It Is a Fallacy to Think That Big Business Organizations Always Make the Most Desirable Buyers.* On the contrary, they sometimes make the *least* desirable buyers because of their emphasis and pressure on price. It is only fair to add that there are many big business organizations that do buy quality merchandise without indulging in chiseling practices. But the salesman who spends all his time trying to knock over the big fellows, and overlooks the medium size accounts, is apt to discover some day that he has a lot of volume with very little profit (or possibly the sales manager will discover it for him). The ideal way to build a permanent business with satisfactory profit is to cater to and build up a customer list of every size of account—small, medium and big—and thus have an outlet for every item in your line regardless of price or quality level. But don't ever get the idea that the big fellow is always the most desirable—unless you are interested in volume alone! Remember that two medium accounts sometimes equal the volume of a large one—and they are more

profitable, much safer, less exacting, and easier to handle all around. Last but not least, two accounts enable you to build up twice as many friendships as one account; and, in the final analysis, it is friendships that build your business just as it is quality that makes the best price argument!

TEST QUESTIONS

1. Why do you think price is futile as a sales argument?
2. Who is usually responsible for the customer's state of price-mindedness, and why?
3. What is the proper place of Price in the process of selling? List some of the things that precede it in importance.
4. Why is it foolish to think that cut prices would hold a buyer?
5. Why bother with advertising and salesmanship if we can have low prices?
6. Isn't it a fact that price-buyers are in the majority?
7. Just what relation does a manufacturer's size have to the quality of his merchandise?
8. Do you think price is always the first thing the buyer considers?
9. Do you think there are enough buyers for high grade merchandise to make it profitable?
10. Why are big business organizations the most desirable buyers? Are they?

STUDY SUGGESTIONS

1. Do you think the appeal of price is becoming more or less futile as business progresses? Why?
2. Name and discuss in detail at least four things that are more important than price in trying to build a permanent customer.
3. What kind of salesman do you think he is who discusses

price more than anything else, and how far do you think
he will go in building up a permanent and profitable
clientele?

4. Why do some salesmen seem to discuss price so readily,
and what do you think would be a good cure for them?

5. If price is so futile as a sales argument, why do we discuss it at all?

CHAPTER XXVI

Non-Stop Selling

For salesmen "on the way up," there are dozens of ways to make the process of selling a system of perpetual motion! Salesmen of the right caliber usually have their eyes and ears tuned in with their brains, and are constantly looking for new ways to cash in on their spare time. Here are three dozen practical ideas that take the "ell" out of selling and put the "man" into salesmanship!

The average salesman spends only a fraction of his time in the presence of his prospects and customers. The greater part of his time is spent in traveling, waiting in reception rooms, standing around in stores, waiting for trains or weather changes or automobile repairs, visiting his factory or main office, looking over territories, and sometimes just plain procrastinating.

How can we utilize all this time?

There are no less than five places—and sometimes more —where the salesman spends his time. . . . 1. on the road; 2. in the prospect's office; 3. in reception rooms; 4. at the main office; 5. in hotel rooms. Let us examine some of these time killers and see what we can do about turning more of our spare time into money—or at least, on the way to making money.

On the Road

When you're delayed in a town and can't get out, why not make the best of it and try to capitalize on the delay? How about looking around for some new leads? Step in at the banks and ask a few questions; ask the officers who are the wide awake business men, the live wires of the town. Walk up and down Main Street and see if some of the stores suggest new outlets, new dealers, new customers, new markets. You might even pick up a new sales promotion idea that you can pass along to a customer. Don't be backward about looking over the newspapers; the leading advertisers have a way of developing into good leads for your line. Even such commonplace things as classified telephone directories and city directories offer possibilities to a good sales detective.

Check into the various communities that surround the principal town and comprise the trading area. Many a good prospect lies off the main road! And many a good prospect is neglected or passed up for that very reason. At the same time, don't forget that the further you get into your territory, the closer you are getting to some of your distant customers; and if you are not going all the way through, it is a good plan to make a few telephone calls to nearby points and keep your contacts alive.

If you are in a town where you have some dealers, you might just as well check over their stocks, their displays, their sales methods, their trade. You might even be able to do a little resale work or put on a few demonstrations, and thus develop the necessary urge and good-will for a good fill-in order! Who knows but there might be a few complaints lying around that you can clean up, or a little servicing that you can do better than the dealer's salesmen. What a splendid way that is to get the customer low-down on your line, and to get some practical ideas on how your product is actually used and what dealers and customers really think of it; to say nothing of the red hot talking points you can pick up that will help you on some other account!

This whole question of utilizing traveling salesmen's time resolves itself into the old familiar wisecrack:—When you're on the road, do you sit and think, or do you just sit?

In the Prospect's Office

Whether you are waiting in his office or in his store, there is frequently an opportunity to put spare time to good use. You might be talking to his assistants or to his salespeople, passing out some ideas on your line that will help them sell it for you. No selling chain is stronger than its weakest link; and occasionally these are the very persons who throw a monkey wrench into the selling machine because of their ignorance of the line, and because they cannot visualize its possibilities. That's where *your* educational work comes in.

Don't forget the endless chain idea when working with your prospect. Get him to give you the names of other prospects, and follow the same plan with every prospect you call on. You will probably get a few turndowns, but you will also get a lot of good names. "Ask and ye shall receive!"

Every now and then your prospect will let loose a good selling idea or a good technical pointer that you can use on someone else. Don't let it go in one ear and out the other. Write it down in your notebook and you'll accumulate a fund of usable ideas that will help you in your selling as you go along. As H. G. Weaver, of General Motors, has so aptly put it: "The buyer's mind is the raw material out of which sales are produced." Keep as close as you can to the practical merchandising mind of the buyer and you'll be surprised at the number of first-grade selling helps you will accumulate.

In talking with your prospect, have you ever *offered* your services on resale work and on store or home demonstrations? An offer of this kind proves that you *know* your product can be sold; and if *you* can sell it, you can show someone else how to sell it, too. That often turns out to be the leverage that pushes an order over the top!

In Reception Rooms

Here is an important place to keep your eyes and ears open. Watch the traffic while you are waiting. People who come and go—both insiders and outsiders—frequently leave important clues. They may be selling a competitive or related line, or a line that doesn't concern you at all; but the "line" they give the receptionist occasionally gives you a line that is worth following.

Speaking of receptionists, don't forget that while salesmen come and go, good-will usually starts or stops right here at the reception desk! Your cleverest tricks and your most important style won't equal the effectiveness of a bright smile and a pleasant manner.

The reception room manner is something worth thinking about, too. It is really a pity how much time is wasted in reception rooms reading newspapers and snappy stories. If you must wait, start thinking. Review your opening statement, your principal idea, your sales presentation, your closing arguments. Have your samples ready; have your place marked in your catalog, or sales manual, or advertising portfolio, so there will be no fumbling when you get the signal to go.

Instead of reading miscellaneous matter, try to find some of the company publications that will give you the company background and a selling tie-up that you may be able to use in your presentation. Digging for sales opportunities in publications of this type is often productive of business-getting ideas; and any ideas you can pick up in your spare time represent a clear gain for you!

A number of reception rooms nowadays contain exhibits of the company's products, and of their advertising and sales promotion campaigns. Many a selling idea is picked up bodily from exhibits of this type. The question is, can you recognize a genuine idea when you see it, even if it has been used by someone else? And are you capable of adapting it to your own selling?

At the Main Office

Visits to the main office or the factory should serve as an inspiration to the man in the field, and should supply him with the ammunition he requires to keep his own personal storage battery charged at full voltage.

These visits are a splendid opportunity to contact the advertising and sales promotion departments for new ideas and new slants that can be put to work in the field. They provide new suggestions on ways to tie in the thoughts of the advertising department with the daily efforts of the man on the firing line.

In the same way, the production department can be visited to learn of new processes, new technical developments, new inventions, new models that can be translated into new talking points at the point of sale. New samples can be acquired that will add freshness to the salesman's presentation, to say nothing of the renewed mental stimulation to an otherwise jaded perspective.

The sales department, naturally, is the salesman's main objective. In his home office he has a first-hand opportunity to check up on shipments, shortages, returns, back orders, etc., and to clean up the little odds and ends of both customer complaints and office complaints. Then, too, it is possible for him to do some constructive planning in the way of going over the office files with the proper assistants, checking up on slow and dormant accounts, and advising with them on ways and means to build them up and bring them back. Last but not least, he has an opportunity to visit with executives and acquire a new understanding of sales and office policies in the light of latest developments and current trends.

The salesman who is so located that he can make these contacts at fairly regular intervals is fortunate indeed. All these are the things that help to rebuild morale and send a man back into the field with new faith, new courage, and a completely revived outlook on the possibilities for more business and on the hitherto unrecognized potentialities of his territory.

In Hotel Rooms

The salesman's calls may be over, but his selling marches on! It is when he returns to the peace and quiet of his temporary home that he has an opportunity to do some really constructive thinking and planning.

Analyze, review and plan for tomorrow! . . . is the star salesman's reply to the troubles of today. Just as the good soldier repairs and renews his equipment and morale after the battles of the day, so does the up-and-coming salesman straighten out his samples, analyze and review his sales presentation in the light of the day's developments, plan new strategy, and build up his courage for tomorrow's offensive. Today, more than ever, he "plans his work and works his plan."

Paper work is cleaned up and mailed into the office. An occasional note is written to some customer friend with a bit of information, a valuable suggestion or an interesting idea picked up during the day. Advance notices of calls may be sent out a few days ahead. A thank-you letter may be sent to a customer, or a letter acknowledging unusual courtesies sent to a prospect.

Not for this salesman is the lure of the billiard room, the movies, the joy ride. Not for this salesman was the phrase written:—"Nothing to do 'til tomorrow." This man's spare time cannot be spared for trivialities. He knows that competition is entirely too keen for any letdown, and that opportunities are not presented on a silver platter, but are *made* by men who plan for them. This man is "on the way up" because he is *always* on the way and he *knows* his way!

TEST QUESTIONS

1. How can we develop our selling process into a system of so-called perpetual motion?
2. How much of a salesman's time do you think is spent in the presence of prospects and customers?
3. Referring to the previous question, what do you think might have an important effect on this?
4. Where do you think salesmen lose a great deal of their time, and why, and how can it be corrected?
5. What do you think is the worst time waster for salesmen who work in the city, and for those who work on the road?
6. What is the "endless chain" idea in selling?
7. If you offered a prospect your services on re-sale work, how could that help your selling?
8. How could you use waiting time in reception rooms to good advantage?

9. When visiting your main office, how could contacts with the advertising department be of help to you?

10. Answer the previous question with regard to the production department, also.

Study Suggestions

1. Attempt to analyze a salesman's trip into an out-of-town territory by either train, automobile, or bus. How do you think the principle time wasters could be converted into time saved for constructive effort, thinking, planning, selling?

2. What do you think is the principal moral suggested by this chapter? Discuss it.

3. What opportunities do you think a salesman on the road has to turn his spare time into constructive effort in making new contacts, building up good-will, friendship, and eventually more sales?

4. Discuss briefly five constructive things that might be done in prospects' offices and reception rooms.

5. Do you think it is worth while for a salesman to leave his territory occasionally to visit his main office? Why, and what are the advantages and disadvantages?

CHAPTER XXVII

Buyer-slants on selling

If *you* were buyer instead of salesman, would you laugh at *you*—or listen?

As a buyer and as a customer of yours, I probably see as many different salesmen each week as you see prospects —if not more. At the end of any average week I can usually count on the fingers of one hand the number of men who stand out in my memory as *uncommon* salesmen. If you were to ask me why this is so, I could give you at least twenty-five different answers . . . and here they are:

1. Do You Know Anything About My Business?

Instead of puffing so much about *your* business, why don't you confine your remarks to *my* business? Instead of trying so hard just to make a sale, why don't you first find out whether your product is any good for my business or for my trade?

2. Why Do You Pester Me to Death?

Don't you think my time is worth anything? And did you ever stop to think I might get tired seeing you so often? If you would make less calls on me, but prepare yourself to make more *intelligent* calls, I might think a lot more of you and you might have a better chance to do business with me!

3. Why Can't You Lose with a Smile?

If there is anything I hate, it is a poor sport. After all, you cannot expect to get every order. Why get peeved when you lose out—and make *me* peeved? Do you think that will help you to get the next order?

4. Why Do You "Speechify" to Me?

Every time you call you talk *at* me as if you were making a speech. What's the idea? Can't you act natural? Or do you think I am unnatural enough to be impressed by your speech-making?

5. What Makes You Think I Am Dumb?

Is it because I don't easily become enthused over being treated and spoken to as if I were a half-wit? What makes you think that your air of superiority makes me anything but tired? Did you ever stop to think that I may *not* be as dumb as your superiority complex?

6. Why Do You Become So Familiar on Short Acquaintance?

You may be an "ambassador of business" in your own estimation, but you are just a peddler to me. Who ever gave you the right to slap me on the back and call me "George" or "buddy" or "old man?" How do you get that way?

7. What Makes You Think You Can High Pressure Me?

I have been high-pressured by experts "way back when!" Surely you don't think you can get away with it, do you . . . or that it would do you any good to try? Haven't you heard that the high pressure days belong to ancient history?

8. Why Complain to Me About Your Sales Manager?

I have troubles of my own. Anyway, I have no use for people who cannot be loyal to their own organizations. That certainly doesn't increase my respect for you!

9. Why Should I Give You My Business?

I have yet to hear a single good reason why I should switch over to you. All you've told me so far is a lot of baloney. Let's get down to brass tacks and talk about things that really count—such as advertising and sales promotion helps, shipping facilities, quality and prestige, service guarantees, complaints and returns, etc.

10. Why Shouldn't I Talk Price?

You fellows don't give me anything else to talk about! Lord knows, I'd give my right arm to run across a real merchandiser among you salesmen, but all I seem to hear from is a bunch of peddlers who talk price, price, price. Is it any wonder that I fall into a price complex myself?

11. What Have You Ever Done for Me?

Suppose I did give you one order. So what? Do I ever hear any more of you after you get the order? Did you ever show even the slightest interest in whether I received the merchandise, or whether it was satisfactory or whether I was disappointed in part of the shipment? And now you seem to feel that I should give you every order I have!

12. Why Don't You Keep Your Shirt On?

How do you expect to get anywhere if you haven't any patience? Your short temper may be temperament to you, but it's just a pain in the neck to me. It certainly won't open any doors for you on future calls.

13. Why Don't You Tell Me the Whole Story?

Forcing me to cross-examine you in order to get all the facts, doesn't build up my respect for you. Or my confidence, either. If you don't know the whole story about your product, why don't you learn it before you call on me and waste my time?

14. What Makes You Think I Don't Want to Do Business with You?

Just because I am inclined to be cagey about committing myself, doesn't mean that I don't want to give you an order. You know, some of us like to take a little time to think things over, and we like to be "sold." We don't all "rush in where angels fear to tread." We may buy more cautiously at the start, but we are apt to be more solid buyers in the long run.

15. Why Don't You Tell Me the Profit Story?

What I would like to know is, how much money can I make selling *your* merchandise as against your competitor's line. Don't be bashful about telling me the profit story; that's just what I'm eager to hear, even though I may discount a large part of what you tell me.

16. Why Do You Try to High-hat My Assistants?

Don't you realize that I pay them good money to work with fellows like you so as to save time and money for me? When you start high-hatting my assistants, you're just cutting your own throat. Get wise to yourself, young fellow!

17. Why Don't You Keep Your Promises?

How can you expect me to believe *anything* you say when you forget to do the things you say you will do? The only basis I can have for future confidence in you is the reputation you build up with me today. You know, I don't have to take too many chances with you fellows; there are always plenty more of you waiting outside my door!

18. You Wouldn't Kid Me, Much, Would You?

Don't forget that I see a lot of salesmen in the course of a few days, and I have to listen to a lot of wild and overly optimistic statements. If you want to tell me something unusual, or make some extravagant claim, it isn't a bad idea to have the proof of it along with you.

19. Why Don't You Stick to Business?

I know you are trying to establish a more friendly personal contact with me; but there's plenty of time for that on future calls. Stick to business on your first call, and I may give you a little more leeway later on. Right now, I am much more interested in facts than in sociable conversation.

20. Why Don't You Give Me a Chance to Say Something?

You've got me so dizzy with your continuous conversation that I am not only tired, but slightly irritated as well. Is it too much to expect that I might want to get a word in edgewise? You know, *I* might want to ask a few questions, also. Or do you think you can convince me solely with a torrent of language?

21. Why Act Like Such a "Smart Aleck"?

Do you think that "wisecracking" me to death is going to pull me over to your side of the fence? Yes, I know *you're* smart; what I want to know is, is your merchandise smart? Has it ever occurred to you that I might think more of a straightforward presentation of facts than a lot of smart conversation?

22. Why Don't You Give Me a New Interest in Your Line?

I have heard the same old story so many times that I literally yawn myself to sleep when you start talking. Why not try to inject a new angle into an old story and tell me something I haven't heard before? Do you mean to tell me that no one in your organization ever sends you any new ideas?

23. Why Don't You Report on That Lead I Gave You?

That's a courtesy that is due me, isn't it, after all I did for you? You see, I might be curious to know just how you came out with my friend, Bill Thompson, as long as I sent you to him. You would be surprised how I eat up that kind of courtesy and consideration. If you don't believe it, try me!

24. Why Don't You Look and Act Like a Successful Salesman?

A calm, confident, optimistic manner and a neat, trim-looking appearance would not make me think any less of you. Not that I expect you to dress like an actor, or to talk like a politician. But a considerable improvement over your present style certainly wouldn't hurt you.

25. *Why Don't You "Sell" Instead of "Peddle"?*

The real salesman does a lot of "creative selling." He not only suggests ideas, but frequently creates opportunities for the successful use and presentation of the ideas. The peddler is nothing but an order-taker; his vision and capacity are limited to the old chestnut: "Do you want anything today?" The one salesman creates his own openings and forces his own issues out in the field. The other man might just as well stay at home and try to pick his orders out of the mail, if any! It is what you have above the eye-line that builds up your sky-line!

TEST QUESTIONS

1. Why should a salesman know anything much about his customer's business?
2. Should a salesman discount his prospect's intelligence? Why?
3. Why is loyalty a desirable quality, and to whom?
4. What about the salesman who always talks price?
5. Is temperament a desirable quality in a salesman?
6. Is there any advantage in discussing profit with the prospect? What?
7. How about the salesman who doesn't keep his promises?
8. What would be your suggestion to the salesman who talks constantly?
9. Of what advantage is a successful appearance to a salesman?
10. Compare the "peddler" with the "creative salesman." Which is the better type, and why?

STUDY SUGGESTIONS

1. In making a preliminary call on a good prospect, discuss some of the things you would do to learn about

his business and to decide just how your product could be of benefit to him.

2. What would be your reaction, your attitude, your manner in places where you occasionally lost an order; and what would you do to keep yourself in line for the next order?

3. What do you think is the value of discussing the profit angle of your line with your prospect? How would you do it in order to impress him with its desirability?

4. If you were a salesman with an inferiority complex, how would you go about building up your self-confidence?

5. What would you do to give your prospect or customer a new interest in your line? Where would you get your information, and how would you handle it?

CHAPTER XXVIII

Ten Tips on Quality Selling

QUALITY tells a story that is stranger than cut-price fiction —and it has the added advantage of being the truth!

There is no resisting the quality appeal; but many an attempt is made to avoid paying the price for quality merchandise. Unfortunately, the man who buys cheap merchandise doesn't realize that eventually he pays the quality price without getting the quality!

The price buyer doesn't analyze his purchase from the viewpoint of greatest value received over a period of time, but from the "penny-wise pound-foolish" angle of how little he can pay today for something that he *thinks* will be "just as good" tomorrow.

It is up to the salesman—the quality salesman, if you please—to try to lead this prospect to the quality counter and to teach him better economics.

It is up to the salesman to offer his sales presentation in the form of an interesting, coaxing, persuasive *quality* story—that will induce the prospect to enter the charmed circle of quality. Once in, he will never come out. At least, he will never *want* to come out.

It is up to the salesman! Here are a number of ways to get his quality message across. These will merely get him started and interested. In the fire of day-to-day selling he will develop many more ideas to add to this list.

It is up to the salesman!

1. Strip for Action

Get the "you" angle into your opening sentence, and the average man will listen to *your* angle. The main thing is, strip for action and go right into your dance. The prospect's time means money to him, and he cannot take offense if you act as though you appreciate it.

Once you have gotten into his presence, get down to business. If you are carrying a hat or coat, get rid of them. If you have a briefcase or arm portfolio, use your eyes to locate a good place to set it down and open it up.

Take it for granted that so long as you're in, you have an unspoken invitation to tell your story. The average businessman won't object; he will be satisfied to see that you look as though you intend to make it snappy. What he wants to do is to let you in, have it over with, and get you out. All you want to do is to get in and get a chance to tell your story. It's up to you!

Start opening your case and, at the same time, tell your man what you're doing:—"You'll want to see the blueprints of this new motor." Or . . . "Here's a picture of that new model we wrote you about." Or . . . "If you want to increase the efficiency of your salesmen, here are several ways to do it." Or . . . "This new method of keeping tax records will save you clerical time and money." Or . . . "I just want you to see this set of new handy containers."

2. Be A Good Listener

A one-sided sales presentation doesn't require a salesman; a phonograph record can do the trick. It is the process of give and take that puts life and reason into your selling process.

Speak your piece; give your prospect plenty of openings to give you his reactions; and thus allow yourself an opportunity to come back with a rebuttal that answers his objections.

Quality selling calls for a presentation of facts and reasons-why that may present an entirely new aspect to the prospect's mind. A hundred to one, he won't take it lying down. He will have something to say; and if you don't give him a chance to say it, the hard luck will be your own.

The more you can get the prospect to talk and unload his mind, the more chances he gives you to find out what's bothering him. Then you can go to work on him intelligently, answer all his objections, and try to sell him.

God help the salesman who thinks he is the only star performer! There are always two sides to a sales performance—the salesman and his audience—and if the audience doesn't get a chance to react properly, he may react improperly!

3. Pat Him on the Back

Flattery that is too obvious weakens your own cause. But the occasional compliment with a sensible basis frequently creates an opening in the prospect's armor.

Why not tell him frankly:—"I'm not trying to kid you, but I know you appreciate unusual quality. How is this model for something out of the ordinary?" Or . . . "After all, you didn't build your business on a shoddy basis, and it really deserves high quality merchandise." Or . . . "You're to be complimented on the quality of your clientele, and I'm sure they will appreciate products as good as this." Or . . . "You know you can sell anything you want to; why not hold up your reputation for higher quality?" Or . . . "You're a good businessman because you have always believed in building prestige and profit at the same time; that's why you should consider this higher grade."

4. Quality Selling Starts at the Bottom

From the very moment of your entrance, remember that you are the apostle of quality. Everything that you are, everything that you do, everything that you say must reflect that quality attitude. Your appearance, your personality, your manner, every detail of your presentation will speak volumes either for or against the kind of quality you have on your mind.

No salesman can sell quality merchandise and be sloppy, or careless, or unmannerly. And certainly no salesman of quality merchandise can overlook the slightest opening into which he can wedge the quality appeal.

Everything about the prospect's store, or business, or trade, or stock, or organization that can be tied up with the quality motif puts you that much ahead. For instance: —"This store certainly carries a quality appeal." Or . . . "A business of this kind is a natural for our quality line." Or . . . "You certainly have a quality trade, the kind that you have to play up to." Or . . . "You have a good looking stock, the kind that talks quality out loud." Or . . . "You seem to have a high grade organization, the kind of people that appreciate quality merchandise."

5. Paint in the Quality Picture

A salesman's job is like an artist's—he paints in the picture of his quality merchandise on the broad receptive canvas of his prospect's mind—and the more of an artist he is, the more of a salesman he proves to be.

In your discussion with the prospect, paint in the quality picture with fine, delicate, subtle strokes—an insinuation here, a suggestion there—just enough to leave the thought of quality without bearing down too hard or becoming too obvious. Such as:—"Yes, indeed, business is picking up rapidly and money is coming much easier." Or . . . "There was a day when price was everything, but now the trend is entirely to quality." Or . . . "Business runs in cycles, you know, and now the quality cycle is having its turn." Or . . . "No matter what the masses of people go through, they always retain their desires for the finer things of life." Or . . . "One of the outstanding features of the American standard of living is the constant desire for something better."

6. Stress the Delusion of Cheapness

A real salesman is a man who can open the eyes of his prospect and enable him to see things in their true light— the light of quality as against cheapness.

The delusion of cheapness is a hangover from the days of scrimping and scraping. With good times on the way back and the stress of depression receding into the distance, it becomes increasingly simple to unmask the snare and delusion of cheap merchandise and cheap buying. After all, a thing that is cheap is worth no more than it costs—sometimes not as much; and the word cheapness itself becomes increasingly distasteful to a people accustomed to the best.

Cheap buying breeds cheap selling and cheap living. Quality selling works in exactly the opposite direction: and quality merchandise—made well, bought well, and sold well—brings greater satisfaction to the customer, increased profit to the buyer, and more commissions to the salesman.

Place the mirror of quality before the delusion of cheapness, and cheapness evaporates into thin air!

7. *Use Competitor Motivation*

The prospect to the contrary notwithstanding, the fact remains that he will always be interested in what his competitors are doing—yesterday, today and tomorrow.

Motivate your quality sales presentation wherever you can with reliable examples of competitive buying; and regardless of whether the prospect admits it then and there, he will most assuredly do some heavy thinking.

There is nothing tricky or difficult about this. It is very simple and oh, so effective. For instance:—"Now, Mr. Brown, you wouldn't want Jones & Ellis to get the jump on you, would you? They just ordered two gross of these." Or . . . "Of course, you'll probably want a different color than Jones & Ellis ordered; they are getting them in green." Or . . . "Here's a recent Jones & Ellis advertisement featurng these in a new green ensemble." Or . . . "By the way, have you heard that Jones & Ellis sold out their entire trial order and are now reordering?" Or . . . "Here's a letter from the biggest dealer in the territory telling what he thinks about it."

8. *Keep Feeding the Quality Lure*

Everybody enjoys the luxury of quality—and your prospect is no exception. Despite the fact that he says he cannot afford it, you know very well that he cannot afford to be without it. Can you convince him?

Tantalize him with the feel of your quality product. Let him handle it, see it in action, try it out, use it. Like this: —"Here, Mr. Brown, won't you keep this on your desk for a few days and just see how beautifully it works?" Or . . .

"Tell you what I'll do, I'll send you a few samples for your salespeople to play around with. Then see what they think of it." Or . . . "You know the difference between price and quality merchandise; take this and make your own comparisons, and I'll abide by the verdict." Or . . . "I know you like to cater to your quality trade; here's another way to make a hit."

9. Suggest High Quality First

Did you ever ask for a suit of clothes in a good store and have the salesman show you, first, the best suit in stock?

If he is a smart salesman, he will do that without asking you what you want to pay. He knows human nature. He knows that a customer hates to back down from a quality garment; that he dislikes admitting he doesn't want anything so good. As a matter of fact, he does want it, although he may not be able to afford it; and many times he wants it so badly after seeing it, and after seeing cheaper merchandise in comparison, that he figures out a way to buy it regardless.

The same applies to every product. When showing your line, start at the top. Get your quick quality impression across with your top number. It will cast a quality glow over the rest of your line, and you'll be surprised how many times your prospect will come back to the quality item. "The recollection of quality remains long after the price is forgotten." And after he has seen your best numbers, the prospect will be consciously or unconsciously discontented with everything else until he can lay his hands on the top quality you first showed him.

After all, the only art in quality selling is the ability to make your prospect wretchedly discontented with anything else but the best you have shown him. That's where the fine finesse of salesmanship does its best work!

10. Speak Softly of Price

It is mentioned here in the position it properly belongs—last! Price is the least important element in the quality picture—and even your hard-boiled prospect knows it, though he won't admit it.

The intelligent salesman has so many other things to talk about that most of the time he forgets the subject of price entirely. And if he does have to mention it, in response to repeated questions, he mentions it so casually and in so off-hand a manner that he minimizes its importance.

There are many ways of doing this. For example:—"Oh, the price doesn't amount to much; you can see for yourself that this is the most inexpensive product on the market." Or . . . "Why worry about the price; the important thing is the quality satisfaction and the service it will give you." Or . . . "As you know yourself, price isn't all-important; it's the value that counts. Do you know of anything with a greater value than this?" Or . . . "Oh yes, naturally it's a few cents more than the other grade, but the value and quality are so much greater that it is actually more inexpensive than the cheaper grade." Or . . . "Price takes care of itself; it's the quality impression that sells this to your trade at any price." Or . . . "Quality, satisfaction and service considered, this is almost as cheap as the lowest price number in the line." Or . . . "In the last analysis, Mr. Brown, what you are interested in is the suitability of this product to your requirements. If it's the thing you need, it is cheap at any price; if it's not, it is expensive no matter how low the price!"

TEST QUESTIONS

1. What do we mean by the "you" angle in talking to a prospect?
2. Is there any advantage in letting the prospect state his objections?
3. How could you compliment a prospect without seeming to flatter him too much?
4. What can you say about a salesman's personal appearance and manners?
5. In what way is a salesman like an artist? So what?
6. What do you think is the difference between "cheapness" and "inexpensiveness"?
7. What do we mean by "competitor motivation"?
8. Demonstrate what we mean by the "quality lure."
9. Is it advisable to make your prospect discontented? In what way, and why?
10. What place does Price occupy in the quality picture?

STUDY SUGGESTIONS

1. Discuss in detail the principal advantages, as you see them, of quality selling as against price selling.
2. Even if the article is very low in price, do you think you could give it a quality atmosphere in your selling? How?
3. If you were told to be "a good listener," how would you get a chance to do your selling? Demonstrate by an actual example.
4. Discuss the subject of "competitor motivation" in detail, and show us just how it can affect your selling.
5. Write down as many of these 10 Tips as you can remember; then number them consecutively in their order of importance for your future use.

CHAPTER XXIX

57 Sales Reminders

1

DON'T forget that friendliness pays the world's biggest dividends. Why not grow rich on your friendships?

2

Don't forget that Price is the least important of your selling points. Quality, convenience, novelty, satisfaction, durability—are all 'way ahead of price in order of importance to your customer.

3

Don't overlook the power of suggestion. More mountains of sales resistance have been moved by suggestion than have ever been forced by pressure.

4

Don't lose track of your customer's interests—personal or otherwise. The more you think of him, the more he will think of you.

5

Don't forget that loyalty is one of the greatest virtues in the business of selling. Give me a man who is loyal, and you may have the other fellow's cleverness!

6

Don't forget that a good sales talk is never wasted. Some part of it may remain in the prospect's mind long after you have forgotten him, and may result in an order you never thought you could get.

7

Don't be too aggressive—unless you are looking for a fight. There is always a happy medium between high pressure and a flat tire.

8

Don't overlook the law of averages—the most inexorable law in selling. Just so many calls, so much effort, so much selling—all inevitably average up to a sale—sometimes when you least expect it. So why let down and break the chain?

9

Don't forget that enthusiasm breeds enthusiasm. The salesman who sells with a dead-pan attitude might just as well work in the cemetery. *Your* customer wants vim, vigor and vitality!

10

Don't argue with your customer, unless you are tired of taking orders. If *you* want the pleasure of arguing, let someone else have the pleasure of selling.

11

Don't expect too much cooperation from your prospect —especially at first. He is naturally against you, anyway, and it is up to you to travel at least three-fourths of the way to bring him the remaining distance.

12

Don't alibi to anyone—your customers are not interested and your firm prefers orders, anyway. So why put yourself on the defensive?

13

Don't forget that the prospect you just left is going to be sold by someone. Is there any real reason for leaving the order to the other fellow?

14

Don't cut yourself off from a return call on your prospect—either next week or next year. This is a small world and you never know when conditions will change in your favor.

15

Don't let yourself get too thin-skinned. It takes a tough hide to make a salesman who can "take it" and bounce back smiling.

16

Don't be afraid to ask for the order! What do you think you're doing—making a social call? If business interferes with your pleasure, who do you think is going to draw down your next pay check?

17

Don't forget to try persuasion once in a while. It might help to change your salesmanship into buymanship and bring your prospect into your own back yard.

18

Don't be too sure that your prospect is a dumbbell. He may turn the tables on you and prove to be as dumb as a fox.

19

Don't leave your prospect with any unpleasantness in his memory. If you ever hope to get an order from him in the future, he may be willing to "cut his nose off to spite his face" rather than buy from you.

20

Don't forget that sales resistance is cut down by sales persistence, just as surely as dropping water wears away the stone.

21

Don't think only of the commissions you are going to get. Think mainly of the friendships you are going to make; the commissions will take care of themselves.

22

Don't ever say or do anything to embarrass your prospect. He may not say anything today—but you can depend upon his remembering it tomorrow.

23

Don't try to sell something you know nothing about. If you don't know, find out. If you don't find out, you'll know about it later—unpleasantly.

24

Don't be afraid to make more calls. There is no substitute for calls and no alibi for lack of footwork. If you don't believe it, study the law of averages, and watch your sales go up as your calls increase.

25

Don't be afraid of a fight—but don't get into one! It is impossible to get out of a fight with your skin whole and your reputation sound—and both are precious possessions.

26

Don't lack confidence! If you haven't got it, at least simulate it. One of you has to have it, and if you don't, your prospect will. Or who do you think is going to make a sale?

27

Don't waste your time! Selling is a constant race against every moment of time. The time you lose today may cost you big business tomorrow by cutting down the number of calls you can make.

28

Don't forget that the most satisfying daily report is the order you send in. Do you know of any sweeter way to prove to your sales manager that you're on the job?

29

Don't distract your prospect's attention with anything you do or wear. Give him a chance to concentrate on your sales talk instead of on your person.

30

Don't knock a competitor! The chances are always in favor of falling over yourself if you do.

31

Don't forget your terminal facilities. If you haven't any, you better get some before you talk yourself out of your prospect's office.

32

Don't talk to your prospect as if you were making a speech. Remember that he is a potential friend. Are you in the habit of making speeches to your friends?

33

Don't fail to keep your word—whatever you do or whatever you promise. One failure raises doubt—the next one raises the roof.

34

Don't be afraid to tell your prospect all about your product. Do you expect him to guess the points you left out and buy from you just because you have an order book in your hand?

35

Don't forget that there are four steps to every sale—Attraction, Interest, Conviction, Desire. Have you built them up to the only logical climax?

36

Don't knock off and celebrate just because you got a big order today. Make hay while the sun shines and while the spirit sparkles—it may rain tomorrow.

37

Don't forget the tremendous value of the endless chain. Get every new customer to suggest another. That is one way to make your head-work save you footwork.

38

Don't pass up a chance to talk quality. There's a definite return to quality buying in every line of business, and every bit of it affects you directly and indirectly.

39

Don't try to bluff your way through an unfamiliar situation. It is much better to *offer* in advance to get the actual facts than to be found wanting later on and be *forced* to get them.

40

Don't be afraid to put a little showmanship into your selling. Dramatize your samples, your written material, your sales talk, all your opportunities as f- as you can. You won't regret it, and neither will your prospect.

41

Don't forget to talk merchandising and profits to your prospect; that means more to him than your merchandise —and you'll mean more to him if you do.

42

Don't cry on your prospect's shoulder—you're there to cheer him up, not to break him down.

43

Don't forget that a self-starter generates his own optimism; he doesn't have to be recharged by the home office.

44

Don't forget that the more supervision you require, the more overhead expense you run up; and the more expense you run up, the more commissions you run down.

45

Don't worry about more territory. Spend your time building up what you now have and you'll have all the worry you can properly take care of. A territory gives you only what you put into it; if you want more, put in more!

46

Don't be afraid to show evidence of activity. Every customer not only admires it, but demands it. After all, he is the boss!

47

Don't drop a good prospect too soon. You may have worked him up to the very point where the other fellow gets the business. Is that what you want?

48

Don't take a regular customer too much for granted; he is liable to give you the shock of your life. Keep on selling, no matter how long you know him. Never give him a chance to catch cold.

49

Don't forget that the hard-to-get prospect is usually the hard-to-lose customer. Who wouldn't work a little harder to get a customer that he will keep a little longer?

50

Don't forget the old saying that "New salesmen are easier to find than new customers." Watch your step, old boy, watch your step!

51

Don't "yes" your customer to death. A salesman who is too much of a yes-man eventually turns a customer into pretty much of a no-man!

52

Don't belittle your competitor. He may be just as good a man as you—possibly better; and if you don't keep your eyes open, you may give him a chance to prove it!

53

Don't overlook the value of imagination. Visualize your objective so that your prospect can see it more clearly—and he will buy more surely.

54

Don't *force* your salesmanship on your prospect. You can do more and go farther with your service-ability!

55

Don't forget the word "you" in talking to your prospect. It is a thousand per cent more effective and more interesting to him than the personal pronoun "I"!

56

Don't forget that the customer is always right—and when he's a good customer, he is perfect!

57

Don't fail to keep in touch with your prospect and to keep your prospect in touch with your business. That's the only way to develop your business.

CHAPTER XXX

100 Selling Maxims

HERE are 100 short, snappy, practical sales tips that "talk turkey" in few words. It is possible that we can all find these of practical help and occasional inspiration in the constant effort to speed sales momentum and to encourage continuous effort.

1. He who hesitates is lost—what are you waiting for and whom do you fear?

2. Strike while the prospect is hot—if you don't, someone else will.

3. Look before you leap—and then make it snappy.

4. 'Tis human to err—but not twice in the same place.

5. There are people that call a spade a spade—why beat about the bush in trying to sell a prospect?

6. Silence is golden, speech is silvern—do you ever listen, or do you like to talk too well?

7. Let no act be done at haphazard—plan your work and work your plan.

8. When men are arrived at the goal, they should not turn back—follow through on your follow-up.

9. A man should *be* upright, not be *kept* upright—what does your customer think of you?

10. Be good . . . and let who will be clever—better for your customer to think that you are *good*, than that you are only clever.

11. Water continually dropping will wear hard rocks hollow—repetition (with variations) will eventually convince the toughest prospects.

12. Pardon one offense and you encourage the commission of many—let a customer slip once and he is liable to get into the habit.

13. Know thyself—know your capabilities and follow them to the utmost.

14. Bad news travels fast—so does the good news that the customer is yours.

15. A bird in the hand is worth two in the bush—a good customer today is worth a whole list of prospects tomorrow.

16. Time is the soul of the world—waste not, want not.

17. Difficulties are things that show what men are—did you expect to find selling a soft snap?

18. Appear to know only this, never to fail nor fall—stick to your prospect and your prospect may stick to you.

19. Find time still to be learning somewhat good, and give up being desultory—do you know your job, your merchandise, your territory?

20. If it is not seemly, do it not; if it is not true, speak it not—remember that your prospect judges you and your company by your actions and by your words.

21. Opportunity knocks but once—pass it up and you may pass out of the picture.

22. There are two sides to every question—do you know your customer's side as well as your own?

23. Nothing can be produced out of nothing—and no one knows it better than the prospect you are trying to convince.

24. Appearances are often deceitful—that "dead-pan" prospect may be listening harder than you think.

25. He that has patience may compass anything—you may even sell that hard-to-please prospect.

26. Fair and softly goes far—do you make the mistake of blustering at your customer?

27. Let us make hay while the sun shines—in tomorrow's rain your prospect may not feel so optimistic.

28. Never leave until tomorrow what you can do today—your competitor may beat you to it.

29. Faint heart ne'er won fair lady—don't be afraid to ask for the order, and ask for plenty.

30. The proof of the pudding is the eating—do you prove your salesmanship by alibis or by orders?

31. Honesty is the best policy—you cannot get repeat business any other way.

32. A good name is better than riches—the reputation you have with your prospects today is what switches them into customers tomorrow.

33. Diligence is the mother of good fortune—there is still no substitute for calls, and more calls.

34. Don't count your chickens before they are hatched —nor discount your competitor before you have the name on the dotted line.

35. Rome was not built in a day—neither is a good customer made in one visit.

36. There's many a slip 'twixt the cup and the lip—just the same as between promise and performance.

37. Hell is full of good intentions—did you call on that prospect you heard about?

38. Talk of nothing but business, and dispatch that business quickly—your prospect's time and temper are just as valuable as your own; possibly more so.

at the flood, leads on to fortune—and the same applies to your dealings with your customer.

68. Let every man be master of his time—and let him be master of his interview also.

69. Brevity is the soul of wit—make it short and snappy.

70. Knowledge is power—the man who knows, and knows that he knows, has the prospect in the palm of his hand.

71. Hitch your wagon to a star—but keep your feet close to the ground.

72. Second thoughts, they say, are best—just like counting ten before losing your temper.

73. The better the day, the better the deed—today is always a good day to do something for your customer.

74. Procrastination is the thief of time—why put it off, when you can just as well do it now and have it over with?

75. Too low they build who build beneath the stars—aim high and you'll go far; aim low and you'll falter.

76. Time and tide wait for no man—neither does your restless customer.

77. While there is life, there is hope—many a customer has said yes, even after he has said no.

78. Style is the dress of thoughts—are you one of the "Oh yeah" type of talkers, or can you hand out a pretty good line?

79. Confidence is a plant of slow growth—and the customer who develops confidence in you is slow to slip away.

80. A man used to vicissitudes is not easily dejected —when you fall down, do you go "boom" or do you bounce right up again?

81. Few things are impossible to diligence and skill—and no one appreciates it so well as a good salesman.

82. Knowledge is more than equivalent to force—which do you think goes farther to sell your prospect?

83. Example is always more efficacious than prospect—and samples are always much more effective than conversation. Have you your sample case with you?

84. One swallow doesn't make a summer—neither does one small order make up your sales quota.

85. One good turn deserves another—if you do something for your customer, why can't he do something for you? Ever ask him to suggest a prospect?

86. A rolling stone gathers no moss—neither does a traveling salesman who travels *past* his prospects.

87. There's more than one way to kill a cat—and there's more than one way to sell a prospect. Have you tried the other way?

88. Time flies—have you made your mark today?

89. Trust that man in nothing who has not a conscience in everything—no matter how much you may smile, there is still a conscience in business, *good* business.

90. Where ignorance is bliss, 'tis folly to be wise—not even a good friend will always thank you for your advice.

91. Charity begins at home—maybe that's the way your customer feels about it, too. Have you sold him properly?

92. Handsome is that handsome does—what have you ever done for your customer that he should do something for you?

93. Fools rush in where angels fear to tread—no wonder that new man is signing up so many customers that his predecessor said were hopeless.

94. Ask, and ye shall receive—even the order, my boy, even the order!

95. Necessity is the mother of invention—how many different ways can *you* figure to get your man?

96. Tall oaks from little acorns grow—many a good customer has grown from small beginnings.

97. Pride goeth before destruction, and an haughty spirit before a fall—even as you and I.

98. Distance lends enchantment—the prospects in the next town always look better until you get there.

99. A soft answer turneth away wrath—and frequently brings home the bacon.

100. He laughs best who laughs last—particularly when you are mailing the signed order in to the home office.

Index